Understanding Burnout Recovery Among Native-Born Korean Missionaries

Evangelical Missiological Society Monograph Series

Anthony Casey, Allen Yeh, Mark Kreitzer, and Edward L. Smither
SERIES EDITORS

A Project of the Evangelical Missiological Society
www.emsweb.org

Understanding Burnout Recovery Among Native-Born Korean Missionaries

Hannah Kyong-Jin Cho

☙PICKWICK *Publications* • Eugene, Oregon

UNDERSTANDING BURNOUT RECOVERY AMONG NATIVE-BORN KOREAN MISSIONARIES

Evangelical Missiological Society Monograph Series 3

Copyright © 2020 Hannah Kyong-Jin Cho. All rights reserved. Except for brief quotations in critical publications or reviews, no part of this book may be reproduced in any manner without prior written permission from the publisher. Write: Permissions, Wipf and Stock Publishers, 199 W. 8th Ave., Suite 3, Eugene, OR 97401.

Pickwick Publications
An Imprint of Wipf and Stock Publishers
199 W. 8th Ave., Suite 3
Eugene, OR 97401

www.wipfandstock.com

PAPERBACK ISBN: 978-1-5326-7498-3
HARDCOVER ISBN: 978-1-5326-7499-0
EBOOK ISBN: 978-1-5326-7500-3

Cataloguing-in-Publication data:

Names: Cho, Hannah Kyong-Jin.

Title: Understanding burnout recovery among native-born Korean missionaries. / by Hannah Kyong-Jin Cho.

Description: Eugene, OR: Pickwick Publications, 2020. | Series: Evangelical Missiological Society Monograph Series 3. | Includes bibliographical references.

Identifiers: ISBN 978-1-5326-7498-3 (paperback) | ISBN 978-1-5326-7499-0 (hardcover) | ISBN 978-1-5326-7500-3 (ebook)

Subjects: LCSH: Missions, South Korean | Evangelism—Korea (South) | Burn out (Psychology)—Religious aspects—Christianity.

Classification: BV2470.K6 C56 2020 (print) | BV2470.K6 (ebook)

Manufactured in the U.S.A.   01/23/20

Abstract

THE KOREAN MISSIONARY MOVEMENT continues to grow quantitatively, sending missionaries all over the world. While in the past it was efficient to send out a great number of Native-born Korean missionaries, today a greater level of quality is required by global mission societies not only to reduce attrition but also to achieve the level of measurable success their supporters demand as a result of their performance-based cultural worldview. While research has been undertaken on Korean missionary burnout prevention, this study sought to understand Korean missionary burnout recovery. Burnout need not spell the end of a missionary's career in global mission.

This study on Korean missionary burnout recovery included thirty-nine research participants who had experienced burnout in missionary service and subsequently recovered. Study participants reported a variety of physical, emotional, and spiritual symptoms, as well as relational difficulties experienced during burnout. This study describes how their self-help approach, characterized by independent, religious self-effort brought only temporary relief. However, through self-care they experienced genuine recovery from burnout. Self-care is holistic and grace-based, characterized by a correct understanding of the roles of God and others in their lives and engagement in authentic community for interdependent care. The path to lasting recovery is characterized by self-care that fosters holistically healthy relationships with God, others, and self.

Keywords: Attrition, burnout, member care, Native-born Korean Missionaries, Korean culture, Korean worldview, culture and psychology, spirituality, emotions, religious philosophies, Self-Help, and Self-Care.

Contents

List of Figures and Tables | x
Acknowledgments | xi

1. **Introduction** | 1
   Problem Statement   4
   Purpose Statement   5
   Research Questions   5
   Definitions   6
   Scope   7
   Significance Statement   7

2. **Literature Review** | 9
   Historical Background of Major Korean Religions   9
   Historical Background of Korean Christianity   11
   The Importance of Member Care   15
   Definition   18
   The Development of Member Care   21
   Korean Member Care   26
   Global Perspectives on Missionary Member Care   30
   Overview of Burnout   42
   Overview of Burnout among Missionaries   48
   Causes of Burnout among Missionaries   50
   Factors Contributing to NBKM Burnout   52
   Overcoming Burnout   73
   Conclusion   73

CONTENTS

3. Methods and Procedures | 75
Why Qualitative Research?   75
Assumptions, Worldview, Paradigms   78
My Philosophical Assumptions and Biases   79
Grounded Theory   81
Participants' Demographics   86
Ethical Considerations   86
Data Analysis Strategies   87
Validation and Verification   88
Conclusion   90

4. Sources and Consequences of Burnout | 92
Sources of Burnout   94
Consequences of Burnout   100
Chapter Four Summary   107

5. Paths to Recovery | 108
Self-Help: Leading to Relapse   109
Self-Initiated Care: Leading to Recovery   112
Chapter Five Summary   131

6. Signs of Recovery | 133
Spiritual Wellness   133
Psychological Wellness   135
Physical Wellness   136
Transformed Mindset   137
Chapter Six Summary   139

7. Discussion, Implications, Applications, and Recommendations | 140
Summary of Findings   140
Discussion of Findings   143
Implications   150
Application: Member Care   156
Chapter Seven Summary   162
Recommendations for Further Research   163
Study Conclusion   164

Appendices

    Appendix A: The Semi-Structured Interviews | 165

    Appendix B: Informed Consent Form | 167

    Appendix C: The Protection of Human Rights in Research Committee (PHRRC) | 169

    Appendix D: Gender Influences | 174

    Appendix E: Group Mentoring and Counseling | 177

    Appendix F: Education as an Aid to Burnout Recovery | 180

Curriculum Vitae | 185

References | 187

List of Figures

1. History of the major religions in Korea | 10
2. The increasing number of Korean missionaries | 14
3. Cross-cultural worker's life time line | 20
4. Conditional patterns leading to culture stress | 21
5. Member care needs and resources (with field examples) | 22
6. A member care model | 24
7. Attrition of single missionaries | 27
8. Attrition of female single missionaries | 27
9. Interaction church–agency | 32
10. Pre-field phases | 33
11. On-field phase | 35
12. Re-entry phase | 36
13. Most important causes of attrition | 54
14. Change of organizational culture for the influx of younger missionaries | 67
15. Three general types of families, and their distinct features: disengagement, differentiation, and enmeshment | 71
16. Recovery approaches: Chart of data self-reported by NBKMs | 93
17. The synergistic influences of being | 145

List of Tables

1. Hart's Comparison of Burnout and Stress | 43

Acknowledgments

I AM FOREVER GRATEFUL to God for His faithfulness and goodness throughout my journey in relationship with Him. On every step of my path, I have been faithfully guided by His ever-present love and peace. As His plan for my life in service to Him unfolds, I am continuously in awe of His grace and mercy. He is a constant Father, eternal friend, and magnificent savior.

I am filled with gratitude to many people for their unique contributions to this dissertation. I am grateful with all of my heart for the contributions of the participants in this research for sharing their experiences, thoughts, and minds so willingly, even though it was not always easy. I also appreciate my committee members, Dr. Richard Starcher, Dr. Rhonda McEwen, and Dr. Tomas Sappington for their careful reading and advice.

I have a special appreciation for Dr. Richard Starcher, my committee chair, who guided me throughout this process and provided constant, patient support. Dr. Starcher's character, leadership, and teaching inspire me and provide me an example of how to be a spiritually and intellectually mature professor. Dr. Rhonda McEwen was another fantastic mentor who gave me careful advice and insightful perspectives on member care. I am grateful for Dr. Thomas Sappington who gave me insights on cross-cultural missionary perspectives. I am also grateful to Dr. Bruce Narramore, founder of Rosemead School of Psychology, and Dr. Nancy Crawford for their encouragement and direction as I pursued my Korean and Asian member care research. In addition, two incredible mission experts Dr. Moon S. S. C. and Lee, T. W., were especially helpful in sharing their Korean resources. I also appreciate the comments of Kelly O'Donnell, Neal Pirolo and Marina Prins as global member care specialists.

My spiritual mentors, Chul Min and Myung Ja Kim are also my spiritual parents and together with the leaders at CMF, they supported me in finding adequate participants and being involved in the practice of member care. The CMF community support members and missionaries were

ACKNOWLEDGMENTS

likewise invaluable as associates in ministry and provided support through prayer and encouragement. I want to also acknowledge the Evangelical Free church mission staff, Pastor Dan, and especially my missionary care prayer members, George and Rosemary in particular. I also want to thank Rev. Park who is director of Interserve USA mission organization, for his character and leadership.

I must also express the deepest gratitude for my three sisters, all of whom deserve my heartfelt thanks. Pastor Won also showed me much kindness through his practical assistance in finishing this study. I am so blessed by Joy People Church, led by senior pastors Taechong Lee and SeongJi Kim, as well as my friends who stood by my side with patience and love. I am also grateful for my colleagues and esteemed friends who also provided guidance and advice in the writing of this dissertation, including Mary Kay, Pauline, Eunyoung, Inhyo, Joseph and Lydia, Jongtae, Amy, and Julia.

Most importantly, I have my family to thank. I want to express my gratitude to my husband who trusted and supported me with his indescribable love and care, without which I could not have finished this study. I also appreciate how my daughter, Grace Yang, has sacrificed by having a mother who is in academia. Their support was irreplaceable, and I could not have done it without them.

1

Introduction

FROM 1997 TO 1999, when I was in my mid-twenties, I worked on one of Youth With a Mission's Mercy Ships. As usual among young Korean missionaries, I set out having little more than a fervent zeal to devote my life to missions—I had no church partnership, a lack of financial support, and no cross-cultural training. Living on board for two years, I found it difficult to adjust to the Westerners surrounding me. At first, I could barely speak any English and was scared I would make serious communication errors and offend my coworkers.

While I was growing up in the traditional Korean church, my pastors taught me to pray hard, read scripture diligently, and be filled with the Holy Spirit. I did not know how to process my experience in cross-cultural ministry. About nine months into my two years on board, my inability to fit in with the ship's American community led me to become emotionally and spiritually burned out. I felt that I was completely alone and had no one other than God who understood me and with whom I could talk.

The Westerners on the ship really seemed to enjoy serving God, whereas as a Korean Christian I thought that in order to serve God I had to work very hard and exercise strict discipline in fulfilling my duty to God. I did not know how to move on to the next step. I felt depressed and my heart was wounded. Not knowing how to solve the cross-cultural problems or understand other people's perspectives, I felt that my efforts and abilities were useless.

While I was looking for emotional and spiritual healing, my pastor encouraged me to study in the U.S. to get to know the Bible better, so I went to a Bible college. Truly knowing God, I gained confidence in being myself, rather than only pleasing pastors and leaders, to fulfill my duty to serve God. I also met my mentor and volunteered in Christian Marriage and Family Ministry (CMF). My mentor helped me to be disciplined and influenced me with his spiritual leadership. Because I had a mentorship with trust and communication and had openness within the close relationships among prayer-community members, I began to see God's plan and myself more clearly. I found love and care through the dynamic sharing of the community. This was a healing process. I was reenergized to move forward to serve God.

My story is not unique; there are many other Korean missionaries who experience burnout, and future missionaries will also. Research shows that "the missionary movement in Korea keeps growing faster than any other national missionary movements in the world."[1] Yet many Korean missionaries face numerous challenges that can lead to burnout: overwork, dutiful obedience, hierarchical structure, and suppression of emotions. According to the following studies on burnout among Korean ministers, cultural values are key influences. Burnout is extremely common among Korean ministers.[2] Moon pointed out that it seems to be a common condition among missionaries as well.[3] S. S. Kang noted: "74.2% of Korean missionaries are pastors and 25.8% are laymen, or tent-maker missionaries."[4] In a more recent study, Moon demonstrated a similar trend: pastor missionaries make up 70.4 percent (including spouses), while 29.6 percent are lay missionaries.[5] S. S. Kang concluded that Korean missions are heavily focused on evangelism and church planting.[6] In light of the fact that more than two thirds of the Native-Born Korean Missionaries (NBKMs) in this study are pastors, D. S. Kim's observations are vital: "Korean pastors of authoritative and demanding traditional backgrounds think that rest and taking care of themselves are the ways of liberal pastors, and that causes burnout to deepen."[7] One reason for this attitude can be found in the culture of Korean ministries. Pan stated, "Coexistence of collectivism and individualism forces the Korean pastors to overload themselves, and confront conflicts of values in their ministry."[8] He further remarked that in Korea the traditionally collectivistic culture "produces conflicts of roles, and forces them to accept their inability to bring about 'win-win' conflict

---

1. Moon, "Recent Korean Missionary Movement," 11.
2. Pan, "Pastoral Counseling."
3. Moon, "Protestant Missionary Movement."
4. Kang, "Korean World Missions," 247.
5. Moon, *Missions from Korea 2013*, 3.
6. Kang, "Korean World Missions."
7. Dong Sung Kim, "Burnout Among Presbyterian," 1.
8. Pan, "Pastoral Counseling," 242.

resolutions."[9] The Korean expects dutiful obedience and strict adherence to the tradition of hierarchy, and thus many ministers not only believe that they have to suppress emotions, but they also attempt to escape personal problems by overworking themselves.

Many pastors who suffer burnout exhibit characteristics of perfectionism and may be seen as workaholics—idealistic, obsessive, narcissistic, and authoritarian.[10] Few have clearly defined boundaries in a context where the clergy is called upon to be involved in a wide variety of activities.[11] They push themselves to exhaustion seeking success, as if implementing a business model. Their drive often fosters unwitting perfectionism that leaves ministers discouraged and disillusioned if they cannot achieve their high standards for themselves and their ministry. When they finally become tired they also become discouraged and depressed.

In seeking to understand their burnout, E. Kim recognized the importance of how missionaries form relationships in the early part of their cross-cultural ministries. Their views of self, others, and society are the most influential factors in their adjustment as missionaries.[12]

Moon, director of the Korea Research Institute for Missions, stated, "Korean missionaries love the romance and adventure of pioneering mission work" based on the example of early Protestant missionaries.[13] Korean missionaries are "strong in starting new projects," but [their] entrepreneurial spirit produces "many lone rangers" who will "start their own ministry instead of joining a team."[14] Additionally, Koreans often lack cross-cultural competency; unlike American missionaries, who have both missionary experience and cross-cultural opportunities in their own country, "Koreans come from a monocultural, monolingual country."[15]

S. O. Lee was concerned that Korean missionaries frequently impose their own culture, which is deeply rooted in Confucianism, on others in their cross-cultural ministries.[16] Cultural values can distort missionary efforts, as seen in such values as obedience; Confucian culture is understood

---

9. Pan, "Pastoral Counseling," 242.
10. Pan, "Pastoral Counseling."
11. Kim, "Attachment Styles."
12. Kim, "Attachment Styles," 2.
13. Moll, "Missions Incredible," 28.
14. Moon as cited in Moll, "Missions Incredible," 28.
15. Moon as cited in Moll, "Missions Incredible," 28.
16. Lee, "Korean Mission."

as duty in social roles that require submission of one category of people to another.[17]

Today's Korean missionaries do not come from a society whose culture is traditionally Christian, and they are not immune to the pressures of following non-Christian values. Four aspects of such pressures are particularly powerful: overwork, dutiful obedience, hierarchical structure, and suppression of emotions. Silzer remarked, "the downside of Confucianism was not being able to deal with conflict, address authorities appropriately, resolve resentment and bitterness," or resist controlling others.[18] They do not discuss their problems and instead keep it all inside. Reflecting on her own experience of Confucian cultural hierarchy and its influence on her behavior as a Christian missionary, Silzer identified several enduring problems:

> I was to consider myself unequal or not as good as men in God's eyes, second, was to do a lot of things in order to please God, and third was to try to control others. These responses were all unconscious.[19]

Furthermore, while there have been efforts to address the lack of oversight by older veteran missionaries, "more systematic efforts are needed . . . .to care for and support younger missionaries."[20]

Like me, many Korean missionaries experience burnout but have no idea how to find the help and healing they need. I received good counsel and mentoring and eventually found help and healing. However, others simply end up leaving ministry altogether.

Problem Statement

Many mission professionals and mission psychologists in the West, within the scope of their member-care efforts, have developed coping strategies to help Western missionaries in cross-cultural ministry to better understand the target culture in order to reduce attrition resulting from burnout. Furthermore, burnout recovery among Western missionaries has been explored. However, it is unknown whether Western approaches are helpful

---

17. Silzer, "Confessions of a Confucianist," 9–10.
18. Silzer, "Confessions of a Confucianist," 7.
19. Silzer, "Confessions of a Confucianist," 7.
20. Moon, "Protestant Missionary Movement," 60.

to Korean missionaries. In the shame-based society of Korea, with its tendency to conceal failure and focus on success, it may be difficult to enable missionaries to be open to constructive ways of dealing with burnout. While common causes of burnout among Korean missionaries have been identified, no qualitative studies have been conducted on how burned out Korean missionaries recover from burnout.

Purpose Statement

The purpose of this grounded theory study is to understand how native-born Korean missionaries recover from burnout. For the purposes of this study *burnout recovery* is defined as overcoming severe emotional, spiritual, and physical fatigue with the result of being fit to reengage in Christian ministry.

Research Questions

This study's central research question is, "How do Korean missionaries describe their recovery from burnout?" The sub-questions are as follows:

1. How do participants describe the role mission organizations play in burnout recovery?
2. How do participants describe the role church organizations play in burnout recovery?
3. How do participants describe the role counseling plays in burnout recovery?
4. How do participants describe the role mentorship plays in burnout recovery?
5. How do participants describe the role a missionary's family plays in burnout recovery?
6. How do participants describe the role spiritual disciplines play in burnout recovery?
7. How do participants describe the role educational efforts play in burnout recovery?

Definitions

Burnout refers to a state in which someone becomes uninterested or depressed and stops functioning effectively, due to the fatigue and frustration of extended stress and overwork.

Native Born Korean (NBK): For the purposes of this study NBK refers to a first-generation Korean, born and educated at least through high school in Korea, and people who are 1.5 generation: Korean born but educated in the United States from middle school or later.

Member Care: The Global Member Care Network suggests that member care refers to the ongoing preparation, equipping, and empowering of missionaries for effective and sustainable life, ministry, and work:

> Member care is the ongoing investment of resources by mission agencies, churches and other mission organizations for the nurture and development of missionary personnel. It focuses on everyone in missions (missionaries, support staff, children and families) and does so over the course of the missionary life cycle, from recruitment through retirement.[21]

More recently, O'Donnell stated:

> Member care is an interdisciplinary field, drawing on the concepts and contributions from behavioral and mental health sciences. It has a growing recognized body of literature, specific types of practitioners/helpers, and various techniques for effecting staff development.[22]

Attrition: For the purposes of this study, attrition refers to missionaries disengaging from missionary service for reasons that deviate from normal expectations. It can include sickness resulting from stress, debilitating and long-lasting personal trauma, or public failure and embarrassment.

Implied definitions used in this study. These definitions come from the data collected from 39 recovered Native-Born Korean Missionaries (NBKMs). They described recovery, what it means to overcome, and features of the *recovery* process:

---

21. O'Donnell, "Going Global," in *Doing Member Care*, 4.
22. O'Donnell, *Global Member Care*, 12.

a. *Recovery:* When one is completely free from the burnout stage and symptoms.
b. *Overcome:* Used more in regards to spiritual burnout, or overcoming spiritual warfare, resulting in the strengthening of their faith.
c. *Recovery process:* Focusing on one's past (emotional trauma, relational conflicts, family upbringing), which affects their current state. Thus, a process of recovery, not only from the issue at hand, but also the need to address issues of the past.

Most missionaries interviewed in this study were for Korean Protestant churches pioneers in the mission field. Regarding the word choice referring to the end of burnout, of the 39 people, only four responded that they *overcame* their burnout, while the rest asserted that they *recovered* from their burnout.

Scope

This study focuses on NBK mission personnel, including lay mission personnel and lay mission directors. It did not include second-generation Korean missionaries.

Significance Statement

This study is significant for at least three reasons. First, it provides Korean missionaries with insights leading to cross-cultural educational strategies for burnout recovery. Most importantly, it reveals the need for missionaries to transform their thinking with regard to how they relate to and serve God.

Second, it helps counselors and home churches provide better member care for burned out Korean missionaries. It reveals the need for a greater understanding of missionary life and service on the part of those who send and those who care for missionaries. This study enables sending churches to resist the temptation to focus wholly on sending by expanding that focus to include care of missionaries and prevention of missionary burnout through systematic support.

Finally, in terms of scholarly research, it advances research into contextually appropriate paradigms and strategies helpful to cross-cultural missionaries. It reveals specifically Korean issues with regard to burnout causes and effects that inform a Korean approach to burnout recovery. In so doing, this study serves as a model for other non-Western studies in missionary member care.

2

Literature Review

THIS CHAPTER SEEKS TO frame the current study by reviewing the theoretical literature shedding light on Korean missionary engagement, missionary burnout, and missionaries' efforts to overcome burnout. In the first section, I recount the history and background of major Korean religions—focusing on Korean Christianity—which is necessary to an adequate understanding of Korean missionary burnout. In the second section I explore the relevant member care literature, which is the larger framework into which a discussion of missionary burnout recovery fits. In the third section I discuss general causes and effects of burnout as a background to understanding missionary burnout in particular. In the fourth section I discuss the literature specifically on missionary burnout. Finally, I explain general strategies non-Korean missionaries have employed to overcome burnout. While Korean missionaries' strategies remain unknown, looking at non-Korean missionaries' strategies will provide a frame of reference for this study of Korean missionaries' journey toward burnout recovery.

Historical Background of Major Korean Religions

For a long time, Korean pastors did not want to admit that Korean Christianity made concessions to Korean culture.[1] However, the influence of the major Korean religions of Shamanism, Buddhism, and Confucianism is clear (see Figure 1). Lee pointed out that Shamanism (e.g., prayer mountains, seeking blessing, faith healing, spiritual exorcism, expectation of miracles) influenced Korean Christianity and made it easier for Koreans to accept the Christian God and the spiritual world.[2] According to Ryu,

---

1. Grayson, "Elements of Protestant Accomodation."
2. Lee, *Holy Spirit Movement*; Chung, *Syncretism*; Lee, "Pentecostal Face of Korean Protestantism;" Park, "Korean Protestant Christianity."

Shamanism, which has continued throughout history, remains at the root of Korean religions, embracing imported religions, and blending with them.³ "Shamanism is the key element in understanding the religious mentality of the Korean people."⁴

In contrast, Buddhist futuristic asceticism corresponds with the unfortunate tendency within Christian eschatology to discount the value of life in this world while over-emphasizing the next. Consequently, those influenced by this perspective may discount the relevance of daily life and society.⁵

Confucianism, too, has impacted Koreans' understanding of Christianity. Confucian ethics are generalized in all areas of Korean society and determine the behavior at all levels, from the individual to the family and community.⁶ The upper middle classes' ethos has been strongly influenced by Confucianism, while the mental outlook of the lower middle classes has been influenced by Shamanism.

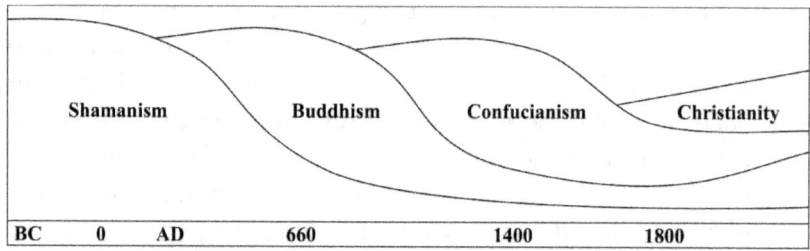

Figure 1. History of the Major Religions in Korea. From Young Hoon Lee, *The Holy Spirit Movement in Korea: Its Historical and Theological Development*, 10. Oxford, UK: Regnum, 2009. Copyright 2009 by Y. H. Lee. Reprinted with permission.

"All the religions took root in the context of the Korean religious soil, and influenced one another."⁷ Together, they have intermingled and formed the background for Christianity in Korea.

Koreans desire to live by the cultural values and religious beliefs in their collective culture. While North Americans tend to conceive of

---

3. Ryu as cited in Lee, *Holy Spirit Movement*.
4. Park as cited in Lee, *Holy Spirit Movement*.
5. Lee, *Holy Spirit Movement*, 16.
6. Park and Cho, "Confucianism."
7. Lee, *Holy Spirit Movement*, 11.

self-identity as individual, rather than collective, Koreans find their concept of identity in their relationships, based on family and community in the social structure.[8] Hofstede explained, "Values are held by individuals as well as by collectivities; culture presupposes a collectivity."[9] Influencing Korean cultural values, Shamanism, Buddhism, and Confucianism have impacted the behavioral patterns and structure of the Korean Christian family and community.

Historical Background of Korean Christianity

Catholicism was introduced to the Korean ruling class in the 18th century, suffered persecution, and saw no substantial growth due to the theological tensions between Catholicism and Confucian tradition.[10] In the late nineteenth century Western missionaries introduced Protestantism to Korea during the expansion of European power and influence in Asia.[11] The Christianity of the American Protestant missionaries strongly influenced the upper classes, particularly the hierarchical ruling class: "Protestantism would not destroy traditional religious heritages, but fulfill their spiritual longings."[12] The Protestant missionary workers set up churches, schools, and hospitals during the late *Chosun Dynasty*, while Korea was in political, cultural, social, and spiritual chaos.[13] J. S. Park argued "the early receptivity by Koreans to Christian faith and the ensuing church growth distracted Korean churches from the need to continue working for the conversion of Korean culture."[14]

Grayson wrote of four factors creating an environment conducive to the rapid acceptance of the Protestant form of Christianity.[15] One, the younger members of the *Chosun Dynasty* were interested in novel and non-traditional ideas. Two, there were many parallels between Christianity and the key values of Korean society, as well as certain elements of the folk religions. Three, the upper class and elite tolerated Christianity and related it to Korean

---

8. Song, "Korean Cultural Family Therapy."
9. Hofstede, *Culture's Consequences*, 5.
10. Lee, *Holy Spirit Movement*; Grayson, "Quarter-Millenium."
11. Yoon Sung-Bum as cited in Lee, *Holy Spirit Movement*.
12. Oak, "Chinese Protestant Literature," 89.
13. Lee, *Holy Spirit Movement*.
14. Park, "Korean Protestant Christianity," 60.
15. Grayson, "Elements of Protestant Accommodation."

nationalism during the Japanese colonial era (1910-1945). Four, there was a lack of any organized religious resistance from other religions.

Pentecostalism influenced early Korean Christianity as well. Pentecostalism ignited in The Great Revival of 1907, which supplied the cornerstone of the Korean Church. "The Movement was based on the Word-centeredness and Penitence."[16] It elevated "the ethical standards of Korean Christians to a notable degree . . . [enacting] changes in their lives."[17]

The period from the 1960s to the 1980s, known as "the period of the unfolding of Korean theology," saw Korean theology "bursting into bloom."[18] It was a period of rapid social change as the nation labored to reconstruct itself after the Korean War (1950-1953) and build an industrial base.

Nation building took place under strict military rule on the basis of national security. These conditions effectively served to suppress human rights.

> Acute feelings of despair and alienation engendered by the interminable social and national ills, i.e., Japanese colonial rule, the Korean War and dire poverty, as well as, anomie [sic] arising from rapid industrialization and urbanization provided psychological impetus for a large segment of the Korean population to seek a satisfying response in the Christian faith. Churches, in turn, served as welfare agencies and as points of contact for displaced individuals, including millions of refugees from North Korea, seeking an identity, comfort and fellowship.[19]

According to A. E. Kim, "Korea's long history of vulnerability to Chinese and Japanese control, Japanese colonialism and the Korean War afforded Christianity a unique opportunity to offer a compelling salvation ethos and promise of both personal and national empowerment."[20] Therefore most churches supported a strong government, which they saw as necessary for national survival and growth. This ethos also resulted in the most rapid period of church growth.[21]

---

16. Park, "Great Revival Movement," 3.
17. Lee, *Holy Spirit Movement*, 30.
18. Kim, "History of Christianity in Korea," 48.
19. Kim, "Korean Religious Culture," 118.
20. Kim, "History of Christianity in Korea," 34.
21. Kim, "Minjung Theology's Biblical Hermeneutics"; Grayson, "Christianity in Korea;" Buswell and Lee, *Christianity in Korea*.

LITERATURE REVIEW

The history of Christianity in Korea is relatively short. The Korean church has experienced continual growth since the revival of 1907, and this growth has been the "driving force for the mission movement."[22] As the church has grown, the nature of its development has been to grow quantitatively as a national movement rather than through spiritual transformation.[23] According to the Korean Statistics Department, nearly 19.7 percent of the population claims to be Protestant Christian.[24] The spread of Christianity in Korea rapidly developed in a short time as many Koreans were in crisis due to wars and persecution.[25] The external pressure placed on the growing Christian movement catalyzed its growth.

In the global context of missions, Jenkins stated, "the center of gravity in the Christian world" is shifting, and the number of African, Asian, and Latin American missionaries is progressively increasing.[26] South Korea, which has become the second-largest missionary sending country next to the United States,[27] sends missionaries "all over the globe."[28] There are over 19,798 Korean missionaries around the world.[29] Lim noted, "the potentiality of Korean churches in the area of world mission is considerable."[30] David Tai-Wong Lee, the dean of the Global Missionary Training Center (GMTC) in Korea, offered at least three reasons he believes the Korean church will increase its number of missionaries:

> First, awareness of the need to be sending out missionaries from local churches; second, efforts of Korean churches working hard to find creative ways to build international partnerships; last, collaboration of the political and economical situation to sending out missionaries."[31]

---

22. Han, "Korean Sending," 372.
23. Clark, "Christianity in Modern Korea"; Lee, *Shift the Paradigm*.
24. Korean Statistics Department, "Statistical Office of the Christians."
25. Kim, "Korean Religious Culture," 118.
26. Jenkins, *Next Christendom*, 2.
27. W. and D. Welliver as cited in Moon, *Korean Missionary Movement*, 2.
28. Whiteman, "Anthropology and Mission," 81.
29. KRIM 2012 as cited in Moon, *Missions from Korea 2013*, para. 1.
30. Lim, *Korea Missionary Training Model*, 3.
31. Lee as cited in Lim, *Korea Missionary Training Model*, 3.

Korean missionaries' involvement in global mission involvement continues to grow exponentially, as shown in Figure 2.[32] By the end of 2008 there were 18,035 Korean missionaries, which marked a 193-fold growth since 1979.

Moon remarked on one important factor contributing to the tremendous growth in the number of Korean missionaries during the last three decades:

> A surplus of seminary graduates is another factor explaining the increase of expatriate Christian workers. Many young Christians who commit themselves whole heartedly to the cause of Christ's Kingdom decide to enter seminary, and then, since there are not enough ministry positions in Korea for all graduates from seminary, many look overseas for their future service. There are negative sides of this phenomenon, but one positive is that it is desirable that more qualified people go to the mission field.[33]

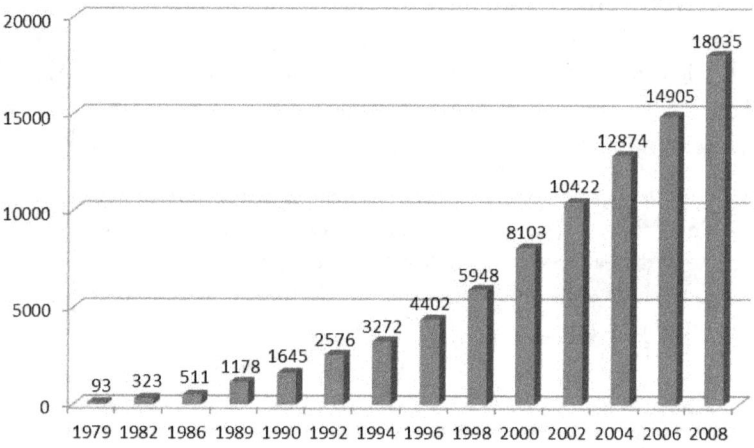

Figure 2. The Increasing Number of Korean Missionaries. From Steve Sang-Cheol Moon, *The Korean Missionary Movement and Leadership Issues* [PDF], 1, retrieved from www.krim.org Copyright 2010 by Author. Reprinted with permission.

According to the *Korean World Mission Association* (KWMA), the Korean church and mission agencies made a commitment to send one million

32. Moon, *Korean Missionary Movement*.
33. Moon, "Protestant Missionary Movement," 60.

tent-making missionaries by 2020 and 100,000 missionaries by 2030.[34] The number of Korean mission agencies has grown steadily also. However, not all have seen this remarkable growth as positive.[35] Moon asserted, "the size of missions agencies keeps growing, but it is legitimate for us to raise questions about their functionality. Rather than competing over numbers, mission agencies need to compete over service. They need to pursue cooperation rather than competition."[36]

> In 2008 there was one agency with members over 2000, three agencies with over 1000 members, nine with over 500 members, and 36 with over 100 members . . . In 1979 Korean missionaries were serving in 26 countries around globe. This number more than tripled by 1990, and then doubled to a total of 177 countries by 2008. For a traditionally monolingual and monocultural people, this phenomenon is quite remarkable.[37]

However, many problems that were anticipated then are now realities.[38] Y. K. Lee noted that the most pressing problem areas that need solutions, in order to improve the quality of missions, are management and missionary care.[39] Another scholar, H. K. Choi, asserted, "Today the Korean Protestant church . . . is facing various problems and difficulties in the area of missional infra-structure unlike her quantitative growth. Support and care of missionaries lie at the center of the problems."[40] He underscored the need for the Korean church to shift from *survival mode* to *developmental* and *growth modes* in order to support missionaries effectively.[41] The next section discusses the importance of member care.

The Importance of Member Care

Missionaries are commonly subjected to stressors that may negatively impact them and their families, leading to burnout and sometimes driving

---

34. KWMA as cited in Ma, "Growth of Christianity in Asia," 4.
35. Ma, "Critical Appraisal," para. 5.
36. Moon, *Korean Missionary Movement*, 3.
37. Moon, *Korean Missionary Movement*, 3.
38. Moon, *Korean Missionary Movement*, 10.
39. Lee, "Study on Stress."
40. Choi, "Construction," 112.
41. Choi, "Construction," 112.

them to seek mental health services. Dodds and Dodds reported that the average cross-cultural worker has approximately 600 points of stress per year on the Holmes/Rahe scale, while 300 points is considered to be the danger zone for potential physical illness.[42] In a more recent study, Dodds and Gardner confirmed these results in their examination of stress levels in cross-cultural workers.[43] According to L. Lindquist, the "mission community needs the ministries and services of both pastoral care and psychological care."[44]

According to Prins and Willemse missionaries' effectiveness in ministering to less reached groups is often diminished by lack of care for the missionary.[45] Responsible not only to God but also to good practice codes and regulatory bodies, missionaries, local churches, mission organizations, and field support must understand the role of missionary care.[46] According to Dodds and Dodds, the combination of long-term stress and a lack of support from their associated organizations have led to startling rates of attrition.[47] Attrition generally refers to premature departure from the field, whether unpreventable (as in cases of health issues or retirement), or, in this case, preventable (as in cases of moral or financial failure).[48]

A comprehensive research project by the World Evangelical Alliance (WEA) Mission Commission—Reducing Missionary Attrition Project (ReMap)—studied mission attrition to determine how many missionaries return early and for what reason.[49] Taylor found, "47% of missionaries leave the field during the first five years; 71% of them do so for preventable reasons."[50] The top five causes of Old Sending Country (OSC) "preventable" attrition involve relationship and character issues, which are not typically the focus of missionary preparation.[51] Recently, researchers for ReMap II have examined missionary retention rates and agency practices,

---

42. Dodds and Dodds as cited in Carter, "Missionary Stressors," 177.
43. Dodds and Gardner, *Global Servants*, 2:140–41.
44. Lindquist, "Pastoral and Psychological Caregivers," 53.
45. Prins and Willemse, *Member Care for Missionaries*, 12.
46. O'Donnell and O'Donnell, *Crossing Sectors*.
47. Dodds and Dodds, "Caring for People in Missions," para. 3.
48. Steffen and Douglas, *Encountering Missionary Life*, 39.
49. Blöecher, "What ReMap I Said."
50. Taylor, "Prologue," 13.
51. Taylor, "Prologue," 13.

identifying which practices contribute most to the retention of missionaries and the prevention of attrition.[52]

Examining the causes of missionary attrition, the Korea Research Institute for Missions (KRIM), discovered that of the 18 percent attrition rate during the first term, 12 percent was for preventable reasons.[53] Moon noted that missionary care would benefit from more systemic efforts.[54]

Commenting on the recent growing inclusion of member care as an essential part of cross-cultural missions in Korea, H. K. Choi asserted that it is essential that all those associated with missions should have an increased awareness of the need for missionary member care.[55] He further noted that in "the 2000s the Korean church and Korean World Missions Association (KWMA) were concerned about a practical approach to missionary member care. Denominations and non-denominational mission agencies established member care departments in their organizational structure."[56] Although statistical records of member care budgets and results of increased efforts toward member care and its effect on attrition among Korean missionaries are indeterminate, it is expected that, as Choi's comments imply, future analysis will be similar to what Western researchers have found.[57]

In 2007, Blöecher found that agencies dedicating more than 20 percent of their budget to member care lowered their attrition rate by one third when compared with those agencies that spent less.[58] Blöecher asserted,

> Member care helps mission workers in so many areas: to grow spiritually and in their personal development, learn new skills, give and receive mutual support, develop a consultative leadership style, practice open communication, build trusted relationships, and increase their flexibility to go through transitions and adjustment."[59]

Tucker and Andrews stated, "Preventive pastoral care of field missionaries is one way in which missions are addressing the increasingly complex spiritual, emotional, and psychological needs of their missionary personnel.

52. Hay et al., "ReMap II Project Methodology," 24–25.
53. Moon, "Missionary Attrition in Korea" PowerPoint, 20.
54. Moon, "Missionary Attrition in Korea" PowerPoint, 20.
55. Choi, "Construction."
56. Choi, "Construction," 112–13.
57. Choi, "Construction"; cf. Hay et al., "ReMap II Project Methodology."
58. O'Donnell, *Global Member Care*.
59. Blöecher as cited in O'Donnell, *Global Member Care*, 44.

One mission identified pastoral care as the most prominent need facing its missionaries."[60]

Definition

O'Donnell and O'Donnell were some of the early pioneers who influenced much of today's thinking regarding member care.[61] While "member care was originally a secular term used in the business world," they believed it also "connotes the mutual responsibility that the people (members) in a group have to each other."[62] After twenty-five years of reflection, O'Donnell defined member care as:

> the ongoing *investment of resources* by sending groups, service organizations, and workers themselves for *the nurture and development* of personnel. It focuses on *every member* of the organization, including children and home office staff. It includes preventative, developmental, supportive, and restorative care . . . to develop resilience, skills, and virtue, which are key to helping personnel stay healthy and effective in their work. Member care thus involves both developing inner resources (e.g. perseverance, stress tolerance) and providing external resources (e.g., team building, logistical support, skill training).[63]

O'Donnell stated that, as a field of study, member care concentrates on embracing diversity in mission through the efforts of trained personnel.[64] Succinctly, O'Donnell asserted that member care supports both mission organizations and their members.[65] Additionally, B. Lindquist urged consideration of issues implicit in or absent from such a definition, which he believed had been developed within the limited context of a North American model of therapy and care.[66] He asserted, "Member care should mean providing a wide variety of services necessary for the development of effectiveness in cross–cultural ministry."[67] B. Lindquist preferred the term

---

60. Tucker and Andrews, "Historical Notes," 31.
61. O'Donnell and O'Donnell, "Perspectives."
62. O'Donnell, *Global Member Care*, 9.
63. O'Donnell, *Global Member Care*, 10.
64. O'Donnell, *Global Member Care*, xv.
65. O'Donnell as cited in Mathis, "Missioning Care Model," 178.
66. Lindquist, "Member Care."
67. Lindquist, "Member Care," 35.

member health, rather than *member care,* because it "starts from prevention rather than remediation."[68]

According to B. Lindquist's complementary view,

> Member care is not about providing counseling services to missionaries on the field. It means coming alongside an organization, understanding the organization's culture and climate, the target culture and climate and what missionaries are supposed to be doing, developing strategies to bring workers to greater effectiveness."[69]

B. Lindquist believes the overarching goal of member care is not help alone, but making people more effective, moving them in an intentional direction[70] and avoiding "creating a member care system that is not complementary with the overall strategy of mission."[71]

In 2002, the idea resurfaced in B. Lindquist's cautions that the tendency in missionary member care scholarship is to see caring for missionaries only in terms of Western psychotherapy. He argued that scholarship on missionary member care must consider the mission agency's unique culture, mission, climate, and strategy for the purpose of empowering the agency's missionaries, as organization members, to achieve greater effectiveness in missions.[72] He suggested, "caring for missionaries needs to be multifaceted" and "take into account not just the personal/psychological, but the interpersonal/social/cultural as well."[73]

Effective missionary member care must not be ignorant of a sending agency's "mission, strategy, culture, and climate," each of which profoundly forms member missionaries.[74] Member care involves linguistic, cultural, emotional, and administrative coaching.[75]

Mathis discussed "the implications of the suggested new connotations in relation to member care's extant models, definitions, and current 'missions ethos,' that is, the basic assumptions, beliefs, and values that

---

68. Lindquist, *Member Health?*, 20.
69. Lindquist, "Member Care," 35.
70. Lindquist, "Caring for Members," 203.
71. Lindquist, "Member Care," 35.
72. Mathis, "Missioning Care Model," 172.
73. Lindquist, "Member Care," 35.
74. Mathis, "Missioning Care Model," 16.
75. Lindquist, "Member Care," 30.

ground its interdisciplinary professional activities."[76] He stated, "the new definition incorporates several fresh ideas (relationships, attitudes, actions, covering, missioning/member care system, missioning capacities, and effectively advancing the organization's missions ethos) and accentuates old ones (health and well-being)."[77]

Prins and Willemse underscored that individual missionaries are also team members:

> As such, their care should be handled in a way that also builds up the team on the field as a whole. Member care is therefore a combination of pastoral care, Christian counseling and human resource development. The aim is to care for and build up the missionary as a total person, so that he will be able to live and minister as a spiritually healthy and effective individual.[78]

Pirolo charted the cross-cultural worker's life time-line (see Figure 3), depicting the physical, emotional, mental, and spiritual lifecycle of cross-cultural workers during their missionary experiences.[79]

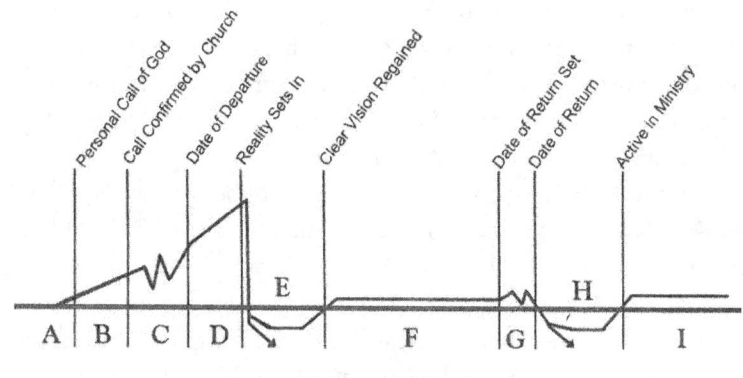

Cross-Cultural Worker's Life Time-Line

Figure 3. Cross-Cultural Worker's Life Time-Line. From Neal Pirolo, *Serving as Senders Today: How to Care for Your Missionaries as They Prepare to Go, are On the Field and Return Home*, rev. ed., 6. San Diego,

76. Mathis, "Missioning Care Model," 177.
77. Mathis, "Missioning Care Model," 182.
78. Prins and Willemse, *Member Care for Missionaries*, 15.
79. Pirolo, *Serving as Senders Today*, 6.

CA: Emmaus Road International, 2012. Copyright 2012 by Author. Reprinted with permission.

Figure 3 shows that periods F to G require prolonged cultural adjustment. Prins and Willemse believed cultural fatigue and stagnation (important precursors of burnout) can occur at the same time.[80] Pirolo saw care for missionaries as extending from before their calling through reentry.[81]

In Figure 4, Dye illustrates conditional patterns leading to cultural stress.[82] Schulz noted that the "formula explains on-going culture stress,"[83] and she referred to Dye's observation that "The different elements on the top line increase the level of stress missionaries experience on the field, while increasing the elements on the second line decreases the level of stress experienced."[84]

Involvement	+	Value Differences	+	Frustration	+	Temperament Differences	+	Unknown Factors	=	Culture Stress
Acceptance	+	Communication	+	Emotional Security	+	Spiritual Resources				

Figure 4. Conditional Patterns Leading to Culture Stress. From T. Wayne Dye, "Cross-Cultural Stress: Stress-Producing Factors in Cultural Adjustment," in *Helping Missionaries Grow: Readings in Mental Health and Mission*, eds. Kelly O'Donnell and Michele Lewis O'Donnell, 336. Pasadena, CA: William Carey Library, 1988. Copyright 1988 by William Carey Library. Reprinted with permission.

The literature just reviewed affirms that member care must intentionally engage not only psychological and cognitive issues, as is often the case in the prevalent understanding of member care, but also the whole being in order to provide holistic care and healing for missionaries experiencing burnout.

The Development of Member Care

O'Donnell offered a widely used model for developing member care, integrating four parameters—*types of staff, type of stages, types of services,* and

80. Prins and Willemse, *Member Care for Missionaries*, 37.
81. Pirolo, *Serving as Senders Today*.
82. Dye as cited in O'Donnell and O'Donnell, *Helping Missionaries Grow*.
83. Schulz, *Why Do Missionary Care?*, 6.
84. Dye as cited in Schulz, *Why Do Missionary Care?*, 7.

types of stressors—as a picture of the needs of, and resources for, the field staff (see Figure 5).[85]

THE MEMBER CARE NEEDS AND RESOURCES GRID (WITH FIELD EXAMPLES)					
Types of Staff	Types of Services				Types of Stages
	Prevention	Development	Support	Restoration	
People: singles, couples, children, families	A. Children's special needs		B. Single women		Mission, family, and individual life cycles
Small group: teams, departments		C. Relief teams		D. Church planting team	Team/group stages
Large group: center, region, agency	E. Organization quality of life		F. Retreat for agencies		Organizational phases
Partnerships: country, people group region, global		G. Partnership training		H. Partnership conflict	Partnership phases
Types of Stressors (each stressor can affect any matrix)					
	Cultural Crises	Historical Human	Occupational Organizational	Physical Psychological	Support Spiritual

Figure 5. Member Care Needs and Resources (with Field Examples). From Kelly O'Donnell, "Member Care on the Field: Taking the Longer Road: Perspective of the Old Sending Countries," in *Too Valuable to Lose: Exploring the Causes and Cures of Missionary Attrition*, ed. William David Taylor, 292. Pasadena, CA: William Carey Library, 1997. Copyright 1997 by William Carey Library. Reprinted with permission.

O'Donnell and Pollock suggested five spheres of care for good practice in member care in *Going Global: A Member Care Model for Best Practice* (Figure 6) *Master care* (the flow of Christ), 2) *Self care* (the flow of community), 3) *Sender care* (the flow of commitment), 4) *Specialist care* (the flow of caregivers), and 5) *Network care* (the flow of connections).[86]

With this in mind, O'Donnell and Pollock provided a visual of five permeable spheres, flowing into and influencing each other (Figure 6). Each sphere included a summarized best practice principle related to the overall "flow of care" needed for staff longevity:[87]

> Sphere 1—Master Care: care from and for the Master—the heart of member care.

---

85. O'Donnell, "Member Care on the Field," 287.
86. O'Donnell, "Going Global," in *Doing Member Care*, 16.
87. Pollock as cited in O'Donnell, "Going Global," in *Doing Member Care*, 16.

Sphere 2—Self and Mutual Care: intentional self-awareness and care for oneself and from supportive and encouraging relationships within the expatriate, home, and national communities—the backbone of member care.

Sphere 3—Sender Care: care by sending groups (churches and agencies) for all mission personnel, from recruitment through retirement—the sustainers of member care.

Sphere 4—Specialist Care: care from professional, personal, and practical specialists—the equippers of member care. There are eight specialist domains of care: Pastoral/Spiritual, Physical/Medical, Training/Career, Team building/Interpersonal, Family/MK, Financial/Logistical, Crisis/Contingency, and Counseling/Psychological.

Sphere 5—Network Care: care from international member care networks to help provide and develop strategic, supportive resources—the facilitators of member care.[88]

---

88. O'Donnell, "Going Global," in *Doing Member Care*, 17-19; cf. O'Donnell, *Global Member Care*, 17.

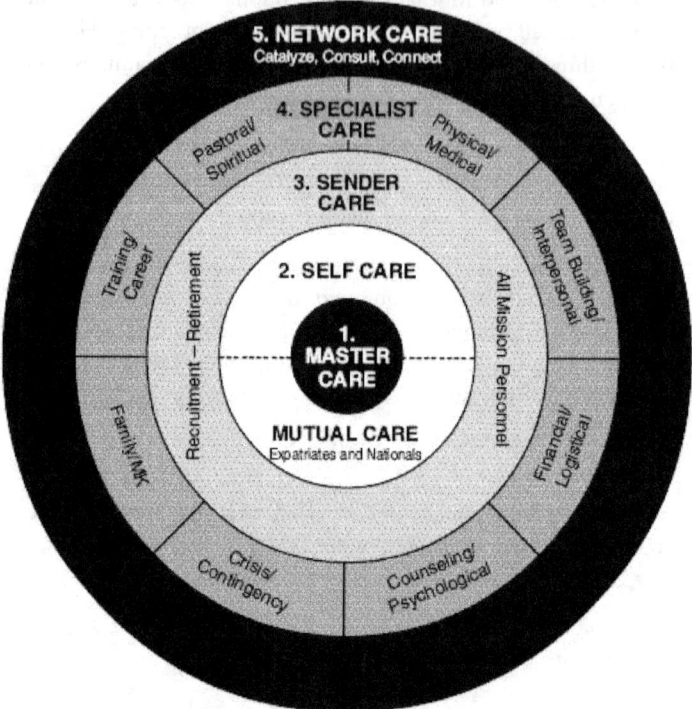

Figure 6. A Member Care Model. From Kelly O'Donnell, "Going Global: A Member Care Model for Best Practice," in *Doing Member Care Well: Perspectives and Practices From Around the World*, eds. Kelly O'Donnell and Michele Lewis O'Donnell, 16. Pasadena, CA: William Carey Library, 2002. Copyright 2002 by William Carey Library. Reprinted with permission.

However, O'Donnell has since expanded this model to include sector care as a sixth sphere:

> People with member care responsibility in mission/aid stay in touch with sectors that are relevant for their work. They are willing to cross into new areas—emphases, projects, disciplines, and fields within related sectors—for mutual learning, exchanging resources, and developing skills. Crossing sectors includes a continuum of involvement which is carefully considered in view of one's primary focus in member care: being informed by, integrating with, and/or immersing in a given sector or part of a sector.[89]

---

89. O'Donnell and O'Donnell, *Global Member Care*, 7.

The expanded model includes "Special Care" replacing "Specialist Care," emphasizing the skills necessary for both specialists as well as those with member care responsibilities in the field. Another change was an added emphasis on the need for member care networks. "Sender Care" was also expanded to include member care for Christian workers not sent by a particular agency, yet still in need of member care. Spheres four and five significantly overlap and contribute to member care in areas such as human resources and health sciences. The updated model maintains its firm emphasis on growth and development as well as holistic care.[90]

Steffen and McKinney Douglas wrote that sending bodies, responsible for the well-being of the missionary, need a "system view of the life cycle of the cross-cultural worker" and require sober "recruitment, selection, funding, pre-field training, geographical placement, selection of teammates, and training provided on field, while on . . . home assignment (including re-entry), and during retirement."[91] This must also include care specialists at home and abroad, to "help reduce preventable attrition" since missionaries can be overwhelmed by the strenuous duties of their cross-cultural labors.[92]

Gardner made clear the layered purpose of member care: members receive care while preserving the efficacy of the organization.[93] Similarly, H. K. Choi asserted, "An organization must . . . respect human value in the relationship with God."[94] D. C. Kim underscores the idea of "*missio Dei*"—the *mission is God's*.[95] That mission involves facilitating personal relationships with God. Consequently, the Korean perspective on missionary care must be rooted in spiritual considerations and not merely psychological. H. K. Choi further affirmed, "Member care must be constructed and applied in a holistic form . . . throughout the missionary life and be applied to all mission personnel participating in God's mission."[96] Holistic transformation must include spiritual and cognitive aspects.

---

90. O'Donnell, *Global Member Care*.
91. Steffen and Douglas, *Encountering Missionary Life*, 156.
92. Steffen and Douglas, *Encountering Missionary Life*, 156.
93. Gardner, "Member Care and Missions."
94. Choi, "Missionary Member Care System," 113.
95. Bosch as cited in Kim, "Missiological Study," 10.
96. Choi, "Missionary Member Care System," 113.

Korean Member Care

In the context of Korea, it is only since the middle of the 1990s that Korea has been able to network with Western mission organizations regarding member care. It was through David Tai-Woong Lee, who had been serving as a committee member of WEA for the sake of Korean missionary development, that the concept of member care was introduced into the arena of Korean missions.[97] The awareness of the importance of member care has only just begun in Korea, and thus there is still need for development in the area.

Lack of Korean Member Care

According to Moon, director of the Korea Research Institute for Missions, Korean mission agencies have focused on numeric growth.[98] Moon quantified the rate of attrition for Korean family missionaries:

> First, roughly 833 units (new families/singles) went to the mission field during the period 1992-1994. Secondly, roughly 153 families/singles came back home during the same period. Thirdly, roughly 101 units came back home for preventable reasons.... The attrition rate of the 153 units out of the 833 units is 18.4%, implying that if 100 missionaries go out, 18 will come back early.... Twelve of these would come back for undesirable reasons.[99]

The attrition rate for single male and female Korean missionaries is 46 percent. However, of greater significance is that over twice as many single (never been married) female missionaries (63 percent) returned home as single males, most due to marriage pressures from their own families.[100] See Figures 7 and 8.

---

97. Choi, "Missionary Member Care System," 93.
98. Moon, *Acts of Koreans*.
99. Moon, "Missionary Attrition in Korea: Opinions of Agency Executives," 135.
100. Moon, "Missionary Attrition in Korea: Opinions of Agency Executives," 135–36.

LITERATURE REVIEW

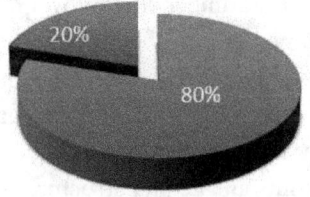 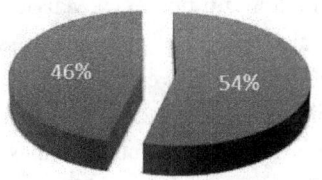

■ Married Missionaries 80%
■ Single Missionaries 20%

■ Attrition/Married 54%
■ Attrition/Single 46%

Figure 7. Attrition of Single Missionaries. From Steve Sang-Cheol Moon, "Missionary Attrition in Korea: Opinions of Agency Executives," in *Too Valuable to Lose: Exploring the Causes and Cures of Missionary Attrition*, ed. William David Taylor, 135. Pasadena, CA: William Carey Library, 1997. Copyright 1997 by William Carey Library. Reprinted with permission.

From 1992 to 1994, Moon reports a perennially high attrition rate (73 percent) among single female missionaries, underscoring the need for more training and specialized care.[101]

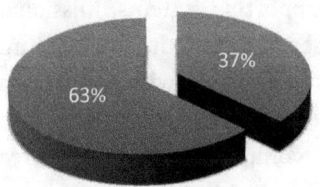 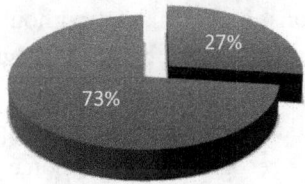

■ Male in Single Total 37%
■ Female in Single Total 63%

■ Male in Single Attrition 27%
■ Female in Single Attrition 73%

Figure 8. Attrition of Female Single Missionaries. From Steve Sang-Cheol Moon, "Missionary Attrition in Korea: Opinions of Agency Executives," in *Too Valuable to Lose: Exploring the Causes and Cures of Missionary Attrition*, ed. William David Taylor, 135-36. Pasadena, CA: William Carey Library, 1997. Copyright 1997 by William Carey Library. Reprinted with permission.

101. Moon, "Missionary Attrition in Korea: Opinions of Agency Executives."

Moon noted, "Slightly more than half of all Korean missionaries are female (52.0 percent). Married missionaries outnumber singles by a ratio of almost 9 to 1."[102] Single missionaries as a percentage of all missionaries fell by half between 1994 and 2008. The membership of denominational mission agencies consists mostly of married seminary graduates and large interdenominational agencies prefer married members over singles.[103] Within the traditional Korean patriarchal family and gender structure, Korean churches, almost universally, have left women "subordinated within the church hierarchy and authority structure."[104]

J. S. Park noted, regarding Korean women within the Korean Christian church, that the unmarried female missionary faces issues of status, gender, and authority.[105] They are often excluded or discouraged from any leadership role, including any teaching roles.[106] However, Lee observed that missionary wives are not primarily helpers, but are *missionaries, called by God*, along with their husbands.[107] He asserted that their spirituality, as well as mission training, should be enhanced. Unmarried female missionaries as well are called by God and should be supported in this identity.

Need for Korean Member Care Support Systems

In addition to gender concerns, Moon reported: "As a weakness for Korean missions, it is clear that without proper supporting systems, missionary movement cannot continue its growth. Agencies must therefore commit themselves to establishing better support systems both within Korea and abroad."[108] MK hostels and camps have been developed as a result of a greater recognition of missionary families' complex needs: "The Korean mission community has been slow in moving beyond stereotypes of the rugged, individualistic missionary or missionary family and truly grasping the significant needs that member care addresses."[109] In 1993 KWMA, in an attempt to help missionary children develop a secure identity, established

---

102. Moon, *Korean Missionary Movement*, 4.
103. Moon, *Korean Missionary Movement*, 4.
104. Park, "Korean Protestant Christianity," 59.
105. Park, "Unmarried Single Women," 29.
106. Park, "Unmarried Single Women," 29.
107. Lee as cited in Park, "Missionary Member Care," 56.
108. Moon, "Protestant Missionary Movement," 62.
109. Moon, "Mission from 2012," 85.

their definition of the purpose of education for Korean missionary children: "to be citizens of God, citizens of the world, and citizens of Korea."[110] Their intention was to help missionary children secure this identity through education, often by sending them to Korean universities.[111]

These family concerns were included by Moon when he identified seven specific areas requiring effective member care support systems:[112]

1. Marriage status and gender
2. Communication skills
3. Marriage and Family issues
4. On-field care
5. Education
6. Screening
7. Quality Control: churches and agencies to maintain the quality of missionary work[113]

Korean leadership's managerial capacity is lacking in strong member care support, and "numerical growth alone does not guarantee maturity and stability of missionary movement."[114] Passion alone is insufficient to sustain a missionary; the missionary candidate must have the appropriate character and characteristics.[115] The expectation is that with the increase of culturally appropriate member care, both at home and on the field, NBKM burnout will decrease. Awareness of and ethos for the quality control of missions should be generated and raised in church and mission agencies. Korean Christians tend to view missionaries unrealistically as spiritual giants who have no emotional problems.[116] Therefore, they fail to recognize that missionaries are vulnerable to stress and need holistic care, including emotional, spiritual, cultural, relational, and psychological member care in order to prevent burnout. While Korean churches pray for their missionaries' safety and peace, they subconsciously also have high expectations for them to lead unrealistic

110. Park as cited in Youn and Muller, "Discussion about Difficulties," 272.
111. Back as cited in Youn and Muller, "Discussion about Difficulties," 277.
112. Moon, "Missionary Attrition in Korea: Opinions of Agency Executives," 137.
113. Moon, "Missionary Attrition in Korea: Opinions of Agency Executives," 139–40.
114. Moon, *Korean Missionary Movement*, 2.
115. Moon, "Missionary Attrition in Korea: Opinions of Agency Executives," 139–40.
116. Kim, "Attachment Styles."

lives of sacrifice and "to miraculously further the outcome of the gospel."[117] Rather than placing unattainable goals upon these missionaries, congregations need to transform their expectations and shift their focus from the missionary himself to God's work through that missionary. Focusing almost exclusively on the growth and mobilization of mission, the Korean church has often suffered from a lack of self-reflection and attention to potential mission reform.[118] Y. K. Park argued that the Korean church should consequently seek to sustain their widespread growth through a heightened sense of self-reflection and pursuit of necessary reform.[119]

Global Perspectives on Missionary Member Care

Member care is about aiding in the development of the resiliency and godliness needed to do missionary work.[120] Yet too often missionaries who ask for help from a member care worker are perceived as "unspiritual or weak, and not trusting the Lord enough."[121] Effective member care, however, helps to "balance the realistic demands of suffering and sacrifice with the realistic needs for support and nurture in our lives."[122] Mental health professionals have been the primary developers of missionary member care. Among them, B. Lindquist focuses on mentoring, coaching, and internationalizing[123] while Lewis and Lewis focus on both personal and professional development—strategy related coaching for further equipping workers.[124] The ReMap II researchers found that "training is not theoretical alone, but that the whole person should be transformed. Character-building is an essential element to the success of training and is the basis for life-long-learning that is so needed on the mission field."[125] Discussion follows on (a) the models of church and the agency member care, (b) missionary life cycles member care and (c) various support systems from member care models. Also, mission professionals who are researching

117. Choi, "Missionary Member Care System," 95–96.
118. Park, "Historical Overview," 16.
119. Park, "Historical Overview."
120. O'Donnell, "International Model"; O'Donnell, *Global Member Care*.
121. O'Donnell, "Staying Healthy," 3.
122. O'Donnell, "Staying Healthy," 3.
123. Lindquist, "Member Care," 36.
124. Lewis and Lewis, "Coaching Missionary Teams."
125. Hay et al., "ReMap II Project Methodology," 59.

missionary care will be introduced. Examining these strategies and issues of global member care is important to this study because Korean missionaries, who often have inadequate missionary support systems, can benefit from the contextualization of these methods.

Models of Member Care within the Church and the Agency

To set the stage for the discussion of various models of member care, it is important to understand how missionaries interact with the sending church. W. D. Taylor's research, presented in the book, *Too Valuable to Lose*, tells us, "Our long-term focus was and is pastoral and is directed to the global mission force in the areas of selecting and screening, preparing and training, sending strategizing and shepherding and encouraging missionaries."[126] Similarly, Girón suggested a missionary model (see Figure 9) that integrates "selection, training, sending, and the pastoral care and supervision of the missionary."[127] Such a model could help committed career missionaries stay where God has called them.

Herr stated concisely, "The missionary is an extension of his local church."[128] Consequently, the mission organization and the local church must cooperatively share expertise and take responsibility for offering effective support to a missionary.[129] O'Donnell suggested, "Sending churches can support workers in the areas of logistics, finances, prayer, communication, reentry."[130] Just like *support teams*, the sending church must be trained to send and serve their workers well.

---

126. Taylor, "Prologue," xiv.
127. Girón, "Integrated Model," 28.
128. Herr, "Doing Your Job?," 43.
129. Prins and Willemse, *Member Care for Missionaries*, 29.
130. O'Donnell, "Staying Healthy," 16.

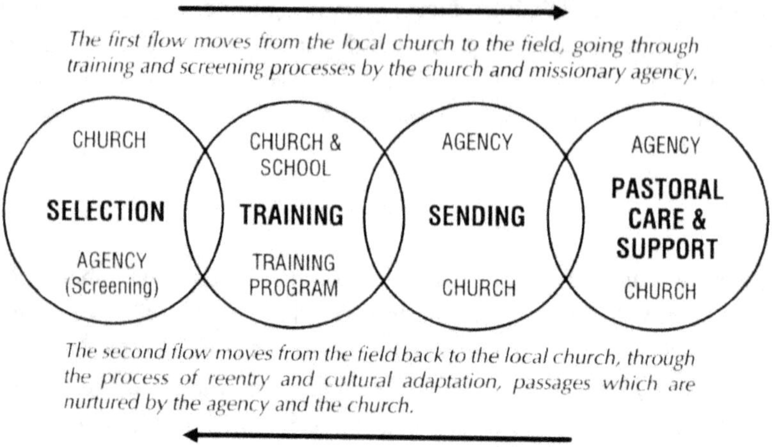

The first flow moves from the local church to the field, going through training and screening processes by the church and missionary agency.

```
    CHURCH         CHURCH &         AGENCY          AGENCY
                    SCHOOL
                                                  PASTORAL
  SELECTION        TRAINING        SENDING         CARE &
                                                   SUPPORT
    AGENCY         TRAINING
  (Screening)      PROGRAM         CHURCH          CHURCH
```

The second flow moves from the field back to the local church, through the process of reentry and cultural adaptation, passages which are nurtured by the agency and the church.

Figure 3-1. An Integrated Model of Missions

Figure 9. Interaction Church—Agency. From Rodolfo "Rudy" Giron, "An Integrated Model of Mission," in *Too Valuable to Lose: Exploring the Causes and Cures of Missionary Attrition*, ed. William David Taylor, 26. Pasadena, CA: William Carey Library, 1997. Copyright 1997 by William Carey Library. Reprinted with permission.

As mentioned previously, in order for sending churches to develop a proper member care strategy, they need to understand the stages and challenges of missionary life. From the pre-field period to re-entry, the goal for sending churches should not only be to send more missionaries, but to be certain that they are cared for effectively.[131]

The Missionary Life Cycle Member Care

I will explain specific member care strategies suggested by various professional missionary member care scholars and psychologists, according to the flow of the pre-field, on field, and re-entry categories.[132] The pre-field, on-field, and re-entry models are based on research by Prins and Willemse.[133]

---

131. O'Donnell, "International Model," 38.
132. Prins and Willemse, *Member Care for Missionaries*; O'Donnell, "International Model."
133. Prins and Willemse, *Member Care for Missionaries*, 41–53.

The pre-field phase

This phase includes selection, personal preparation, formation of the support team, and field orientation.[134] They facilitate the cataloging of a candidate's behavior, personality, and practical skills. This information can be used to identify emotional problems and personality disorders, address areas of personal development, and assist in career planning to determine candidate suitability for a specific environment, culture, or position. The missionary should be well prepared spiritually and emotionally, and additional skills should be acquired where needed. Schubert suggested, "The key to wise selection is in the testing and pre-field evaluation."[135]

Likewise, B. Lindquist evaluates missionary candidates by looking for evidence of stability in their home culture. He defines stability as the ability to remain stable in an unstable environment. "Should the mission be a hospital for dysfunctional missionaries? Or, a coaching, or fitness training center?"[136] The pre-field phase has four categories: selection, personal preparation, the support team, and field orientation.

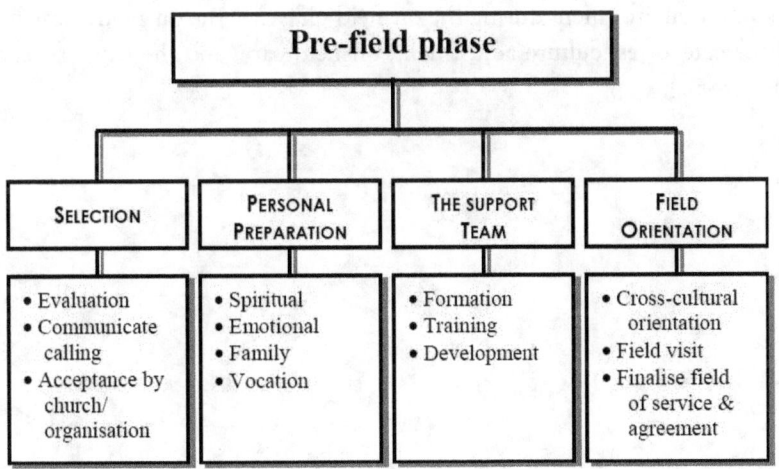

Figure 10. Pre-Field Phases. From Marina Prins and Braam Willemse, *Member Care for Missionaries: A Practical Guide for Senders,* 2nd ed.

---

134. Prins and Willemse, *Member Care for Missionaries.*
135. Schubert, "Current Issues," 87.
136. Lindquist, "Member Care," 40.

[PDF], 42. Brackenfell, South Africa: Member Care Southern Africa, 2009. Copyright 2009 by Authors. Reprinted with permission.

In the pre-field phase, a family evaluation should include the wife and children, allowing them to express their calling to the sending church leadership. Discussion and prayer should precede their acceptance as missionaries by the sending church. During this process, the support team should be formed within the sending church, equipped, and begin functioning.[137] O'Donnell describes the kind of training needed to equip the support team: "Training includes such areas as: counseling, crisis care/debriefing, organizational systems/dysfunction, interpersonal skills, personnel development, and family/marriage."[138]

The on-field phase

During a missionary's time of adjustment, it is important for the support team back home to understand what the missionary is experiencing. They must be able to give him the necessary support, as he has become a part of a new environment during the on-field phase.[139] The on-field phase has three categories: culture adjustment, on-field care, and the support team (Figure 11).

---

137. Prins and Willemse, *Member Care for Missionaries*, 70–71.
138. O'Donnell, "Staying Healthy," 19.
139. Prins and Willemse, *Member Care for Missionaries*, 49.

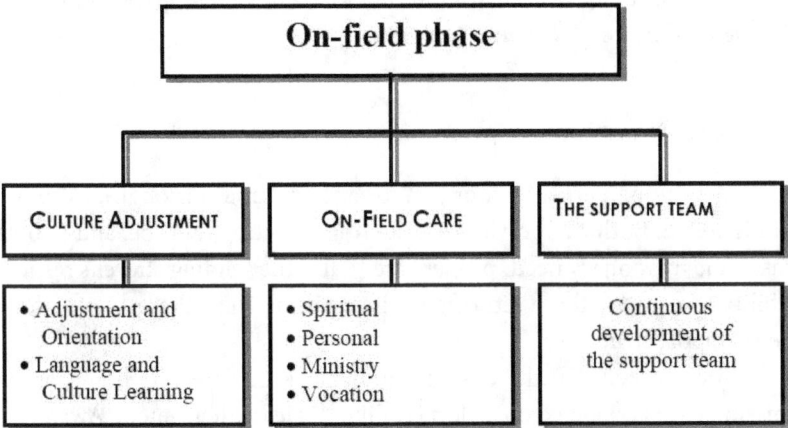

Figure 11. On-Field Phase. From Marina Prins and Braam Willemse, *Member Care for Missionaries: A Practical Guide for Senders*, 2nd ed. [PDF], 48. Brackenfell, South Africa: Member Care Southern Africa, 2009. Copyright 2009 by Authors. Reprinted with permission.

During the on-field phase, it is advisable for the missionary to engage in full time study of the language and culture. Personal care includes aspects such as physical and emotional care and the continuous development of missionaries.[140]

Steffen and McKinney Douglas urged the recognition of an important challenge in missions work: "Burnout and posttraumatic stress disorder (PTSD) occur, and missionaries need help and support to face them."[141] The relationship between psychological symptoms and the everyday stresses of the mission field likewise has been noted by Foyle.[142] Duhe recommended that these field-based missionaries receive member care.[143] For example, *the Mobile Member Care Team (MMCT) model is designed to facilitate community development in the field. The driving force in this model is the development and education of peer response teams and mentoring leadership, sending out competent professionals equipped to provide member care to missionaries.*[144] This vision is executed through seminars covering

140. Prins and Willemse, *Member Care for Missionaries*, 50.
141. Steffen and Douglas, *Encountering Missionary Life*, xv.
142. Foyle, *Honorably Wounded Stress*, 70.
143. Duhe, "When There is No Shepherd."
144. Mobile Member Care Team, www.mmct.org.

important issues for missionaries in the field: transitions, grief, team building, debriefing, and burnout prevention.

The re-entry phase

Re-entry can be permanent, or just for a short time (furlough), as shown in Figure 12. Both can prove a disorienting and stressful time, and in both cases, the missionary needs proper care.[145] It is the sending church's responsibility to care for these returning missionaries. Thus, there is need for a new support structure.

Pirolo noted that there is an initial shock in returning home, as the missionary has changed on all levels of life.[146] He further stated, "Awareness of factors of reentry can prepare you to become a strongly supportive friend in the "coming back home" process.[147]

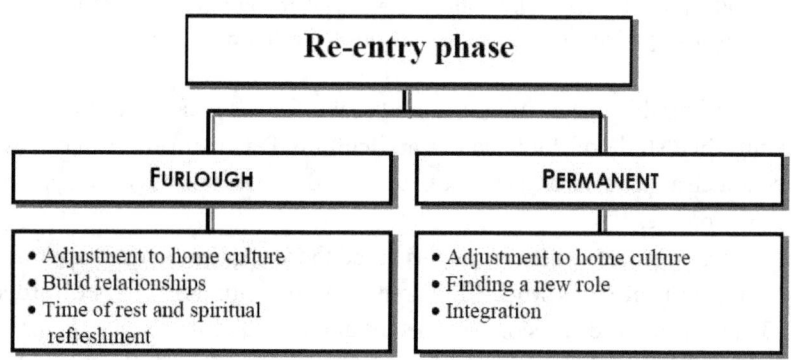

Figure 12. Re-Entry Phase. From Marina Prins and Braam Willemse, *Member Care for Missionaries: A Practical Guide for Senders*, 2nd ed. [PDF], 52. Brackenfell, South Africa: Member Care Southern Africa, 2009. Copyright 2009 by Authors. Reprinted with permission.

---

145. Jordan, *Re-Entry*, 17–18.
146. Pirolo, *Serving as Senders*, 138; cf. Pirolo, *Serving as Senders Today*.
147. Pirolo, *Serving as Senders*, 139; cf. Pirolo, *Serving as Senders Today*.

Various Supporting Systems

There are several varieties of member care support systems, three of which are addressed here: online member care, organizational member care, and spiritual and psychological member care. This section also deals with member care strategy challenges.

Online member care

With missionaries placed in different geographical locations, "missionary member care begins with the missionary. Field leadership soon becomes an integral part of missionary care through email."[148] An expanding member care service is e-consultation, using technology to allow the mental health practitioner to reach a distant missionary without leaving his country. Missionary Outreach Support Services (MOSS) provides mental health services via e-mail.[149] MOSS services offer "psycho-educational information to increase a missionary's well-being and act as a preventative service by providing both support and information catered to the missionary's individual need."[150]

Organizational member care

Understanding organizational factors and leaders is also important to reducing burnout by providing member care. William Taylor of World Evangelical Alliance (WEA) Missions Commission helped publish research on missionary members. Among the major contributors, Kelly O'Donnell has helped introduce to the evangelical circle a model for *best practice*. This practice, spearheaded by the humanitarian community, can be also termed "good practice" and refers to "recognized principles and performance standards for the management and support of staff."[151] These principles can be written and essentially are public statements "formed, adopted, distributed, and reviewed by organizations."[152] O' Donnell's *Global Member Care* goes

---

148. Steffen and Douglas, *Encountering Missionary Life*, 157.
149. Schwandt, "Missionary Outreach Support Services," 208.
150. Schwandt, "Missionary Outreach Support Services," 28.
151. O'Donnell, "Going Global," in *EMQ*, 212.
152. O'Donnell, "Going Global," in *EMQ*, 212.

further and features human rights, along with Scripture and healthy practice codes, as a critical foundation for good practice in member care.[153]

Aid organizations desiring to support their staff need to consider the combined effects that the environment, tasks, and personal experience have on their international staff members. Such staff members often work in areas where they are under-resourced, exposed to trauma, and faced with the realities of human suffering.[154] "Organizational leaders are responsible to select and adequately train their staff."[155] It is critical that mission organizations have discerning and professional staff to aid the selection and pre-field evaluation process, sending out missionaries who have shown competence for the field through psychological testing and screening.[156]

A key role in preparing staff to deal with stress is performed by mission agency support—providing the four types of appropriate member care services described by O'Donnell:

1. Prevention approaches: Decrease stressors. Eliminate problems before they arise: choose healthy candidates, less prone to problems on the field, and do reasonable person-job matching to decrease work frustrations.

2. Development approaches: Help missionaries acquire and improve important coping skills: conflict resolution training to help team members work through inevitable tensions, or pre-field instruction in language-learning techniques to help missionaries with language mastery.

3. Supportive approaches: Encourage missionaries experiencing stress: pray together, offer brief counseling, or send field coaches. Mission agencies play a crucial role in staff preparation for dealing with stress and providing mutual care.

4. Restoration approaches: Debilitating stress and problem reduction: crisis intervention team sent to missionaries needing immediate care. These efforts may not undo damage, but they will hopefully minimize the effects of potential continuing problems.[157]

---

153. O'Donnell, *Global Member Care*.
154. Eriksson et al., "Expatriate Humanitarian Aid Workers."
155. Eriksson et al., "Expatriate Humanitarian Aid Workers," 671.
156. Schubert, "Current Issues," 87.
157. O'Donnell and O'Donnell, "Understanding and Managing Stress," 116–17.

A balanced approach to member care includes "prevention, personal development, and ongoing supportive service."[158] Understanding the interdependent nature of these aspects of member care is essential for ensuring that member care be ethically developed and executed through the mission agency.[159]

Missionary care should be holistic. Mathis supported this idea when he emphasized "Missions ethos" as the combination of calling, beliefs, assumptions, and values shared by a mission organization's members as their reason for existing.[160] Similarly, B. Lindquist asserted that *Member health* (Member care) continues to become an organic component in organizational life: "By organic, the concepts, mindsets, stances, activities inherent in member health flow throughout all the components of the organization, the team, the sending and receiving organizations and entities such that everyone is playing a part."[161]

Spiritual and psychological member care

In contrast to Korean missions, Western member care generally emphasizes psychology and counseling to prevent burnout. However, holistic healing of cross-cultural burnout also demands a focus on spiritual maturity. Spiritually healthy missionaries appear more likely to stay on the field longer. Bergaas studied 240 Norwegian missionaries and discovered that burnout rates were lower among missionaries who exhibited spiritual maturity.[162] Strauss and Narramore pointed to the importance of the sending church being recognized as central to identifying, preparing, and developing broad spiritual and emotional support systems for its missionaries at the time the missionary is first selected.[163] Without this support system, burnout becomes an imminent possibility.

The preeminent attribute of successful missionaries may be Christian character, but, as former missionaries and missionary caregivers Dodds and Dodds, found: "Spiritual growth happens co-incidentally for most missionaries, as they are pressed to God by the extreme stresses. But the lack

---

158. Lindquist, "Counseling and Clinical Care," 71.
159. O'Donnell and O'Donnell, "Ethical Concerns," 260, 267.
160. Mathis, "Missioning Care Model."
161. Lindquist, *Member Health?*, 44.
162. Bergaas, "Relationship of Spirituality to Burnout."
163. Strauss and Narramore, "Increasing Role," 303.

of care also pushes some out of mission work and leads to disillusionment, discouragement and even estrangement from God."[164] The stressful life in the field opens many wounds, but the pressure to press on for fear of admitting weakness simply magnifies the stress, as noted by Foyle.[165] Many missionaries go on living spiritually vital lives, but for others, spiritual mentors joining alongside them would benefit the spiritual dimension of their lives. On the field, missionaries may primarily focus on the volume of work rather than personal growth, and "easily lose sight of the Spirit's direction."[166] According to Stirling, "Missions should be ready to provide mentors for their younger missionaries because this group expects spiritual mentors."[167]

Missionary member care must focus on both the psychological and spiritual aspects, together contributing to greater productivity. According to Coe, when the Christian life is lived in autonomy—that is, not dependent on the work of the Spirit in the believer's heart—the result is a continuous striving in moralism, which ends in burnout.[168] This development underscores the necessity for nurturing of the missionary's soul and deepening of his relationship with God. Foyle concluded that relationship with God allows the individual to gain their spiritual strength from direct relationship with him.[169] The spiritual health of a missionary will determine the effectiveness of their adjustment to the culture and the effectiveness of their ministry.[170] Also critical to the healing of a missionary from burnout is community: "Healing is best promoted in the loving, caring, body of Christ in intentional community."[171] Leslie's research concluded, "satisfaction with one's spiritual life is nurtured and supported in the context of caring relationships and the practice of the spiritual disciplines."[172] O'Donnell and Pollock's model likewise "places 'Master Care' at its core—that is the relationship with God, care from/for the Master."[173]

---

164. Dodds and Dodds, "Caring for People in Missions," 5.
165. Foyle, *Honorably Wounded Stress*, 26.
166. Tidwell as cited in Nichols, "Spiritual Mentoring Program," 4.
167. Stirling as cited in Nichols, "Spiritual Mentoring Program," 47.
168. Coe, "Resisting the Temptation," 55–56.
169. Foyle, *Honorably Wounded Stress*, 270–71.
170. Barnett et al., "Psychological and Spiritual Predictors," 29.
171. Dodds and Dodds, "Caring for People in Missions," 14.
172. Andrews, "Ministry Satisfaction," 110.
173. O'Donnell, "Going Global," in *Doing Member Care*, 17.

Challenges in Implementing Member Care Strategies

It is an open question whether Western strategies to overcome burnout are also applicable to the member care of non-Western organizations and cultures. Korean missionaries, suspicious of counseling, are educated to believe that if they pray hard, without ceasing, and cry out to God, the Holy Spirit is obligated to give help. They believe spirituality is like a contract. This understanding is prevalent and is often deeply rooted in their belief system. There is a great need for comprehending the various distinctions of Christian spirituality and formation in cross-cultural conditions. According to Augsburger,

> The intercultural person is not culture-free (a hypothetical and undesirable state). Rather, the person is culturally aware. Awareness of one's own culture can free one to disconnect identity from cultural externals and to live on the boundary, crossing over and coming back with increasing freedom.[174]

O'Donnell noted, "Psychosocial support is increasingly being recognized as a necessary and ethical organizational resource."[175] He wrote that the strategies of member care from all people groups need to "be raised up and trained . . . to work both within their own cultures and cross-culturally" and suggested a two-fold strategy for such member care: supporting the diversity of people involved in Christian mission and training others from various cultures to be quality care providers.[176]

A major reason for the lack of preventative care against burnout is that people fail to understand they have gone through burnout themselves. In order for intervening and healing care to be effective, it is necessary to first understand one's own condition. However, many times the concept of burnout is not even grasped and understood in Korean society. Koreans understand symptoms of burnout, but often cannot define it. Therefore it is important to be explicitly informed regarding the condition of burnout.

---

174. Augsburger, *Pastoral Counseling Across Cultures*, 13.
175. O'Donnell, "Staying Healthy," 17.
176. O'Donnell, "Staying Healthy," 21.

Overview of Burnout

Maslach and Leiter stated, "Burnout is reaching epidemic proportions among North American workers today."[177] There is a notable difference between burnout and the general symptoms of stress; an examination will presently be made of the possible physical, spiritual, emotional, cultural, and psychological factors inherent in burnout.

According to Y. H. Kim, the closest Korean concept of physical and spiritual burnout is *Tal-jeen* (탈진).[178] K. J. Lee brought up an issue of primary importance: Koreans generally misunderstand the concept of *Taljin* (burnout).[179] Perceiving it in measurable degrees and evaluating the condition at any one point in time, they compare their level of endurance to their perceived level of *Taljin*. Consequently, this *Taljin* can go undiagnosed so long as endurance outweighs burnout. Lee concludes that *Taljin is not an event, but a process*. This process can thus go unnoticed until the point of total breakdown, when *Taljin* finally overcomes endurance. Therefore, it is better understood in terms of frequency and duration: the symptoms of *Taljin* are the consequences of a process that takes place over time.[180]

Definition

Schubert noted that burnout is usually a precursor to depression. The term burnout has been used in occupational fields: Western society describes victims of excessive stress in the business world as burning out, and this term "can be applied to pastors and missionaries, as well."[181] According to psychologist Maslach, burnout is "a syndrome of emotional exhaustion, depersonalization, and reduced personal accomplishment that can occur among individuals who 'do people work' of some kind."[182] Further, Maslach and Leiter's definition brings to light some of the symptoms and implications of burnout:

> Burnout is the index of the dislocation between what people are and what they have to do. It represents erosion in values, dignity, spirit, and will—an erosion of the human soul. It is a malady that

---

177. Maslach and Leiter, *Truth about Burnout*, 1.
178. Kim, "Depression of Korean Missionaries," 60.
179. Lee, "Pastor, Why Pastor Burnout?"
180. Lee, "Pastor, Why Pastor Burnout?"
181. Schubert, *What Missionaries Need to Know*, 2.
182. Maslach, *Burnout*, 3.

spreads gradually and continuously over time, putting people into a downward spiral from which it's hard to recover. What might happen if you begin to burnout? Actually three things happen: you become chronically exhausted; you become cynical and detached from your work; and you feel increasingly ineffective on the job.[183]

They consider burnout to be a state of exhaustion resulting from excessive and prolonged stress. Minirth, Hawkins, Meier, and Flournoy offer some balance to the concept of stress and its link to burnout, stating: "some stress is common, perhaps inevitable, and some stress is positive, too much stress over too long a time can result in burnout. Too much burnout, without learning and applying certain coping techniques, can lead to clinical depression."[184] To summarize: stress leads to burnout, which then leads to depression.[185]

BURNOUT	STRESS
defense characterized by disengagement	characterized by over-engagement
emotions become blunted	emotions become over-reactive
emotional damage is primary	physical damage is primary
exhaustion affects motivation and drive	affects physical energy
demoralization	disintegration
loss of ideals and hope	loss of fuel and energy
depression caused by grief engendered by loss of ideals and hope	depression produced by the body's need to protect itself and conserve energy
sense of helplessness and hopelessness	sense of urgency and hyperactivity
paranoia, depersonalization, detachment	panic, phobic, and anxiety-type disorders
may never kill you, but life may not seem worth living	may kill you prematurely, and you won't have time to finish what you started

Table 1. Hart's Comparison of Burnout and Stress. From Archibald D. Hart, "Depressed, Stressed, and Burned Out: What's Going on in My Life?," 21. In *Enrichment* Journal, 2006, retrieved from www.enrichmentjournal.ag.org. Copyright 2006 by Author. Adapted with permission.

183. Maslach and Leiter, *Truth about Burnout*, 17.
184. Minirth et al., *How to Beat Burnout*, 15.
185. Minirth et al., *How to Beat Burnout*.

Archibald Hart compared burnout and stress (see Table 1).[186] According to Hart, long-term stress seems to be one of the causes of burnout. People involved in the helping professions, such as pastors, are especially vulnerable. Their identities may become fragile, and compassion may be eroded as they involve themselves in activities beyond their capacities.[187] Pines noted "it happens most often among those who work with people and results from the emotional stress that arises during the interaction with them."[188]

Minirth et al. explained further regarding certain personality types:

> One of the tragic paradoxes of burnout is that the people who tend to be most dedicated, devoted, committed, responsible, highly motivated, better educated, enthusiastic, promising, and energetic suffer from burnout. Why? Partially, because those people are idealistic and perfectionistic. They expect too much of themselves as well as of others. Also, since they started out performing above average, others continue to expect from them those early, record-breaking results over the long haul, even though no one would expect a runner in the one hundred-yard dash to keep up that same speed in a cross-country run.[189]

There are internal risk factors for people who are categorized as personality type A, some of whom are ministers. Friedman and Rosenman compared the two personalities types, noting that type A personalities tend to be impatient/time conscious, concerned about status, competitive, aggressive, multitaskers, workaholics, and have difficulty relaxing, while type B personalities tend to be patient, relaxed, easygoing, creative, imaginative, self-analytical, and laid-back.[190] As evidenced by this comparison, Type A characteristics are more conducive to burnout.

In addition to the internal factors favoring burnout, there are externals factors that, when not handled properly, can negatively affect one's emotional wellbeing:

> In addition to occupational stress, inherent characteristics of the individual and his or her behavior also many contribute to occupational . . . interaction . . . which determines either coping or

---

186. Hart, "Depressed Stressed and Burned Out."
187. Hart, *Adrenaline and Stress*, 27.
188. Pines, "Burnout," 387.
189. Minirth et al., *How to Beat Burnout*, 17.
190. Friedman and Roseman as cited in Jackson, *Mad Church Disease*, 63.

maladaptive behavior and stress-related disease: (1) the dimensions or characteristics of the person and (2) the environmental stressor at work.[191]

Sometimes, the person in the field does not recognize burnout because work is unceasingly demanding and the symptoms develop gradually. It may start as mild fatigue and waning enthusiasm for the job, or it may be as extreme as severe exhaustion, severe depression or anxiety, increasing relational conflicts, spiritual crisis, or thoughts of suicide.[192] Rush listed factors contributing to burnout:

> Feeling "driven" to work, not pacing oneself, trying to "do it all yourself," having unrealistic self-expectations, being stuck in too many routines, persisting in a life of unbalanced priorities, being in poor physical condition, and maintaining ongoing and unrelenting contact with other people's problems.[193]

Physical and Emotional Burnout

Wright explained the physical aspect of burnout as the total energy available to accomplish a task. A person who is experiencing burnout is "someone in a state of fatigue or frustration brought about by devotion to a cause, way of life, or relationship that failed to produce the expected reward."[194] According to Wright the emotional aspect then refers to whether a person's emotional life is basically positive or negative: "People with a balanced life of outside interests have a buffer against burnout." [195] O'Donnell likewise added: "Burnout is the incapacitating result of emotional distress and behavioral dysfunction due to chronic, unresolved stress."[196]

Spiritual and Psychological Burnout

A missionary's spiritual development and the influence of religious background often shapes their identity, particularly when it is so natural to

191. Ivancevich et al., "Occupational Stress," 374.
192. Richardson, "Psychopathology in Missionary Personnel."
193. Rush as cited in Richardson, "Psychopathology in Missionary Personnel," 97.
194. Wright, *Winning Over Your Emotions*, 129.
195. Wright, *Winning Over Your Emotions*, 131.
196. O'Donnell, *Global Member Care*, 27.

identify oneself as a servant of others.[197] Minirth et al. suggested that one warning sign for burnout among Christians may be an increase in self-effort instead of reliance on God or others, leading the believer to, "start giving more lip service to their trust in God in order to cover up their decreased dependence on him."[198] Wright wrote that psychological burnout develops slowly and is recognizable when crisis happens, affecting all relationships: "Recreation becomes mechanical. The person is aloof and distant with friends . . . Psychological burnout takes time to develop and time to reverse."[199] The two major causes of burnout are expectations and distribution. Wright asserted,

> Another facet of unrealistic expectations is the belief that "it can't happen to me." Other people collapse, but not me. Other people fail, but not me. The second major contributor to burnout is distribution. You give and give and give, but never receive any replenishment. Soon you are empty.[200]

He states that burnout is "to wear oneself out by excessively striving to reach some unrealistic expectation imposed by oneself or by the values of society."[201]

Cultural and Relational Issues in Burnout

Addressing cultural issues in burnout, Foyle commented that prolonged culture shock exacerbates feelings of homesickness, ultimately leading to disengagement with the surrounding culture as the missionary attempts to run away from the stresses and symptoms of depression.[202] Coming from the perspective of a cultural anthropologist, Hiebert asserted that when entering a new culture, everyone encounters culture shock: "the shock in discovering that all the cultural patterns we have learned are now meaningless."[203] According to Livermore, burnout often ensues when lead-

---

197. See Dodds and Gardner, *Global Servants, Volume 1*.
198. Minirth et al., *How to Beat Burnout*, 34.
199. Wright, *Winning Over Your Emotions*, 131.
200. Wright, *Winning Over Your Emotions*, 133.
201. Wright, *Winning Over Your Emotions*, 129.
202. Foyle, *Honorably Wounded Stress*, 69–71.
203. Hiebert, "Cultural Difference," 375.

ers in cross-cultural situations lack cultural intelligence.[204] Cultural values can similarly cause conflict in interpersonal relationships.[205]

In addition to the cultural aspect of burnout, relational issues also present a significant problem. Croucher noted that Maslach gave "the name *'burn-out'* to the special stressors associated with social and interpersonal pressures."[206] Fawcett asserted that distressed, depressed, and burned-out people have little capacity for creating healthy interpersonal relationships.[207] According to Wright, the social aspect of burnout refers to feelings of isolation compared to feelings of involvement.[208] Reflecting this, as predicted, adult attachment styles correlate with burnout:

> In five different studies, which involved a wide range of participants from different cultures, occupations and social strata, a secure attachment style was found to correlate negatively with burnout, whereas an insecure attachment style, be it anxious ambivalent or avoidant, was found to correlate positively with burnout. In other words, the more secure one's attachment style, the less likely one is to burn out. The less secure one's attachment style, the more likely one is to burn out.[209]

The significance of these cultural and relational issues will be discussed more fully in subsequent sections.

Organizational Issues in Burnout

Studies by Schaufeli and Janczur[210] and Maslach and Leiter[211] have found organizational and work features to be more highly correlated with burnout than personal features. Fawcett asserted that the factors that protect humanitarian workers from developing acute stress and traumatic responses are most likely to be other than individual factors.[212] Job burnout is understood through key aspects of the organizational environment and the six

---

204. Livermore, *Leading with Cultural Intelligence*, 168.
205. Elmer, *Cross-Cultural Conflict*, 54.
206. Croucher, "Stress and Burnout in Ministry," para. 5.
207. Fawcett, *Stress and Trauma Handbook*, 128.
208. Wright, *Winning Over Your Emotions*, 131.
209. Pines, "Adult Attachment Styles," 76.
210. Schaufeli and Janczur as cited in Pines, "Adult Attachment Styles," 67.
211. Maslach and Leiter, *Truth about Burnout*, 188.
212. Fawcett, *Stress and Trauma Handbook*

inherent risk factors for burnout—workload, control, reward, community, fairness, and values:[213]

> The first two areas are reflected in the demand-control model of job stress . . . and reward refers to the power of reinforcements to shape behavior. Community captures all of the work on social support and interpersonal conflict, while fairness emerges from the literature on equity and social justice. Finally, the area of values picks up the cognitive-emotional power of job goals and expectations.[214]

Fawcett asserted,

> Organizational culture needs to affirm in practice any values ascribed to human beings and human community. Discrepancies between agency mission statements relating to communities being assisted and employment practices for staff will be very clear and are often a cause of staff distress.[215]

In one study of expatriate humanitarian aid workers, Eriksson et al. found that lack of organizational support contributed significantly to emotional exhaustion and depersonalization.[216]

Overview of Burnout among Missionaries

Most missionaries have a profound sense of calling and purpose when they leave home; however, a large number of them crash and burn on the mission field. Churches, supporters, and the missionaries themselves are often baffled as to how this happens and what can be done to change this pattern. ReMAP I, which sought to find ways to reduce missionary attrition, shed light on this question, in the article "What ReMAP I said, did, and achieved."[217] Blöecher reported:

> At the 1993 National Mission Congress in Caxambu, Brazil, participants were shocked at the report given by a respected Brazilian missionary leader that 75% of that nation's cross-cultural

---

213. Maslach and Leiter, *Truth about Burnout*.
214. Maslach, "Stress e Qualidade," 43.
215. Fawcett, *Stress and Trauma Handbook*, 188.
216. Eriksson et al., "Social Support," 671.
217. Blöecher, "What ReMap I Said," 9.

missionaries quit their posts during their initial five-year term of service, or don't return after first furlough.[218]

Some studies are helpful to understanding this phenomenon because they identify common characteristics of missionaries and their families,[219] including typical stressors.[220] Family issues in a cross-cultural context contribute to missionary stress. Specifically, "resentment of other people in the mission organization is associated with less marital and family satisfaction, poor conflict resolution, and problems with children, family and friends."[221] Such stressors are numerous. For example, O'Donnell described culture shock as the "incapacitating effects of anxiety, confusion, value dissonance, discouragement, and identity challenges that result from trying to get one's needs (and wishes, preferences) met in unfamiliar or unavailable ways in a new culture(s)."[222] Within cross-cultural contexts, the biggest challenge for new missionaries is adjustment to the mission field, where they struggle with personal, marriage, and family problems. In particular, missionaries with children face unique kinds and levels of stress.[223]

Gish[224] identified five major sources of missionary stress: confrontation, cross-cultural communication, support maintenance, work overload, and establishing work priorities.[225] Foyle noted that the usual reasons missionaries return home after a few months overseas are not strictly medical, but arise from their inability to handle stress.[226]

Burnout can lead to missionary attrition. Attrition refers to all categories of missionaries who return earlier than expected.[227] The book *Too Valuable to Lose* describes several primary causes of "preventable" attrition among missionaries from Old Sending Countries (OSC), Canada and North America. Each of these attrition factors result from conflicts in relationships. Consequently, training which focuses on enabling missionaries

---

218. Blöecher, "What ReMap I Said," 9.

219. O'Donnell, "Developmental Tasks"; O'Donnell and O'Donnell, *Helping Missionaries Grow*.

220. Foyle, *Honorably Wounded Stress*.

221. Dodd, "Missionary Family," 266.

222. O'Donnell, *Global Member Care*, 27.

223. O'Donnell, "Running Well and Resting Well."

224. Gish, "Sources of Missionary Stress."

225. Gish as cited in Corby and Fish, "Missionary Ministry Satisfaction," 10.

226. Foyle, *Honorably Wounded Stress*.

227. Taylor, "Introduction," 6.

to continue in the field must now address issues of character and relationships.[228] ReMap II revealed that decreases in attrition were found among agencies emphasizing more personal strategies such as vacation time, personal spiritual life, health care, and relationships.[229] Increased emphasis on candidate selection, spiritual disciplines, and prayer support also resulted in decreased attrition.

Causes of Burnout among Missionaries

Burnout is complicated by "dropping [one's] spiritual guard" and the expectation of success because of our own effort and within our own time limits.[230] Bitterness too can contribute to burnout: "Freedom from bitterness is necessary for effective recovery."[231] All these factors are exacerbated by workaholism, "neglect of appropriate spiritual priorities, compromise of biblical convictions, weakening of personal commitment to Jesus Christ,"[232] and "lack of proper nourishment."[233] Richardson described burnout as "a phenomenon frequently experienced by missionary personnel . . . when subjected to unrelenting stress that goes beyond a missionary's physical, emotional, and spiritual abilities to cope."[234] O'Donnell wrote, "*Compassion fatigue* is a special type of burnout resulting from dealing with people's problems. Brownout is a middle form of burnout and a precursor to it."[235]

K. O'Donnell also tells us that stress occurs depending on one's response to spiritual, emotional, and social demands. Experiencing too much stress over too long a period of time produces "physical tension and emotional discomfort, relational strains and lower cognitive functioning, and sometimes addictive behaviors, spiritual and relational struggles."[236] The cultural factors found within relationships in organization and family may also contribute to general stress symptoms: loss of hope, feelings of worthlessness and helplessness, discouragement, and depression. In

228. Taylor, "Introduction," 13.
229. Hay et al., "ReMap II Project Methodology."
230. Minirth et al., *How to Beat Burnout*, 46.
231. Minirth et al., *How to Beat Burnout*, 48.
232. Minirth et al., *How to Beat Burnout*, 144.
233. Lewis, "Burnout," para. 2.
234. Richardson, "Psychopathology in Missionary Personnel," 94.
235. O'Donnell, *Global Member Care*, 27.
236. O'Donnell, *Global Member Care*, 27.

addition, K. O'Donnell[237] pointed to organizational factors of burnout and M. O'Donnell[238] offered a list of common causes of stress and burnout among missionaries:[239]

1. Cultural stress: Meeting needs in new ways: language learning, culture shock, reentry.
2. Crises stress: Potentially traumatic events, natural disasters, war, accident, political instability.
3. Historical stress: Unresolved past areas of personal struggle: family of origin issues, personal weaknesses.
4. Human stress: Relationships: with family members, colleagues, and nationals, raising children, couple conflict, struggles with team members, social opposition.
5. Occupational stress: Job-specific challenges and pressures: work load, travel schedule, exposure to people with problems, job dissatisfaction, more social opposition.
6. Organizational stress: Governance and management: incongruence between one's background and the organizational ethos, incompetence or corruption in leadership, dysfunction.
7. Physical stress: Illness, nutrition, aging, adjustment to a new climate and environment, tiredness.
8. Psychological stress: Overall emotional stability and self-esteem: unresolved past hurts, loneliness, frustration, depression, unwanted habits, stage of life issues.
9. Support stress: Raising finances, housing needs, retirement issues, limited clerical and secretarial help, minimal pay, finances limited to survival use.
10. Spiritual stress: God and/or transcendent values: meaning, evil, inner growth, practices/disciplines, maintaining one's devotional life, spiritual warfare, subtle temptations, lack of trust in spiritual leaders.[240]

237. O'Donnell, *Global Member Care*.
238. O'Donnell, "CHOPS Inventory."
239. Cf. O'Donnell and O'Donnell, "Understanding and Managing Stress," 117–18; O'Donnell, *Global Member Care*, 67.
240. O'Donnell, "CHOPS Inventory."

O'Donnell and O'Donnell noted that the most frequent challenge missionaries face is their relationships with other missionaries, followed by cultural adjustment, managing stress, raising children, marriage difficulties, financial pressure, and loneliness. Cross-cultural adjustment and spiritual warfare are stressful to missionaries and tend to amplify unresolved problem areas.[241]

Furthermore, O'Donnell stated that organizational factors cause burnout.[242] All missionaries face issues related to incompatibility with organization values. According to B. Lindquist, a missionary is an integral member of a mission organization.[243] To be effective in missionary member care, one must comprehend the specific agency's "mission, strategy, culture, and climate," all of which significantly impact its members.[244] In the ReMap II project Hay, Lim, Blocher, Ketelaar, and Hay noted, "Agency practices and procedures are generally determined by a composite of an organization's ethos, values, and purposes. The character and worldview of an agency permeate all aspects of its operations."[245] In this sense, missionary member care should be aware of those organizational values, goals, and policies present in their culture that contribute to or cause a missionary's burnout. Mathis claims that member problems are too often treated with "quick fixes" in response to the dysfunction of the agency (e.g., changes in personnel, policy, structure, or activities) with little concern for the missionary ethos.[246]

Factors Contributing to NBKM Burnout

Worldviews are the most fundamental and encompassing views of reality shared by a people in a culture. They incorporate assumptions about the nature of things—about the "given" reality.[247] Challenges to these assumptions threaten the very foundations of our world, and we resist these challenges with deep emotions for they threaten to destroy our understanding

---

241. O'Donnell and O'Donnell, "Understanding and Managing Stress," 112; O'Donnell, *Global Member Care*, 67–68.
242. O'Donnell, *Global Member Care*, 10–18.
243. Lindquist, "Member Care," 33–40.
244. Mathis, "Missioning Care Model," 16.
245. Hay et al., "ReMap II Project Methodology," 33.
246. Mathis, "Missioning Care Model," 2.
247. Hiebert, *Anthropological Reflections*, 38.

of reality.[248] The factors for NBKM burnout reveal how their cultural and Christian worldviews are challenged by their cross-cultural relationships and ministries. Furthermore, B. Kang reported that the health of a person is threatened by the tension created by conflicting worldviews.[249]

Many Korean missionaries leave South Korea in a spirit of complete self-abandonment to Christ, unrealistically promising Jesus that they will give their all to Him and that they are willing to suffer any agony for Him. Many of them, however, return to South Korea within only five to ten years, burned out and unable to continue on in cross-cultural ministry.[250] According to H. J. Kim, "In terms of burnout level with regard to the duration of missionary work, those who were dispatched to carry their missions for more than 5 years and fewer than 12 years showed the highest burnout level."[251] This statistic is consistent with Ko's findings: burnout among long-term Korean missionaries includes the physical, emotional, and social.[252] This conclusion indicates that burnout does not result from isolated events, but is a process, consisting of sometimes complex overlapping stressors, which include language difficulties, lack of social support, geographical remoteness, restrictions, and relationship conflicts—all of which feed into the vulnerability common in the development of adjustment problems.[253] H. J. Kim also identified factors in the marital adjustment of the NBKM that lead to burnout of missionary couples sent abroad.[254]

Another major factor is the continuing generational problem of Korean *pure blood*.[255] Such ethnocentrism and attendant nationalism are contrary to the effective strategy of the cooperative spirit of global missions. According to Augsburger, "Ethnocentrism that makes us captive to our culture-bound socialization and values"[256] can be seen in the way that "the early growth of Korean Christianity . . . became inseparably intertwined with Korean nationalism" and values.[257] Studies on NBKM

---

248. Hiebert, *Anthropological Reflections*.
249. Kang, "In the Mission Field."
250. Moon, "Protestant Missionary Movement;" Kim, "Attachment Styles."
251. Kim, "Burn-Out and Marital Adjustment," 177.
252. Ko, "Long-Term Missionaries' Burnout."
253. Kim, "Attachment Styles."
254. Kim, "Burn-Out and Marital Adjustment."
255. Im, "Incarnational Bonding Process."
256. Augsburger, *Pastoral Counseling Across Cultures*, 7.
257. Park, "Korean Protestant Christianity," 59.

pressures reveal these same adjustment stress factors.[258] For instance, NBKMs often cannot break out of the worldview of Confucianism that places importance on hierarchy. Former missionaries feel entitled because of their pioneering experience and treat succeeding missionaries with authority; later missionaries do not understand and feel obligated to follow without questioning them. Hence there is tension among missionaries, and these tensions keep missionaries from reaching out for help, exacerbating stress, isolation, and depression.[259]

According to Sohn, while performing NBKM medical examinations and counseling, he noticed that many NBKMs had interpersonal relationship and emotional problems, including depression and anxiety.[260] These came from their constant engagement with people in evangelism, discipleship, healing, and mentoring. These problems in relationships are crucial factors in burnout.[261]

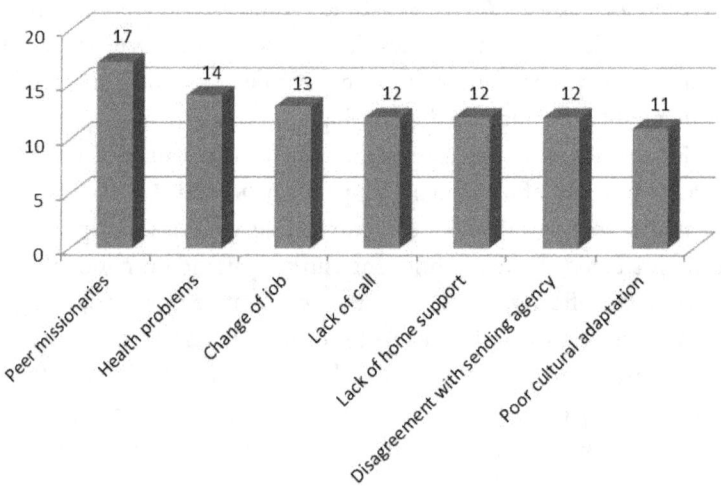

Figure 13. Most Important Causes of Attrition. From Steve Sang-Cheol Moon, "Missionary Attrition in Korea: Opinions of Agency Executives," in *Too Valuable to Lose: Exploring the Causes and Cures of Missionary Attrition*, ed. William David Taylor, 135. Pasadena, CA: William Carey

258. Kim, "Attachment Styles;" Sunkyusacarenet, *Morning of the End*; Kim, "Missionaries' Self-Respect."
259. Kim, "Depression of Korean Missionaries," 61.
260. Sohn as cited in Sunkyusacarenet, *Morning of the End*.
261. Kim, "Attachment Styles."

LITERATURE REVIEW

Library, 1997. Copyright 1997 by William Carey Library. Reprinted with permission.

Moon stated that NBKMs think health should not be an issue if they are called by God.[262] Furthermore, he affirmed that more than *health problems*, the first out of seven major causes of burnout is "problems with peer missionaries" (see Figure 13).[263] Exploring attrition rates indicates potential causes of burnout, particularly those leading to attrition.

There are three types of factors leading to burnout among NBKM: cultural issues, organizational issues, and NBKM family issues.

Cultural Issues

Culture encompasses all human interaction: social practices, values, beliefs, and norms.[264] Culture is a people's mental map of their world—a map for determining action. It provides them with a guide for their decisions and behavior.[265] Hayward asserted that, according to Clifford Geertz, culture, from the perspective of idealists or cognitivist, is "an idea, a perception about the nature of reality, and in response to this perception social patterns of behavior begin to emerge as creative responses to these perceptions."[266]

Hiebert noted, "Culture is external to the individual . . . This gives us emotional security."[267] Additionally, Kraft observed, "Culture (including worldview) is a people's way of life, their design for living, their way of coping with their biological, physical and social environment."[268] Kraft's view is that "Worldview, the deep level of culture, is the culturally structured set of assumptions (including values and commitment/allegiances) underlying how a people perceive and respond to reality."[269] The relationship between religion and worldview, according to Hiebert, is that they are equivalent;

---

262. Moon, "Missionary Attrition in Korea: Opinions of Agency Executives," 136.
263. Moon, "Missionary Attrition in Korea: Opinions of Agency Executives," 136.
264. Hiebert, *Anthropological Insights for Missionaries*.
265. Hiebert, "Cultural Difference," 375.
266. Hayward, "Defining Culture," 185.
267. Hiebert, *Transforming Worldviews*, 29.
268. Kraft, "Culture, Worldview and Contextualization," 401.
269. Kraft, "Culture, Worldview and Contextualization," 401.

"Religion is also based on the person's ability to transcend the self, to step outside" of oneself and contemplate the universe and other humans.[270]

Kraft noted, "contextualization within a new culture risks a *natavistic* kind of syncretism: a Christianity that is dominated by foreign cultural forms with imported meanings is anti-scriptural and just as syncretistic."[271] Tippett observed that Animism and Christianity similarly accept and believe in the spiritual realm.[272] In like manner, Korean Shamanists' acceptance of the Gospel merged traditional Korean religious culture and Korean Christianity.[273] Oak confirms the fact, "The syncretistic fusion between shamanism and other world religions was characteristic of Korea's multi-religious 'identity.'"[274]

In addition, Won identified the chief factor producing the secularization of Korean churches as Confucianism. Confucianism is foundational to Korean thinking, and its power has penetrated Korean Christian culture.[275] Confucianism's patriarchal and authoritarian culture, according to Won, has "aggravated the secularization of churches and brought about the pastoral narcissism . . . stopped growth, and faced with the crisis of stagnation . . . It is hard to find the culture of Christ any longer."[276] These indicate that contemporary Korean missionaries still risk reflecting such syncretistic thinking and practice.

Conflicting worldviews

One contributing factor to NBKM burnout is the conflict resulting from Korean traditional religious philosophies and Christianity having become syncretized. Hiebert stated that just as "people could adapt their behavior to get jobs, win status, and gain power without abandoning their old belief. They could give Christian names to their pagan gods and spirits and so *Christianize* their traditional religions."[277] Moon asserted, "Korean missionaries, especially mission leaders, need to check their actual worldviews

270. Hiebert, *Cultural Anthropology*, 372.
271. Kraft, "Culture, Worldview and Contextualization," 406.
272. Tippett, *Introduction to Missiology*, 329–30.
273. Keum, "Grounded Theory Study."
274. Oak, "Healing and Exorcism," 96.
275. Won, "Secularization of Korean Churches."
276. Won, "Secularization of Korean Churches," 86.
277. Hiebert, *Transforming Worldviews*, 11.

and, as needed, change them" to eliminate "short-termism, obsession with visible results, and exporting prosperity myths, [which] are a few expressions of secular worldviews."[278]

Conflicting spirituality and values

Korean Christianity is, at present, inseparable from Korean culture: "Korean missionaries easily confuse Christian worship with their Korean cultural patterns of worship, so their converts are led to believe that to become a Christian one must also adopt Korean culture."[279] They come from a mono-cultural background that causes difficulty in participating in international Christian missions. The religious historical background of Korea brings with it the syncretism of major religions such as Shamanism, Buddhism, and Confucianism.

SHAMANISM

Shamanism in Korea has influenced not only Christianity, but also Buddhism and Confucianism. NBKMs need to understand how their own culture influences their thinking about other cultures. J. Y. Lee[280] argued, "Shamanism is an internal characteristic of the Korean ethos that will never disappear, but will continue to reappear in different forms in contemporary life, for it is the native religion of the Korean people."[281] Influenced by Shamanism's mentality of focus on spiritual matters, the everyday life of Korean Christians has become imbalanced between vertical prayer with God—seeking blessings—and the horizontal lack of focus on loving and serving others.[282]

One of Shamanism's key influences is found in *Gibok*—seeking relief and prosperity—and relates to "the desire of Koreans to overcome uncontrollable natural phenomena through seeking blessings."[283] Shim observed, "In the development of the Korean new [Christian] religious movement,

---

278. Moon, "Mission from 2012," 84.
279. Whiteman, "Anthropology and Mission," 81.
280. Lee, "Korean Taegeuk Thought."
281. J. Y. Lee as cited in Im, "Incarnational Bonding Process," 159.
282. Keum, "Grounded Theory Study."
283. Lee, *Holy Spirit Movement*, 13.

spiritual exorcism, direct communication with the Holy Spirit, and healing, are largely influenced by Shamanism."[284]

Shamanism influences the Christian view of God and how difficulties are solved—if we learn to pray, and perform other ritualistic acts, all problems will be solved, and God is like a deity whom we manipulate to answer our prayers. For example, one may look at the Korean practice of persistent early-morning prayer: for Korean Christians to solve their own problems, they pray diligently (ideally in the mountains).[285] If problems do not cease, they think it is because of *their* inadequate faith or personal sin, so prayer and ritualistic acts increase. They believe that engaging in these activities ritualistically will solve their immediate problems. This reflects Ryu's explanation that Shamanism functions as a "near-sighted pragmatism . . . present-oriented and focused on how to avoid today's disasters and anxieties and leads to a peaceful and enjoyable life now."[286]

Buddhism

Grayson stated that the form of Buddhism "transmitted initially to Korea was a syncretistic type with shamanistic overtones."[287] Buddhism "deeply infiltrated every aspect of Korean Life."[288] Christianity came later, and Korean Christians adapted self-denial and the attaining of salvation through divine spirits and prayers as part of Christian practice. Buddhists seek to avoid non-virtuous actions and create merit for a happy life and a favorable rebirth: a final escape from the cycle of death and rebirth. "Buddhism does not appreciate the value and meaning of life, but inspires faith in the other world."[289]

Such futuristic asceticism, like Christian eschatology that discounts the importance of life in this world, over-emphasizes the next life and promotes indifference to society.[290] However, *Mahayana* Buddhism, similar to the Christian ethos of self-sacrifice—performing many good acts—leads

---

284. Shim, "New Religious Movements," 103.
285. Pak et al., *Singing the Lord's Song*, 18.
286. Ryu, *Folk Religion and Korean Culture*, 155.
287. Grayson, "Religious Syncretism," 189.
288. Grayson as cited in Im, "Incarnational Bonding Process," 163.
289. Lee as cited in Lee, *Holy Spirit Movement*, 16.
290. Lee, *Holy Spirit Movement*.

duty-driven Christians to burnout in their attempts to please God—a mentality that leads to NBKM burnout.[291]

Confucianism

Cumings described current Korean cultural elements as "Confucian residues."[292] He pointed out the influence of Confucianism in the shaping of Korean culture: "The Confucian heritage has unquestionably stamped Korea as indelibly as it did China."[293] Confucian ethics coincide with Christian ethics, such as the importance of family: "Family cohesion and continuity are taken as the foundation for sustaining the human community and the state."[294]

The Asian self-concept entails social relationships: "Confucianism emphasizes . . . models for what is expected in our behavior toward others . . . . If Koreans fail to do this, they feel fatal shame and disconnected in the relationship."[295] Confucian-based perspectives such as false humility, face-saving, shame-based approaches, and inability to resolve conflict are evident in social relationships: "Social harmony has been cherished in the Korean society and face-saving has been emphasized to tactically defend social harmony and avoid conflicts."[296]

The values of Confucianism have had an overwhelming effect on the social and political aspects of the culture. For example, Confucianism emphasizes the importance of duty and responsibility while deemphasizing the value of women in the hierarchal ruling class. It is hard to distinguish between "the moral and social values of Confucianism prominently in the mental landscape of Koreans and the high moral code taught by the Protestants who converged with what many Confucian-minded Koreans felt and thought."[297]

Confucianism's impact on Korean Christians is far greater than that of Buddhism and Shamanism. Having been a presence longer than Buddhism, Confucianism acts upon Korean thinking and behavior covertly: the idea

---

291. Lee, "Korean Taegeuk Thought."
292. Cumings, *Two Koreas*, 8.
293. Cumings, *Two Koreas*, 8.
294. Park and Cho, "Confucianism," 117.
295. You, "Shame and Guilt Mechanisms," 62.
296. Sohn and Wall as cited in Kim, "Negotiating with Terrorists," 266.
297. Kim, "Korean Religious Culture," 117.

of ruling others has weakened the Christian idea of serving others, human beings are seen through a submissively obedient hierarchal structure, emotions are not revealed or expressed, individuals are dependent beings of equal ability and talent, and all human relationships are vertical.[298] S. O. Lee stated that Korean missionaries, as dutiful ministers, frequently impose their own culture, which is deeply rooted in Confucianism, on others in their cross-cultural ministries.[299]

Contextualized syncretized Korean Christianity beliefs

The syncretism that occurred in the contextualization of Korean Christianity resulted in a Christian culture influenced by the ideals of the previous religious cultures.[300] As with Shamanism, both physical health and material success in the here-and-now have been the drive of Korean Protestantism. A. E. Kim's view of what he calls the basic dynamic of Korean religious practice is,

> The image and the role of Korean clergy also took on many characteristics of the shaman... this way, the distinction between Christianity and Shamanism in general and between church service and shamanic ritual, in particular, became blurred in South Korea."[301]

A. E. Kim's perspective is that throughout Korean Protestant history, God has not only been understood to be the creator of the universe, but also the magical ruler, pouring out grace at will—that He intervenes through miracles to help is popularly accepted among Korean Protestants.[302] His view is that such ideas are deeply and detrimentally enmeshed in the Korean Protestant mentality and worldview. J. S. Park also noted, "a bitter fruit of Confucianism in Korean Christianity has been the development of clericalism, with clergy exercising excessive power in both the faith and the polity of the church."[303]

---

298. Song and Meek, "Impact of Culture."
299. Lee, "Korean Mission."
300. Chung, *Syncretism*; Kim, "Attachment Styles."
301. Kim, "Korean Religious Culture," 129–30.
302. Kim, "Korean Religious Culture."
303. Park, "Korean Protestant Christianity," 10.

As a reflection of Korean church culture, sending churches and agencies compete with each other over the number of missionaries they sponsor and impose unrealistic expectations on NBKM, who strive to fulfill the missionary tasks while pressured to be successful in the visible growth of their ministry projects.[304] In this sense, some applicants might be accepted without a missionary calling or motivation. By implication, NBKMs that are wrongly motivated or lack a clear call, fail in the field, seek personal prestige, or use mission for personal benefit or as a means to another end are candidates for burnout.[305]

Korean church culture has contributed to NBKM burnout. The Korean church has isolated itself from global society, focusing more inwardly towards future life.[306] The Korean church suffered severe persecution during the Japanese colonial reign. This persecution influenced the church "to be more concerned about spiritual matters and made them rather apathetic to political and social matters," leading in turn to a style of *escapism in faith*.[307] The adverse affects of faith tradition were increased by exaggerated national identity.

Historically, *Koreanized* (indigenized) theology exacerbated leader burnout due to its foundation in nationalism and traditional religious heritage as opposed to theological convictions rooted in Scripture alone.[308] This phenomenon has contributed to the trend of a mono-cultural Koreanized worldview among NBKMs.[309] This limited worldview has led to burnout in their cross-cultural ministry.

Organizational Issues

Confucianism's work in modern education reflects its profound reverence for learning. The missionaries' strict moral teachings were seen as "consistent with the austere moral code of Neo-Confucianism."[310] Neo-Confucianist leadership contributed to the rapid growth of the Korean church and mission. However, it came to have a negative influence on the

304. Moon, "Protestant Missionary Movement."
305. Choi, "Preparing Korean Missionaries," 207–8.
306. Lee, *Holy Spirit Movement*, 33.
307. Lee, *Holy Spirit Movement*, 33
308. Keum, "Grounded Theory Study," 32.
309. Keum, "Grounded Theory Study."
310. Park, "Korean Protestant Christianity," 59.

development and maturation of Korean missions. The Korean church and mission agencies have been primarily focused on institutional expansion and growth in numbers.[311] Consequently, there is no holistic support for NBKM. Most mission agencies lack cooperation and a holistic approach to the care of missionaries.[312]

Organization influenced by cultural issues

Even though Korean missionaries "have become known for aggressively going to . . . the hardest-to-evangelize corners of the world,"[313] Korean mission organizations lack proper structures to provide adequate and appropriate pre-field training for NBKMs.[314] Moon notes that some of the significant problems are:

> Insufficient attention being paid to (1) infrastructure development, (2) strategy for field ministries, (3) care of missionary families, (4) leadership development, (5) crisis management, and (6) preparation for missionary retirement. Though the last decade has seen significant progress in all these areas, an increasing number of problems in mission accountability have also been coming to light.[315]

Mission organizations also suffer from leadership issues—for example, authoritarian and perfectionist tendencies. According to S. S. Kang, "The [Korean] church may be in a crisis leadership situation."[316]

Lack of cross-cultural pre-field training

One factor contributing to burnout is the lack of strategic training for cross-cultural ministry prior to leaving for the mission field, a problem evident in the Korean missionary movement. Without effective training focusing on key areas—character building, community-life training, area research, and missiological knowledge—many NBKMs will face worldview conflicts and

311. Park, "Korean Protestant Christianity"; Moon, *Korean Missionary Movement*.
312. Moon, *Korean Missionary Movement*.
313. Onishi, "Korean Missionaries."
314. Moon, *Korean Missionary Movement*.
315. Moon, "Mission from 2012," 84.
316. Kang, "Missionary Attrition Issues," 264.

experience culture shock, which may lead to frustration, stress, depression, and burnout.[317] Consequently, inadequate missionary training and poor cross-cultural adjustment predict a high rate of missionary attrition and burnout.[318] Bong Rin Ro pointed out some problems of inadequately prepared missionaries:

> Most Korean missionaries have not developed good relationships with each other, and demonstrate little cooperation between mission agencies and sending churches . . . [they are] criticized for their use of financial resources . . . being colonialistic, or "military style missionaries" . . . and seldom cooperating with missionaries from other countries or even with fellow Koreans . . . [they also have] various family problems, especially MK (missionary kid) problems, in missionary homes. The lack of adequate missionary preparation . . . through cross-cultural training has produced the most serious problems.[319]

Moon added that *lack of call* is also an important cause of Korean missionary withdrawal from the field.[320]

Leadership Issues within the Organization

Modern Korean missionaries do not come from a society with a traditionally Christian culture. The historical religious background of Korea brings a mixture of Christianity and traditional Korean religious thinking and behavior, leading to a variety of problems. The negative side of Korean values, such as the authoritarian, top-down leadership style, the strong hierarchical social structure, strong competition, emphasis on visible outcome, formalism, and ethnocentricity all lead to burnout.[321] All of these factors significantly impact NBKM leadership.

---

317. Moon, "Protestant Missionary Movement."
318. Choi, "Preparing Korean Missionaries," 19.
319. Bong Rin Ro as cited in Choi, "Preparing Korean Missionaries," 10.
320. Moon, "Missionary Attrition in Korea: Opinions of Agency Executives," 136.
321. Choi, "Preparing Korean Missionaries," 357.

NBKM leaders' character issues

NBKMs do not readily admit their vulnerabilities and weaknesses. They mask their true feelings and focus on reaching success in their ministry. Authoritarian and perfectionist values are expected in the religious leader or pastor. Many NBKMs who were previously pastors are afraid of revealing their personal weaknesses because they believe that weakness threatens their superior self-image.[322] However, mission leaders emphasize personal and spiritual maturity as more important qualities of mission leadership than experience, knowledge, or managerial ability.[323] J. U. Kim argues that Confucian values are still valid today in the national character.[324]

Hierarchical structure

Hierarchy and patriarchy are characteristics of Confucianism: there is still a distinct leadership structure defining who is above whom; those who are younger serve those who are older, and women serve men. Wagner discusses the distorted thinking that is prevalent:

> If we think of ourselves primarily as leaders or big shots, it is easy to start looking down on those who follow us . . . . But when we start thinking of ourselves as leaders, humility tends to evaporate—sometimes, along with our ministry."[325]

Excessive authoritarianism appears to be another cultural tendency of Koreans, featuring displays of humility for the sake of appearances, as opposed to true humility (e.g., when a person chooses not to make his or her opinions known to avoid potential conflict or embarrassment). In Confucian leadership culture, followers tend to obey without questioning. NBKMs follow their leaders without questioning authority when conflict arises. This blind obedience while experiencing conflict in cross-cultural ministry contributes to burnout.

---

322. Creighton, "Revising Shame and Guilt Cultures."
323. Moon, "Protestant Missionary Movement."
324. Kim, *Koreans: Their Mind and Behavior.*
325. Wagner as cited in Lee, "Healthy Leaders, Healthy Households 1," 62.

Hierarchal Leadership Style

The NBKM hierarchal model of leadership is predominant instead of the servant model of leadership that Jesus demonstrated. Korean culture does not embrace the suffering servant model of leadership. Traditionally, because of their level of education, Korean pastors and missionaries believe they rightfully rule over and control others and do not allow their decisions to be questioned.[326]

Shame

Korean society often excludes a person who is perceived to have been shamed—i.e. who has lost the support and confidence of family and community. This occurs when there is a *loss of face*. "If one does not fulfill expectations of the self, then one loses face . . . when one loses face, one feels tremendous shame."[327] Miller argues that shame is an expression of narcissistic distress that can be used defensively.[328]

Narcissism and Perfectionism

In Korean culture, Won attributes the secularization of churches to the Confucian patriarchal, authoritarian tradition, which has produced narcissistic Korean pastors.[329] Churches have faced spiritual stagnation, devoid of the culture of Christ. Narcissism and perfectionism are dominant among Korean ministers in active ministry. According to Pan, narcissism is often found in Korean leaders who perceive themselves to be always on display.[330] If narcissistic tendencies creep into the clergy, they may be continually aware of being noticed and held to high expectations. This awareness often results in fear or anger if they fail to meet expectations.[331] They are likely to become perfectionists and overly conscientious people, to develop one aspect of their ministry excessively, or maybe to identify too closely with

---

326. Park, "Unmarried Single Women."
327. Huang and Yeh as cited in Lee, "Healthy Leaders, Healthy Households 1," 66.
328. Miller, *Shame in Context*.
329. Won, "Secularization of Korean Churches."
330. Pan, "Development of Group Counseling Program."
331. Pan, "Development of Group Counseling Program."

unreasonable expectations. Because of this, they suffer from an overloaded work schedule. According to Pan,

> Narcissistic clergy are likely to pursue huge success as evidence of their superiority. They are always aware of being noticed and strive to display their perfect image. They have no social support system, because their interpersonal relationships are displayed on the stage where they show their positive image . . . Therefore, they are likely to fall into burnout easily.[332]

NBKMs have a tendency to be driven to be successful in their mission projects and to be in competition with their Korean church community. Because of the sending churches' expectations of miracles and extreme sacrifice, missionaries fear sharing their struggles.[333] Hong noted that they are driven to prove to themselves through their work that they aim to please and glorify God.[334] This driven work ethic pervades the culture of Korean ministry, and the clergy experience all these stressors and more.

Inability to Resolve Conflict

Korean Christians have not had sufficient opportunities to practice healthy conflict resolution in their own personal relationships or in the church setting.[335] They "have a tendency not to air their grievances."[336]

NBKMs tend not to set boundaries in terms of balancing their lives. It is hard for Koreans to resolve conflict when opinions may be in opposition. Offending authority figures is highly shameful. In modern society, a more expressive communication style is gradually changing the Korean community, but there are still clashes of traditional and modern ways. Additionally, Moon also confirmed that conflict with the home office and conflict with colleagues, respectively, are among the reasons for burnout–caused attrition of Korean missionaries.[337] The lack of cooperation and support in team ministry can cause burnout in NBKMs. Confucian

---

332. Pan, "Pastoral Counseling," 252.
333. Choi, "Missionary Member Care System."
334. Hong, "Understanding Intergenerational," 136.
335. Lee, "Healthy Leaders, Healthy Households 1," 67.
336. Lee, "Healthy Leaders, Healthy Households 2," 88.
337. Moon, "Protestant Missionary Movement"; Moon, *Korean Missionary Movement*.

thinking among Korean Christian leaders produces undercurrents of conflict throughout the lives of Korean Christians.

According to Moon, there are conflicts among different Korean missionary generations due to the difference in cultural norms: "Younger generations are more horizontal" or egalitarian "in their way of thinking than older generations, [and are] thus often misunderstood as less orderly and even as unspiritual"[338] (see Figure 14).

Moon asserted that the concerns of leadership and organizations are indicative of the unique dynamics of that organization: "We need to diagnose and guide these issues and phenomena wisely to deepen our understanding of the cross-cultural dimensions of Korean people and their ministries."[339]

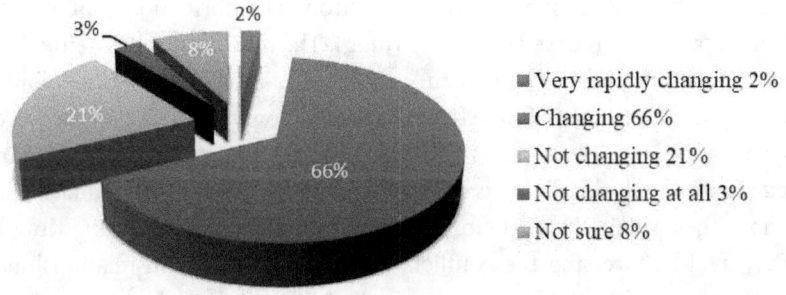

Figure 14. Change of Organizational Culture for the Influx of Younger Missionaries. From Steve Sang-Cheol Moon, *The Korean Missionary Movement and Leadership Issues* [PDF], 9, retrieved from www.krim.org Copyright 2010 by Author. Reprinted with permission.

Emotional Suppression

The Korean concept of *Jung* (human affection) leads to the ability to bond in relationships with others. *Jung* is made of emotional boundaries. There seem to be no clear personal boundaries between the personal and professional according to *Jung*. Gudykunst, Ting-Toomey, and Nishida stated,

338. Moon, *Korean Missionary Movement*, 9.
339. Moon, *Korean Missionary Movement*, 10.

> The psychological basis of interpersonal relationships in Korea is twofold. One is love (or *sa-rang* in Korean), and the other is *jung*. Love, as in Western society . . . is purely affective. *Jung* is a much broader concept than love. In addition to the affective aspect of love, *Jung* comprises the forces of inertia of a relationship . . . Jung is unconscious and voluntary . . . [with] four properties: duration, togetherness, warmth, and solidarity.[340]

According to Choi and Choi, *Jung*

> is non-romantic emotional affection that is imperfectly understood as a [familial bond]. It is not mere love, but more [emotionally holistic] and includes a temporal aspect. It is a deeper concept than mere love but includes a long-term steady relationship of continued affection between people.[341]

Korean culture develops social relations through the formation of practical-individual relations based on *cheong* [Jung]. The role of the self is defined by social relations because of Korean "collective *we-ness*."[342] B. Lee uses Korean's *we-ness* language to frame Korea's anthropology.[343] B. Lee uses the word *uri*, meaning *we*. "Most things—including relationships—are referenced by '*our*' instead of by '*my*.'"[344] It is hard for Koreans to criticize individuals with whom they are in close relationship, due to the concept of *cheong* [Jung]. They avoid addressing the conflicts that inevitably arise in relationships, making relationships a common psychological issue. D. G. Lee, S. Lee, & H. J. Park noted, "In Korean culture where collectivism and Confucianism are salient, clients typically report difficulties in relationships and suffer from various anxiety symptoms."[345] The discomfort with conflict results in psychological difficulties. The emotional suppression so characteristic of their Korean culture magnifies interpersonal relationship conflicts.

---

340. Gudykunst et al., *Communication in Personal Relationships*, 243.
341. Choi and Choi, "Effects of Korean Cultural," 56.
342. Choi and Choi, "Effects of Korean Cultural," 56.
343. Lee, "Philosophical Anthropology."
344. Lee, "Philosophical Anthropology," 60.
345. Choi and Kim as cited in Lee et al., "Validation of Korean Version," 68.

Literature Review

Interpersonal relationships

Choi and Choi explained that Korean culture emphasizes relational harmony. Unlike Western culture, community is emphasized over the individual, and the foundational emphasis is placed on relationships.[346] While the self is acknowledged in Korean culture, it is not foundational, and its role is a function of relational unity, or *we-ness*.[347]

> In Korean culture, the self is a function of the relational culture . . . . [sic] Korean *we-ness* is a relational cultural identity, it is a principle, and the *self* finds its foundation in "collective *we-ness*," this is as opposed to "western *we-ness*," which places the self as the principle of community, resulting in the distribution of the self to form community, or "distributive we-ness."[348]

This cultural framework for interpersonal relationships contributes to psychological stress. According to Korean psychology research reports, unbalanced human relationships account for most of the stress in Korean culture. Koreans are especially distressed by interpersonal relationship problems because of the collective nature of their self-identity.[349] For example, B. Lee stated "one must evaluate one's role and duties lest one's own ambitions undermine the cooperate psyche" (abstract).[350] This cultural problem also manifests in the mission field. Interpersonal conflict for NBKMs (i.e., conflict involving fellow missionaries, locals, and family) is the leading cause of stress, burnout, and spiritual moral crisis for Korean missionaries.[351] The effects of interpersonal relationships also influence leadership ethics and values.

NBKM leadership ethics and values

NBKMs have a traditional Korean value system, which dictates certain behaviors, such as men are never supposed to share their feelings, such as crying. Therefore, they are likely to succumb to burnout easily. Also, many pastors and NBKM are likely to be dominated by the institutional

---

346. Choi and Choi, "Effects of Korean Cultural."
347. Choi and Choi, "Effects of Korean Cultural," 56.
348. Choi and Choi, "Effects of Korean Cultural," 56–57.
349. Kim, Park, and Shin as cited in Choi and Choi, "Effects of Korean Cultural," 57.
350. Lee, "Philosophical Anthropology."
351. H. J. Choi as cited in Kim, "Missiological Study," 10–13.

culture, increasing the potential for burnout.[352] Another factor is the mask of self-pride sometimes fostered by Confucian culture, with its emphasis on performance and tendency toward hypocrisy. Additionally, political and social authorities heavily influence the church's ethics and the behaviors of its clergy.

One concern about these values is that they have the potential to produce self-centered Christians who are primarily concerned about their own interests. For example, Y. H. Lee noted "The exclusivism and conservatism of Confucianism accounted for an exclusive and conservative tendency in Korean protestant Christianity, thus causing the denominations to be divided into a great number."[353] These things become manifest in that there are too many leaders, not enough followers, and a great tendency to show off one's accomplishments.

NBKM Family Issues

One of the most critical factors possibly contributing to burnout is the NBKM family system and their perspective of family unity.[354] Married NBKMs deal with cross-cultural family stress through the lens of their cultural values. This tends toward burnout in the cross-cultural context of their marriage and their communication with their children. Enmeshed family backgrounds cause a lot of stress and burnout among leaders, straining interpersonal relationships and communication with unhealthy thinking patterns and acting in cross-cultural circumstances.

NBKM married women sometimes have a *lack of call*. They are easily burned out in a cross-cultural context. S. E. Lindquist, writing of missionary wives in general, says, "Wives are often the determining factor for families staying or leaving the field."[355] In cross-cultural adjustment, male NBKM leaders have charismatic personality and are authoritarian, while wives who follow their husband's calling without expressing their own opinion experience a lack of personal calling and easily burn out.[356]

---

352. Pan, "Development of Group Counseling Program."
353. Lee, *Holy Spirit Movement*, 18.
354. Jung, "Family Ministry for Missionaries."
355. Lindquist, "Prediction of Success," 22.
356. Kim, "Burn-Out and Marital Adjustment"; Ko, "Long-Term Missionaries' Burnout."

Cohesion refers to a family's degree of closeness to one another. Strong families feature individuated members: "each one possesses a healthy degree of separateness from the others. However the members of an enmeshed family are overly dependent upon the family for identity."[357] An example is when all members make one member's problem their own, becoming too involved. They lose perspective, and the problem worsens, making a solution less likely. The *negatively cohesive* family structure—*enmeshed*—is typical of Korean missionaries.

Figure 15 illustrates three general types of families, and their distinct features, beginning with the disengaged.

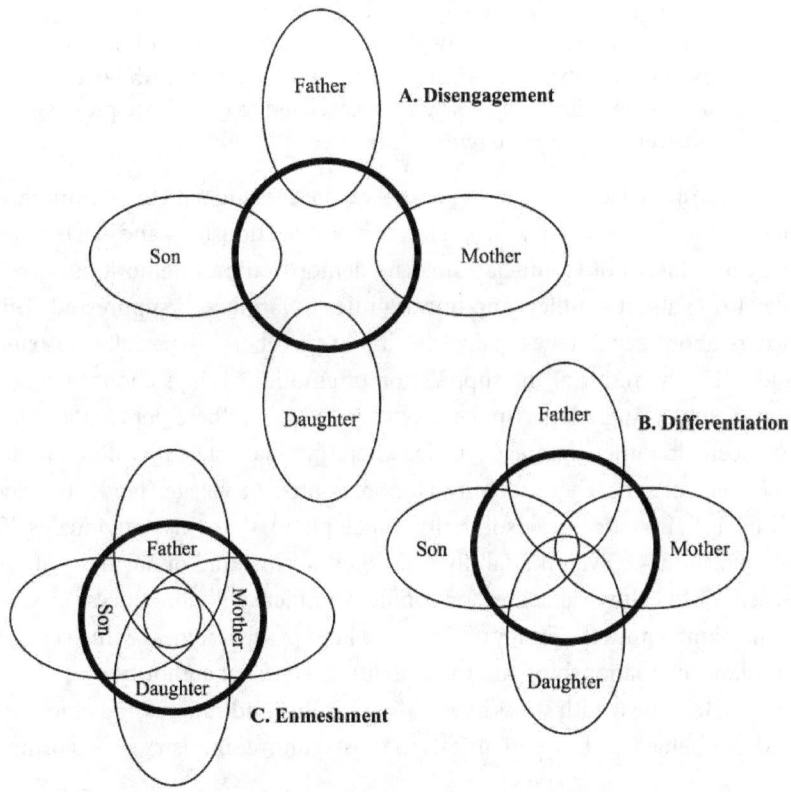

Figure 15. Three General Types of Families, and their Distinct Features: Disengagement, Differentiation, and Enmeshment. From Jack O. Balswick and Judith K. Balswick, *The Family: A Christian Perspective*

357. Balswick and Balswick, *Family*, 44.

on the Contemporary Home. Grand Rapids, MI: Baker Academic, 2007. Copyright 2007 by Authors. Reprinted with permission.

> In the disengaged family (A), the lives of the individual members very rarely touch each other. Cohesion is so low that each person lives in psychological isolation from the others.
>
> In the differentiated family (B) daily lives overlap, but each individual is also involved in activities outside the family. Each member has a separate life and identity and is, therefore, actively and meaningfully engaged with others . . . member's identity and support is found within the family . . . and beyond the family boundary as well.
>
> In the enmeshed family (C) the lives of all are helplessly entwined with each other . . . [with] little identity beyond the boundary of the family. . . . A member of an enmeshed family who tries to separate is likely to be labeled disloyal and to experience pressure from the others to remain enmeshed.[358]

Traditional Korean families are very cohesive, and tend to be enmeshed due to their Confucian values. Harmonious relationships and society are the centerpieces of Confucianism. The demonstration of emotions, which may bring about conflicts and uncertainties in families, is suppressed. This brings about separateness between family members—especially husband and wife. The result of the suppression of emotions brings about burnout. For example, Augsburger spoke about filial piety, "Where personalities are sociocentric rather than egocentric, where familial esteem is more crucial than self-esteem, where identity is more rooted in village (land), in tribe (Kinship), in patrilineal solidarity (filial piety) than in individual self-actualization."[359] Even if a family is devoted to this kind of harmony at the expense of healthy capacities for conflict, conflicts will nonetheless arise at some point within the family.[360] There is a kind of separateness, which causes problems in relationships and the inability to confront authority.

NBKM deal with stress by avoiding conflict and suppressing emotions and this behavior clearly manifests in cross-cultural ministry.[361] According

---

358. Balswick and Balswick as cited in Balswick and Balswick, *Family*, 48–49.
359. Augsburger, *Pastoral Counseling Across Cultures*, 16.
360. Park, "Korean Protestant Christianity," 59.
361. Kang, "Stress of Missionaries."

to Im, NBKM find it difficult to share their emotions, which causes stress and low-self-esteem when exposed to the cross cultural adjustment.[362]

Overcoming Burnout

According to N. Wright, burnout involves all five major areas of life: physical, intellectual, emotional, social, and spiritual.[363] Although Wright is not specifically a psychologist working with missionaries, he—unlike the majority of psychologists who are involved in such work—emphasizes *overcoming* rather than prevention and intervention. He distills some helpful insights regarding basic steps to overcoming burnout.

Physical burnout—debilitating fatigue—can be overcome through effective exercise, nutrition, and stress reduction efforts. Engaging in a hobby or other means of *intellectual* relaxation can neutralize diminished intellectual ability and cynicism. A balanced life of outside interests and self-awareness provides a buffer against burnout characterized by *emotional* states of depression and pessimism, precipitated in part by loss of dreams and wrongly elevated expectations tied to work. *Social* burnout is overcome in the presence of effective support systems in which feelings are freely shared and problems aired. Realistic dreams for life and proper expectations about God's provision enable a person to overcome disappointments and experience *spiritual* health. Sometimes a short vacation, a few days off, or "any type of change, which brings about a new interest or even a variation of his work routine may help."[364] Among global member-care specialists and missiologists who are concerned with member care, a number have proposed strategies and models for effective member care.

Conclusion

Many native born-Korean missionaries have experienced burnout during their early mission work and have quit, considering themselves to be failures. Korean Christian theology has been contextualized and has become syncretized in such a way that it contributes to burnout among NBKMs. Today, member care offers strategies for Western missionaries to overcome

---

362. Im, "Incarnational Bonding Process."
363. Wright, *Winning Over Your Emotions*.
364. Wright, *Winning Over Your Emotions*, 130–33.

burnout. An important question is whether the Western member care strategies will be effective in the NBKM cultural context. Due to a lack of sufficient research, strategies used by the NBKMs remain unknown. Specifically, particular strategies for NBKMs to overcome burnout have not been revealed. Therefore, specific research on the efficacy of the Western strategies being used by NBKMs could help to solve this problem.

This study attempts to open the currently sealed "black box" of Korean missionary experiences with burnout. This qualitative study, based on Korean missionary self-disclosure, is an effort to discover effective strategies to enable Korean missionaries to overcome burnout. This research could also be helpful for improving Korean mission leaders' and agencies' member-care strategies for missionary support systems, including training, mentoring, counseling, and development of global missions leadership.

3

Methods and Procedures

THIS CHAPTER PROVIDES AN overview of the research methods and procedures used in this study of burnout recovery. More specifically, it shows the relevance of the approach employed. The chapter gives specific attention to the selection of the qualitative method, the advantages of that method, the essential elements of *grounded theory*, and data validation methods used in this study.

Why Qualitative Research?

The three reasons I have chosen to use a qualitative approach for this study are: 1) it fits my topic with consideration for the insider point of view—individual experience of human beings, 2) it enables discovery of theory to explain sample values and perspectives, and 3) it relies on listening to subject narratives. This study aims to provide a more exact understanding of native-born Korean missionary (NBKM) efforts to recovery from burnout. Individual experiences cannot be limited to parameters of exact quantitative measurement. According to Denzin and Lincoln,[1] "the role of the researcher . . . and the individuals from whom qualitative data are collected play a more central role in the researcher's design decisions."[2] The qualitative approach tends to better yield an emic view.

Unlike a quantitative project with predetermined limits to an investigation, this study attempts to a discover theory that explains an important phenomenon. The qualitative approach recognizes that researchers bring their own values and perspectives to their research, "as a broad explanation for behavior and attitudes and it may be complete with variables, constructs

---

1. Denzin and Lincoln, *Sage Handbook*.
2. Denzin and Lincoln as cited in Creswell, *Qualitative Inquiry*, 3.

and hypotheses."[3] As Denzin and Lincoln observe, "All research is interpretive: it is guided by the researcher's set of beliefs and feelings about the world and how it should be understood and studied."[4]

According to Creswell, qualitative research is "exploratory and is useful when the researcher does not know the important variables to examine."[5] Qualitative research exposes the underlying values of participants by facilitating the uncovering of predictive theories that can explain phenomena, or at least isolated factors, which contribute to certain phenomena and people groups.

Quantitative research examines the influential factors in relation to their outcomes. The intent is to "reduce the ideas into a small, discrete set of ideals to test, such as the variables that comprise hypotheses and research questions... based on careful observation and measurement of the objective reality."[6] However, this study attempts to identify the *emic* factors inherent to the subject sample, beyond the limits of the quantitative approach.

Denzin & Lincoln described the depth and breadth of qualitative research:

> Qualitative research is a situated activity that locates the observer in the world. It consists of a set of interpretive, material practices that make the world visible. These practices transform the world. They turn the world into a series of representations, including field notes, interviews, conversations, photographs, recordings, and memos to the self. At this level, qualitative research involves an interpretive, naturalistic approach to the world. This means that qualitative researchers study things in their natural settings, attempting to make sense of, or interpret, phenomena in terms of the meanings people bring to them.[7]

The goals of this particular study required the researcher to interact with the participants, a key feature of the qualitative approach, employing "assumptions, a worldview . . . inquiring into the meaning individuals or groups ascribe to a social or human problem."[8]

---

3. Creswell, *Research Design*, 61.
4. Denzin and Lincoln, *Sage Handbook*, 22.
5. Creswell, *Research Design*, 18.
6. Creswell, *Research Design*, 7.
7. Denzin and Lincoln, *Sage Handbook*, 3.
8. Creswell, *Qualitative Inquiry*, 37.

Van Manen described the primary goal of qualitative research as "to transform lived experience into a textual expression of its essence."[9] Thus, the qualitative researcher is a key instrument in the process—researchers are the ones who interactively gather information.

The interview/observation aspect of the qualitative process better captures individual perspectives, and also considers the entire context of the research subject. Creswell reflected on the essential advantages of this approach:

> We conduct qualitative research because a problem or issue needs to be explored . . . . We also conduct qualitative research because we need a complex, detailed understanding of the issue. This detail can only be established by talking directly with people, going to their homes or places of work, and allowing them to tell the stories unencumbered by what we expect to find or what we have read in the literature . . . We use qualitative research to develop theories when partial or inadequate theories exist for certain populations and samples or existing theories do not adequately capture the complexity of the problem we are examining.[10]

A quantitative researcher is distant from those being researched, relying on mathematical models, statistical tables, and graphs, and usually writing about their research in impersonal, third-person prose.[11] In contrast, qualitative research implies that we should be open to culturally different perspectives, discovered primarily through the interactive interview process. Creswell underscored the need to avoid the impersonal power relation of researcher to subject, which is inherent in such quantitative studies, in order to hear the voice of individuals and empower them to share their stories.[12]

The scope of qualitative research encompasses the range of life experiences, where individual belief and actions intertwine with culture.[13] The shared life experiences of cross-cultural missionaries are immeasurably valuable to the broader church's understanding of factors involved in recovery from burnout. Using a qualitative methodology to discover

---

9. Van Manen, *Researching Lived Experience*, 36.
10. Creswell, *Qualitative Inquiry*, 40.
11. Denzin and Lincoln, "Introduction," 10.
12. Creswell, *Qualitative Inquiry*, 40.
13. Denzin and Lincoln, "Introduction."

the elements of their successes will benefit both missionary and sending church member care.

Assumptions, Worldview, Paradigms

To begin the process of designing a qualitative study, researchers should reveal their philosophical assumptions.

> Qualitative research begins with assumptions, a worldview, the possible use of a theoretical lens, and the study of research problems inquiring into the meaning individuals or groups ascribe to social or human problem ... The researcher's interpretations cannot be separated from their own background, history, context, and prior understandings.[14]

Creswell writes of five assumptions: ontological (the nature of reality), epistemological (how the researcher knows what she or he knows), axiological (the role of values in the research), rhetorical (the language of research), and methodological (the methods used in the process).[15] Then, as the inquirer brings their worldviews and beliefs to the process, they must make further decisions regarding the process and presentation of the study. Creswell affirmed, "Good research requires making these assumptions, paradigms, and frameworks explicit in the writing of a study, and, at a minimum, to be aware that they influence the conduct of inquiry."[16] Charmaz concurred:

> We are not scientific observers who can dismiss scrutiny of our values by claiming scientific neutrality or authority. Neither observer nor observed come to a scene untouched by the world. Researchers and research participants make assumptions about what is real, possess stocks of knowledge, occupy social statuses, and pursue purposes that influence their respective views and actions in the presence of each other.[17]

Creswell noted, "The qualitative researcher chooses a stance on each of these assumptions, and the choice has practical implications for designing

---

14. Creswell, *Qualitative Inquiry*, 37–39.
15. Creswell, *Qualitative Inquiry*.
16. Creswell, *Qualitative Inquiry*, 15.
17. Charmaz, *Constructing Grounded Theory*, 15.

and conducting research."[18] Researchers must select from among several research approaches, based on the assumptions they have accepted. Paradigms often used by qualitative researchers are post-positivist, constructivist, advocacy/participators, and pragmatist.[19]

> Post-positivism: reductionist, logical cause-and-effect-oriented research including empirical data collection and deterministic based on a priori theories.
> Constructivism: research directed at identifying subjective patterned meanings from experience through historical and cultural norms.
> Advocacy/Participatory: research aimed to create reform that may change the lives of participants and provide a voice for these participants.
> Pragmatism: outcome-oriented research focusing solely on solutions to problems.

My Philosophical Assumptions and Biases

I acknowledge that my interpretation flowed from my own personal, cultural, and historical experience. As Creswell suggested, "the language of the qualitative researcher becomes personal, literary, and based on definitions that evolve during a study rather than being defined by the researcher."[20] "The researcher's intent, then, is to make sense (or interpret) the meanings others have about the world."[21] Denzin and Lincoln noted that through the use of the multiple methods of qualitative research, "objective reality cannot be captured."[22] The qualitative researcher should, therefore, report the subjective realities of the human participants rather than solely determine what the objective reality is. As Creswell noted:

> When researchers conduct qualitative research, they are embracing the idea of multiple realities. Different researchers embrace different realities, as do also the individuals being studied and the readers of a qualitative study. When studying individuals,

18. Creswell, *Qualitative Inquiry*, 15.
19. Creswell, *Qualitative Inquiry*, 19–23.
20. Creswell, *Qualitative Inquiry*, 19.
21. Creswell, *Qualitative Inquiry*, 21.
22. Denzin and Lincoln, *Sage Handbook*, 5.

qualitative researchers conduct a study with the intent of reporting these multiple realities.[23]

While I am, in some respects, a pragmatist and a constructivist, my biases and assumptions also are influenced by my biblical worldview. I understand reality through biblical lenses and consider myself subject to God's word and to His work in society. This view is not an isolated belief. Christian anthropologist Paul Hiebert expounded what he believed to be the foundational necessity for understanding and incorporating a biblical worldview in evaluating research findings:

> As Christians we hold that this master blueprint is a biblical worldview that *helps us see the big picture of reality* presented in Scripture and in nature. This blueprint begins with the God of the Bible and includes the reality of an orderly creation, human shaped in the image of God, the fall, redemption through the death and resurrection of Christ, and eternal life in him.[24]

I affirm that there is objective reality in the world, but people from different cultures, with different histories, perceive reality through their subjective and relative vantage points. According to Hiebert there are clearly "epistemological assumptions a culture makes about the nature of reality and human knowledge."[25]

In social science research there is a connection between the nature of reality (ontology) and the nature of knowledge (epistemology). I am an NBKM who grew up in South Korea. I experienced burnout and left the mission field, but I have recovered from it. Hence, I am an *emic* to my study. Currently, I am actively involved in a Korean church and mission organization. From a cross-cultural perspective, my contextualized Christianity, as a Korean, influences my biases and philosophical assumptions. I recognize that my own background shapes my pragmatic, constructivist, and biblical interpretation.

---

23. Creswell, *Qualitative Inquiry*, 18.
24. Hiebert, *Transforming Worldviews*, 75.
25. Hiebert, *Transforming Worldviews*, 46.

Grounded Theory

There are at least five different approaches to qualitative research: Narrative, Phenomenology, Ethnography, Case Study, and Grounded Theory.[26] As already noted, this study has adopted Grounded Theory. Strauss and Corbin[27] explained, "Grounded Theory is a qualitative research design in which the inquirer generates a general explanation (a theory) or a process, action, or interaction shaped by the views of a large number of participants."[28] According to Creswell, the intent of a grounded theory study is "to move beyond description and to generate or discover a theory, an abstract analytical schema of a process."[29] Participants in a study will all have experienced the same process (in this case, recovery from burnout). The central idea of a grounded theory study is that theory-development is generated by data gleaned from participants who have gone through the same process. Interaction between the researcher and participants with shared experience will provide a deeper meaning to the data, to be able to understand the "significance of the human experience, in context of the whole human experience."[30]

Grounded theory employs comparative analysis of the data from the earliest stages, fine tuning of the research questions and theoretical sampling, coding of the data to create categories, and re-constructing of the theoretical categories. Essentially, this method follows systematic inductive guidelines for gathering and analyzing data to construct "middle range theoretical frameworks that explain the collected data," in order to discover the values and attitudes of a certain people group, in this case NBKMs, and their strategies (or efforts) for recovery from burnout.[31]

I began by questioning, not by suggesting a hypothesis. I then collected data and, through comparative analysis and theoretical sampling, constructed a theory. The grounded theory approach required constant comparative analysis, interviews, and theoretical sampling. Subsequently, I conducted oral interviews and observations to reach the theoretical saturation point of this study.

26. Creswell, *Qualitative Inquiry*.
27. Strauss and Corbin, *Basics of Qualitative Research: Techniques*.
28. Strauss and Corbin as cited in Creswell, *Qualitative Inquiry*, 63.
29. Creswell, *Qualitative Inquiry*, 63.
30. Van Manen, *Researching Lived Experience*, 62.
31. Charmaz as cited in Denzin and Lincoln, "Introduction," 509.

The Background and Development of Grounded Theory

Grounded theory was developed by Strauss and Glaser in 1967, two sociologists who felt that systematic theories used in research were frequently "inappropriate and ill-suited" for study participants.[32] The two researchers ultimately developed differing approaches, resulting in their separation. Glaser criticized Strauss's approach "as too prescribed and structured."[33] Later, Grounded Theory became synthesized: the more systematic procedures of Strauss and Corbin,[34] with the constructivist approach of Charmaz.[35]

Between the two approaches of Grounded Theory, I have chosen to rely on the systematic approach of Strauss and Corbin[36] in applying Grounded Theory to this research:

> The investigator seeks to systematically develop a theory that explains process, action, or interaction on a topic (e.g. the process of developing a curriculum, the therapeutic benefits of sharing psychological test results with clients). The researcher typically conducts 20-30 interviews based on several visits "to the field" to collect interview data to saturate the categories (or find information that continues to add to them until no more can be found.[37]

I conducted this study with thirty-nine NBKM participants. I observed and collected data until reaching saturation of the emerging theoretical categories. For this, the systematic approach better explains the process, action, and interaction with my topic, because, as Creswell contended, research must "be 'grounded' in data from the field, especially in the actions, interactions, and social processes of people."[38] This approach to research recognizes the value of both the subjective and objective realities of subjects' experiences.

---

32. Creswell, *Qualitative Inquiry*, 63.

33. Creswell, *Qualitative Inquiry*, 63.

34. Strauss and Corbin, *Basics of Qualitative Research: Grounded Theory*; Strauss and Corbin, *Basics of Qualitative Research: Techniques*.

35. Charmaz, *Constructing Grounded Theory*.

36. Strauss and Corbin, *Basics of Qualitative Research: Grounded Theory*; Strauss and Corbin, *Basics of Qualitative Research: Techniques*.

37. Creswell, *Qualitative Inquiry*, 64.

38. Creswell, *Qualitative Inquiry*, 63.

In contrast to this reliance on both subjective and objective reality, the constructivist approach is limiting. Charmaz noted that in

> Constructivist grounded theory . . . the viewer creates the data and ensuing analysis . . . the "discovered" reality arises from the interactive process and its temporal, cultural, and structural context. Researcher and subjects frame that interaction and confer meaning upon it.[39]

I reject the implied value of solely subjective conclusions reached in the relativistic, constructivist approach. However, Charmaz rightly suggested that qualitative traditions are developed by studying experience from the point of view of those who live it, as provided by grounded theory.[40] Yet, there is more to theory development than subjective opinion. It is not so simple, "Constructivists aim to include multiple voices, views, and visions in their rendering of lived experience. How does one accomplish this?"[41] The views, values, beliefs, feelings, assumptions, and ideologies of individuals are important, from Charmaz's standpoint. Even though its interpretive approach has attractive elements (e.g. flexibility in structure),[42] I do not entirely agree with Charmaz, who asserts that any conclusions developed by grounded theorists are suggestive, incomplete, and inconclusive.[43] What is more, I am convinced that the systematic procedure best matches my biblical worldview as the means to research objective reality within the Korean cultural context. Hiebert affirmed that critical realism holds there is a real world outside, and that people from different cultures experience it:[44]

> While different cultures construct different internal maps of reality, all of them must correspond in significant ways to that external world or humans cannot exist . . . all our knowledge is partial and approximate. Knowledge in critical realism is not one or a series of photographs, nor is it individual Rorschachs. It is many complementary maps or blueprints.[45]

---

39. Charmaz, "Grounded Theory," 524.
40. Charmaz, "Grounded Theory," 522.
41. Charmaz, "Grounded Theory," 525.
42. Creswell, *Qualitative Inquiry*, 66.
43. Charmaz as cited in Creswell, *Qualitative Inquiry*, 66
44. Hiebert, *Transforming Worldviews*, 19.
45. Hiebert, *Transforming Worldviews*, 274.

Procedures in Conducting Grounded Theory

This section will discuss: 1) question formation, 2) theoretical sampling, 3) interview and observation data collection, and 4) data analysis and coding.

Forming my questions

Permission was obtained before data were collected via interviews. After initial questioning and analysis of the issues, the researcher asked the participants additional questions to elicit greater detail. The asking of questions and thinking about the range of possible answers is a tool that is useful at every stage of analysis, from the beginning to the final writing.[46]

Theoretical sampling

Glaser and Strauss defined theoretical sampling as

> the process of data collection for generating theory whereby the analyst jointly collects, codes and analyzes his data and then decides what data to collect next and where to find them, in order to develop his theory as it emerges.[47]

Interview and observation data collection

I collected data through participant-observation and interviews. Marshall and Rossman promote the necessity of immersion by the researcher:

> Participant observation demands firsthand involvement in the social world chosen for study. Immersion in the setting permits the researcher to hear, to see, and to begin to experience reality as the participants do . . . this immersion offers the researcher the opportunity to learn directly from his own experience.[48]

I observed and participated in several mission organization gatherings. For more than one year, I established rapport with each organization and church.

---

46. Corbin and Strauss, *Basics of Qualitative Research*, 69.
47. Glaser and Strauss as cited in Dey, "Grounded Theory," 83.
48. Marshall and Rossman, *Design Qualitative Research*, 100.

METHODS AND PROCEDURES

Interviews provided reportable data because an interview goes deeper than casual conversation and reviews earlier events, beliefs, and emotions.[49]

Criteria and number of participants selected for this grounded theory study

According to Creswell, "this process begins with a homogenous sample of individuals who are similar."[50] This research sample consists of NBKMs who have experienced and overcome burnout—participants with worldwide experience who have left mission fields to relocate in and around Los Angeles, CA, and NBKMs attending a Korean World Mission Council conference in Chicago, IL, July 20-24, 2012.

Time frame, number of interviews, length and location, protocol

The sample was purposely selected from first generation Korean missionaries. These thirty-nine participants, individuals who were born and educated up to high school in Korea, both ethnically and culturally "Korean," had experienced the same phenomenon of burnout due to worldview, cultural values and differences. Each interview lasted at least one hour. These individuals were on furlough in the Los Angeles area or were attending a mission conference in Chicago. Though the participants came from different walks of life and different countries, they all shared the experience of being cross-cultural missionaries who had overcome burnout.

I asked the participants open-ended questions about how their experiences with their churches, sending organizations, families, spiritual formation, counseling, mentoring, and inner healing contributed to their strategies for overcoming burnout (See Appendix A). Due to the fact that I am a first generation *female*, it was occasionally difficult to arrange meetings directly with first generation NBK male missionaries. Furthermore, because of cultural reluctance to express failings, my participants shared in a limited manner what occurred during their missionary burnout. Therefore, as needed, I also contacted mission directors to help with my interviews. It was important that the participants knew I was a learner who had shared a similar process of burnout and recovery. In order to gain the trust of the participants, ethical behavior and confidentiality was ensured.

49. Charmaz, *Constructing Grounded Theory*.
50. Creswell, *Qualitative Inquiry*, 240.

Participants' Demographics

The participants included 16 married men, 11 married women, and 12 single women. Sixteen of them were between the ages of 56 and 66, 15 between the ages of 46 and 55, and 8 between the ages of 36 and 45. Among the men, 3 out of 16 were lay workers, not ordained pastors. Most of the married women were theologically educated, with only 3 out of the 11 having no theological education. As for single women, 2 out of the 12 were lay workers, while the rest were theologically educated with a master's degree or above. Study participants were not only well educated but also had five to thirty years of cross-cultural ministry experience. Most were pioneers in the Korean-sending mission field. Every single one them experienced burnout at least once. Yet, all recovered and persevered in ministry.

Ethical Considerations

Gathering data on strategies for overcoming burnout among NBKMs required participants sharing sensitive loss-of-face situations. According to Hofstede and Associates, there is power distance in Korean culture: masculine values are considered more important than feminine values.[51] In a society highly sensitive to shame and conscious of social standing, particularly in church and mission leadership, sharing these sensitive situations is easily perceived as a sign of weakness or failure.

Conducting this study required me to show respect and consideration for participants. I obtained informed consent from them (see Appendix B). They were never required to share any information that they were not comfortable sharing.

All data were kept confidential. To preserve confidentiality, the identity of participants and all affiliated churches and mission organizations and their locations were masked.

Participants shared their personal stories and experiences from the mission field and mission organizations. Their honest reflections could have resulted in awkward situations vis-à-vis their churches and mission organizations. Hence, I was particularly careful to protect the interviewees' privacy. I referred to specific Korean churches and mission organizations by random designation (e.g. Church-A and Organization-M). I used pseudonyms or generic designations in referring to study participants.

51. Hofstede, *Masculinity and Femininity*, 19.

Finally, I obtained permission from the Protection of Human Rights in Research Committee (PHRRC) at Biola University, prior to collecting data (see Appendix C).

Data Analysis Strategies

As a preliminary to analysis, all interviews were transcribed word-for-word. Verbatim transcripts of the interviews were essential data for the next phase of Grounded Theory: coding, analysis, and further theoretical sampling.

Data were analyzed using three phases of coding: open coding, to develop categories of information; axial coding, interconnecting the categories; and selective coding, building a "story" that connects the categories—ending with a set of theoretical positions.[52]

Open Coding

In open coding, "the researcher forms categories of information about the phenomenon being studied by segmenting information."[53] In this study the interviews were coded and analyzed immediately following each interview session. In this step of analysis categories of information were identified from the data: "the process of breaking down, examining, comparing, conceptualizing, and categorizing data."[54] I assigned codes line-by-line; "in vivo" codes were used where possible to keep the analysis close to the actual data. Charmaz emphasized the importance of a systematic approach; "word-by-word and line-by-line coding help you to see the familiar in new light."[55]

Axial Coding

In axial coding, "the investigator compiles the data in new ways after open coding in relation to the phenomenon."[56] I categorized and compared data to determine their contribution to a theoretical category. I grouped coded interview segments as I sought to understand what part each played vis-à-vis

---

52. Strauss and Corbin as cited in Creswell, *Qualitative Inquiry*, 160
53. Creswell, *Qualitative Inquiry*, 67.
54. Strauss and Corbin, *Basics of Qualitative Research: Grounded Theory*, 61.
55. Charmaz, *Constructing Grounded Theory*, 55.
56. Creswell, *Qualitative Inquiry*, 67.

the central phenomenon. As Creswell noted, axial coding (dimensions of a category: a dense texture of relationships) provided "insight into specific coding categories that relate or explain the central phenomenon."[57] I sought to "saturate" the categories using the constant comparative approach.

Selective Coding

In selective coding, "the researcher may write a 'story line' that connects the categories" to elaborate the development and integration of data in comparison to other groups.[58] Once a dominant category is evident from the data, irrelevant data may emerge and be removed. As the data are coded and categories developed, important ideas will be recorded—memos. The result of this process of data collection and analysis is a theory.[59]

In the case of my study, selective coding generated the following theory (to be discussed in subsequent chapters): Native born-Korean Missionaries (NBKMs) who have experienced burnout pass through several stages on their path to recovery. The process begins with a new measure of awareness of their condition and an effort to do something about it. Such efforts are characterized by either works-based Self-Help (leading to relapse), or Self-Care marked by reliance on a source of help other than self (leading to healing).

Validation and Verification

Qualitative research has garnered much criticism in the scientific ranks for its failure to "adhere to canons of reliability and validation" in the traditional sense.[60] Yet, alternative ways of thinking about reliability and replicability have emerged from qualitative methodologists (e.g., Seale) specific to validation of the study: "internal" and "external" reliability, member checks, audit trail, reflexivity; providing a rich, thick description; and peer review, triangulation, and clarifying researcher bias. Internal reliability refers to the extent to which a measure is consistent within itself. External reliability, on the other hand, "concerns the replicability of entire

---

57. Creswell, *Qualitative Inquiry*, 161.
58. Creswell, *Qualitative Inquiry*, 67.
59. Creswell, *Qualitative Inquiry*.
60. Creswell, *Qualitative Inquiry*, 202.

studies: would other researchers studying the same or similar settings generate the same findings?"[61]

For the purposes of this study, I employed the following six validation strategies: 1) member checks, 2) an audit trail, 3) reflexivity, 4) rich, thick description, 5) triangulation, and 6) bias clarification.

Member Checks

Creswell stated that this technique is considered to be "the most critical technique for establishing credibility."[62] I presented my data, analyses, interpretations, and conclusions to participants for them to evaluate the accuracy and credibility of the interpretation—NBKMs were both participants and examiners.

Audit Trail

Merriam and Associates state simply, "The audit trail is dependent upon the researcher keeping a research journal or recording memos throughout the conduct of the study."[63] Accounts of the methods, procedures, and decision points in carrying out this study were detailed and written down.

Reflexivity

Reflexivity is the process of "reflecting critically on the self as researcher, the human as instrument."[64] The researcher describes the thesis, how the participants were chosen, the study context, and values or assumptions brought to the study. I included in the write-up critical analyses of the effects of my interaction as a human instrument.

Providing Rich, Thick Description

To ensure that the findings are transferable between the researcher and those being studied, a rich, thick description is necessary—detailed description

   61. Seale, *Quality of Qualitative Research*, 141.
   62. Creswell, *Qualitative Inquiry*, 208.
   63. Merriam et al., *Qualitative Research in Practice*, 26–27.
   64. Guba and Lincoln, "Paradigmatic Controversies," 210.

of the participants and setting under study.[65] This is especially necessary for "seeing the bigger picture, the dynamics and connections at work between issues/concepts, for dealing with concrete/practical ideas, and for giving thick descriptions."[66] My write up contains rich, thick descriptions of participants' experiences.

Triangulation

In triangulation, researchers make "use of multiple and different sources, methods, investigators, and theories to provide corroborating evidence."[67] In this study, multiple methods of data collection were used. This study confirmed results using data from different sources to clarify specific themes or perspectives. Some of the methods used included audio and video recording, note-taking, and photography.

Researcher Bias

Reflecting on and identifying researcher bias from the outset of the study is important so that the reader understands the researcher's position and any assumptions that may impact the study. The researcher may explain past experiences, biases, prejudices, and worldviews that may have shaped the understanding and approach to the current study.[68]

Because I am a first generation Korean woman (and NBKM) who grew up in Korea, I recognize that there may be biases in this study. I have served previously as a cross-cultural missionary in many countries and recognize that my assumptions, based on past experiences, may have impacted this study.

Conclusion

This chapter discussed the research design and procedures used in conducting this study. I reviewed the philosophical assumptions underlying qualitative research, my choice of the grounded theory approach, and explained

---

65. Creswell, *Qualitative Inquiry*, 209.
66. Enns, "Now I Know in Part," 265.
67. Creswell, *Qualitative Inquiry*, 208.
68. Creswell, *Qualitative Inquiry*.

METHODS AND PROCEDURES

my data collection strategy and data sources. I identified my participants and explained the interview process. I told how I analyzed the collected data using open, axial, and selective coding procedures, while memoing continuously. The data revealed the participants' life experiences and the process of recovering from burnout. The next chapter discusses my findings with regard to burnout recovery.

4

Sources and Consequences of Burnout

THE CENTRAL UNDERSTANDING TO emerge from this study, based on data collected from thirty-nine participants, is that Native born-Korean Missionaries (NBKMs) who experienced burnout passed through several stages on their way to recovery. The process began when burnout forced a new level of awareness of their condition and an effort to do something about it. Such efforts were characterized by either works-based Self-Help (independent help leading to relapse), or grace-based Self-Care marked by humble reliance on a source of help other than self (interdependent care leading to healing through healthy relationships with God and others), as illustrated in Figure 16. This chapter provides a preliminary overview of the important stages on the path to recovery (to which the whole of chapter five is devoted). However, prior to turning to an in-depth discussion of recovery, it was necessary to visit study participants' descriptions of the causes and effects of burnout, which parallel the literature discussed in chapter two. Even though this dissertation focuses on recovering from burnout, study participants were keen to share their perceptions of the causes and effects of burnout because cause and effect informed their understanding of the recovery process. Hence, chapter four is devoted to discussing burnout's causes and effects. After exploring participants' paths to recovery in chapter five, chapter six discusses manifestations (or signs) of recovery.

Before explaining in greater detail NBKMs' paths to recovery, this chapter will discuss (in separate sections) the causes and effects of their burnout. It is necessary to understand these causes and effects in order to comprehend fully the paths to recovery. Lastly, signs of recovery—spiritual, psychological, and physical wellness and transformed thinking—will be discussed.

SOURCES AND CONSEQUENCES OF BURNOUT

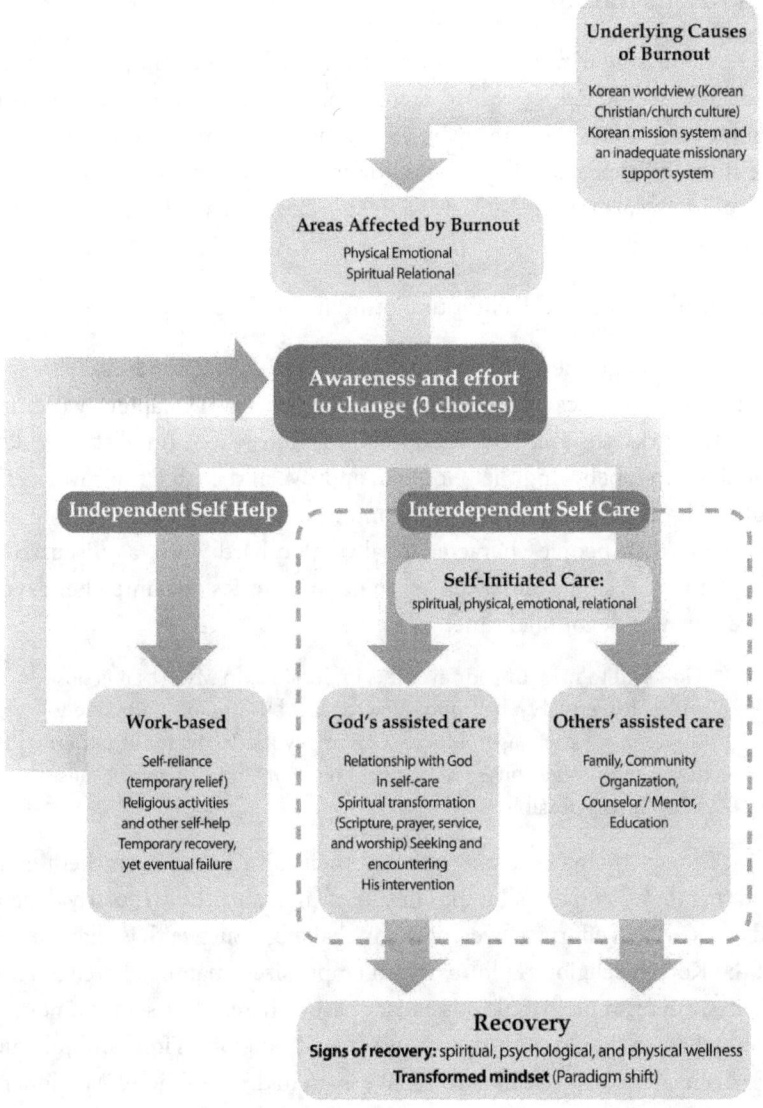

Figure 16. Recovery Approaches: Chart of Data Self-Reported by NBKMs

Sources of Burnout

Korean missionaries are at a disadvantage when adapting to other cultures due to the deeply rooted dictates of their cultural worldview. Three sources of Korean missionary burnout emerged from the research data: 1) a culturally-impacted religious foundation, 2) the Korean mission system, including local churches and mission agencies, and 3) a lack of self-care.

Culturally Impacted Religious Foundation

Due to the engrained Korean Christian, Confucian, Buddhist, Shamanic and other influences on religious practices (as seen in Chapter Two), many Korean Christians are influenced to be religiously and ritualistically dedicated to God, believing that God will approve and enable their work. This culturally-impacted religious foundation shapes the Korean Christian culture, in which people characteristically value hard work, as discussed in chapter two. A single female pastor in her mid-fifties recounted her experience during a devotional time:

> God said to me, "In your eyes it is impossible. In My eyes it is possible." It seemed to be impossible for me, but in God I am able to do it. This is the reason I focused on my work. In my mind I knew it was impossible, but in faith, I kept on *doing* my ministry because I saw it was possible.

Though the participants assumed their faith would keep them going, and that they could do "all things in Christ," in reality they regularly depended on their own efforts to overcome any challenge. Such faith is characteristic of the Korean religious culture, which emphasizes quantifiable religious activities. For example, a male missionary pastor shared, "We set the amount of hours that we should pray, the way we should do Quiet Time, and the number of chapters that we should read. We learn to do all of these." Missionaries reported working very hard to maintain control of their circumstances by acting on their cultural and religious assumptions regarding leadership and the expectation of God's approval of their actions.

These missionaries struggled and continued striving to work until they recognized they had not overcome their burnout. A female pastor realized the limits of her efforts,

> As I spoke with [the locals] and saw they did not understand me, I tried forcing them to accept my thoughts and to follow what I told them to do. But I came to realize I could not change them but only God could do so.

A male lay missionary in his mid-forties realized his own limitations, saying, "I cried many, many times and wondered, 'How can I change my situation?' I really didn't know how, seeing my limitations. How can I serve the locals . . . in what ways?" Although realizing their limits helped these missionaries to reorient themselves, nevertheless, the Korean culture powerfully impacted their view of themselves as potential failures. In Korean Christian culture, strong, independent faith is considered sufficient to meet all difficulties, so any failure suggests personal and spiritual weakness.

Furthermore, the strong work ethic of the NBKMs interviewed—especially of males—put the focus on spiritual life and its practices to the neglect of their physical limitations, often leading to overwork and ill health. This response from one male NBKM leader shows the extent to which he abused his body.

> As a trainer for Korean missionaries, my physical condition became run-down. My body has always lacked stamina, being fatigued easily. For example, I would be so ill that I would not be able to sing all the way to the end of a song. Yet I believed that in such circumstances, the way to heaven was to simply endure. Seeing my students growing and being motivated to become right with God gave me joy, and once again I felt what I am doing was confirmed by God.

The Korean Mission System

The Korean mission system has been likewise impacted by the culture. Study participants perceived that the Korean mission system's focus on sending rather than sustaining missionaries did not fully prepare them for cultural challenges. This problem is twofold: the lack of training and the lack of systematic support.

Lack of training

The interviewees indicated that without sufficient preparation, it was hard for them to adjust to other cultural contexts. A male pastor in his mid-forties commented on his need for preparation:

> I realized that it is important not only to go to Egypt but also how to go. Rather than overcoming my struggles completely through my own effort, God helped me to realize the basics of mission, and I am in the process of determining how I am going to prepare for the mission before I go there again. Without the preparation, it would be really hard to go to mission [field].

Without cross-cultural training, the NBKMs were ill equipped for appropriate cross-cultural adaptation. A female pastor indicated confusion with the multicultural context she served in, "All the culture becomes mixed . . . . As I confronted language barrier difficulties, I thought how can understand this? . . . What am I going to do in this context?" Inadequate mission training and poor cross-cultural adjustment contributed to burnout. For example, a missionary wife in her late fifties shared,

> Having raised my children, honestly, I was burned out in [the field] . . . the primitive environment. Of course, it was not just an environmental problem, but also, the children, who made us annoyed and stressed. I could not handle the stress of childcare, so that I became sick. I thought I would rather give up this mission work and thus prayed. Yet, in that I gave up my self-will and became obedient to His call to go. I decided to go back to the mission field, in spite of my severe emotional and physically sickness, right after my [physical] surgery.

The lack of systematic support

The lack of training in mission organizations points to the underlying problem of its lack of an entire systematic support system. For example, a missionary to Egypt contended that the Korean church and mission system needed to be renewed, and that it was focused on a narrow agenda emphasizing the growth of organization and numbers:

> Do you know why missionaries burn out? The church merely sends missionaries and does nothing else; they provide us no further support in the field, in part because they don't understand

the context of the mission field. However, the church continues to communicate strong expectations for results and success. This is how Korean churches cause missionary burnout.

He saw this lack of proper focus broadly affecting the entire mission effort:

> The Korean church should reflect a [gospel] focus by placing the truth [of Christ] as fundamental, and use this to reestablish the mission system. The structure of the Korean church should be renewed because of this systemic problem . . . The process of the sending church is wrong . . . This is not an individual problem, it is a problem with the system . . . including outside pressure and the cultural system, which influences the Korean sending church . . . there is a lack of communication and relationship between Korean churches and missionaries.

The data indicated a lack of systematic support systems to prepare Korean missionaries for transition to a foreign culture as well as a failure to identify those missionaries who might be predisposed to burnout in the field. Participants noted the missionary agencies' lack of mission support for NBKMs' self-care. A single female pastor in her mid-fifties reported,

> Korean missionary agencies do not have self-care whatsoever. There is not even a concept of self-care. People cannot understand how a missionary can have depression. They say, "What! Depression! How can a missionary have a depression! Doesn't he pray?" or . . . when we return for a sabbatical . . . average layperson does not have any clue . . . when they do not see any results, they cut off their support. In this kind of environment, you can't even imagine such thing as missionary care. There is no concept of caring for missionaries.

For these Korean missionaries, it is not culturally acceptable to be unsuccessful in their struggles, and therefore they do not share problems with the church or with sending agencies that expect either miracles or personal sacrifice in the face of any challenge (as discussed in chapter two).

Similarly, a male pastor and mission leader reported how the viewpoint of the Korean sending church further discourages the practice of self-care and rather reinforces among missionaries a mentality and self-conception of being poor and needy in order to fulfill the church's expectations and receive support. One of the mission directors explained the difficult relationship inherent between the organizations, such as sending churches, and missionaries.

> The Korean [church] thinks that if you are suffering, working under hard conditions, getting by with minimal possessions and with little money, then they think that missionaries are doing their job well. So this causes the missionaries to develop a hypocritical behavior that fulfills church's expectation of the role and agenda of missionaries. When missionaries do not overtly display need and suffering, the church suspects them of being dishonest. This creates an environment where missionaries have no other way to behave.

Furthermore, there are some unhealthy team-leadership problems in the mission field. One missionary director in Eastern Europe described troubles among those with whom he worked,

> Some mission leaders who should be cured or healed in their mental health, consider other co-workers to be personally competitive . . . many problems arise on the mission team in the field . . . the personnel are not in good mental health . . . cooperation is not good . . . causing relational problems . . . fighting with each other, rumors, and miscommunication.

These NBKMs faced a variety of difficulties related to church and personal expectations as well as a lack of rest and of support in relationships. They attempted to meet the mission agenda, while trying to remain strong in the faith that caused them to face undue hardships, including isolation and feeling left out in the mission field.

Without systematic pre-field support and orientation to address the importance of rest and other forms of self-care, burnout will persist. A single female pastor in Indonesia explained,

> Korean people do not know how to rest, this is the disease! . . . I was not wise enough to take care of my health. I never had an orientation about it . . . because I was a forerunner in my mission organization. There were no people before me. I was the first one so I did not have any wisdom about the tropical place.

This pastor claimed that when NBKMs are without one of the most important forms of self-care—having supportive relationships with other Korean missionaries—burnout becomes more likely. A female pastor in her late fifties recalled, "For me there were more hardships caused by missionaries [Korean co-workers] than local people."

This lack of mission support in relationships clearly contributed to burnout. Like this woman, most of the NBKMs interviewed did not want to share their struggles because they would lose face as a missionary. One

NBKM leader told me, "Missionaries do not share unless have trustworthy relationships . . . by not sharing . . . the difficult issues and stories, they cover it up . . . or they try to figure it out case by case . . . this is the biggest cause of NBKMs' burnout." Fostering self-reliance and isolation rather than cooperative reliance on others caused burnout. A single female missionary in her mid-forties recounted the self-reliance that isolated her from conflict and competition among other NBKMs.

> I felt depressed and couldn't share my thoughts . . . we should have been supportive of one another in our missionary community . . . I chose to be isolated, away from conflict and those competitive people. I had to focus on God. Yet I ended up being burnt out due to loneliness and the conflict-driven relationships with my co-workers.

Without a support system, most missionaries relied on themselves to survive. One might expect marital relationships to be a helpful support system. However, as one NBKM wife noted "in the Korean mentality, it is known that 'buy one get one free.' Pastors' wives are like shadows, going after their husbands, and thus, not needing to exercise their own giftings." Participating missionary wives identified with the confusion regarding their callings—which, for them, contributed to burnout.

Lack of Self-Care

Self-care is both necessary and elusive for NBKMs because they often lack a realistic sense of self. Characteristically, NBKMs lack a sense of boundaries and a proper understanding of the importance of spiritual, physical and emotional wellbeing. They overextend themselves with no regard for personal resource management. This weakness was noted by a pastor missionary in his late fifties, "Those who did not overcome burnout tend to stubbornly believe that they have actually overcome burnout. In reality, they should be seriously concerned for their [mental or spiritual] states." This overconfidence, among other perceptions, is consistent with Korean beliefs about missionaries.

Korean missionary family life promotes a specific conception of the roles of men and women, which does not include proper emotional boundaries. One's own needs as an individual may often go unexpressed and unattended, in an effort to maintain group harmony. Saving face is primary, so emotional expression is discouraged. One participant in his mid-forties recounted a consequence of growing up in the traditional family:

> My father pushed me. I have tendency of being a perfectionist. Although I would do 90 out of 100, if I did not get a perfect score, I imagined my father's thoughts [i.e., reaction] and tried to make him feel better. I think the image that I had of my father, which was perfectionism, was reflected in my image of God, so I tried to make Him happy.

This participant represents a typical example of Korean perfectionist missionary burnout. His family background greatly influenced his personality and character. Perfectionism, expectations of strong leadership, and suppression of emotions and desires created an elitist personality that struggles in a cross-cultural context, characterized by difficulties leading to burnout in four major areas of the NBKM's life: physical, emotional, spiritual, and relational.

Consequences of Burnout

Based on the study findings, burnout appears to affect Korean missionaries in four areas of their wellbeing: physical, spiritual, emotional, and relational. While burnout generally affects some combination of the four areas, I will discuss each individually.

Physical Wellbeing

Physical wellbeing includes proper nutrition, exercise, and taking time off. Most study participants mentioned burnout affecting their physical wellbeing. For example, one missionary wife explained the deterioration of her health in these terms:

> I was really persevering with my sick condition. Even though filled with the Holy Spirit in my prayer . . . my prayer became weaker. I realized my physical condition worsened . . . . It took five years for me to recover and gain energy. In the underdeveloped environment [of the mission field] my condition weakened. But, when I went back to Korea for a break, my physical condition slowly recovered.

This missionary wife thought that her trust in the Holy Spirit, alone, would help her get better. She deferred dealing with her physical condition, confessing that her biggest mistake was that she had waited too long to take a break and therefore her body could not recover right away. She regretted the delay, waiting for God to intervene, rather than taking care of the issue as she was capable of doing. However, she realized in retrospect the importance of self-care and proper treatment when it was needed. It is evident from the data that men, too, are subject to physical burnout, perhaps to a greater degree and more commonly because of the compulsion to achieve approval. For example, one pastor in his late fifties described his experience:

> Yeah, I was very unwise, and kept on pursuing ministry without rest. But after a while, I became very exhausted and run down and all the energy was sucked out of me when I was doing ministry in [Asia]. It made me very tense. There was this one time that I fainted and collapsed due to weariness.

A lay participant in his mid-forties recounted the confusion and loss of health stemming from lack of self-awareness and right relationship with God:

> I focused on the work. You know, a Korean man focuses on his work—it is all about ministry. I did not work as God wanted me to do; I did what I wanted to do. With my agenda . . . I thought it was God's will . . . I burned out [physically] because I had been a workaholic for two years without realizing it. I did not know myself. I burned out.

Without self-awareness, these NBKMs reinforced the behaviors and attitudes that lead to physical burnout. The approval of others and need for accomplishment made it hard for them to see their limits.

Spiritual Wellbeing

In contrast, the symptoms of burnout related to spiritual wellbeing include exhaustion in one's prayer life and lack of intimacy with God. On the surface, the NBKMs interviewed looked spiritually healthy, but on the inside their spiritual practice did not lead to genuine, intimate connection with God. One late-forties male missionary to Egypt stated:

> There is no one to check on me. My spirituality feels dry, like a rice field without water. I thought I could manage my spiritual

dryness with my own strength. I kept driving myself to participate in worship and other formal spiritual duties, but I still felt spiritual dryness.

Other reported spiritual symptoms of burnout included emptiness and exhaustion in one's prayer life. Most participants recognized the deterioration of spiritual health as their most important loss. One mid-forties male NBKM went through heavy spiritual suffering and became completely spiritually exhausted:

> I became physically, mentally, spiritually, completely exhausted . . . being spiritually empty. My strength was completely sapped as I was lying down . . . at that time, I felt complete burnout . . . I wanted to kill myself several times. I was completely burnt out spiritually, completely exhausted . . . . At that time faintly I was saying that God, You are taking me, I will go. I was worshipping like that.

Even repeated and increased spiritual practices, such as continuous prayer, failed to fill his spiritual emptiness. Suicide, the ultimate physical escape, seemed to be his best solution for ending his exhaustion. This burnout affected not only his spiritual wellbeing but also his emotional wellbeing.

Emotional Wellbeing

Emotional wellbeing involves having an emotionally healthy view of oneself and others. Emotional balance is critical: NBKMs, like all people, are affected by negative emotions, often accompanied by identity crises. Female participants, more often and with greater detail and expressiveness than males, reported that the most obvious symptoms of burnout were the disturbing emotions that appeared—anger, depression, bitterness, feelings of betrayal, and loneliness, among others.

A female pastor missionary in her fifties identified some of the attitudes, emotions and distorted perceptions that accompany burnout:

> I did my best for one year, putting out all my energy—I burned out. Do you know why Korean pastors are burned out? That is, not only feeling depressed, but [we] are tired of the people to whom we minister because we always help them, but with no result, no gaining salvation. There is no spiritual growth among the local believers. We feel betrayed.

Her negative perspective of those around her was not unique to her. Another single female missionary also experienced the signs of emotional ill health.

> The symptom was that I became very angry and was easily offended by people. I then questioned myself, "Do those people really make me angry?" Suddenly I realized my part and I repented in the evening for the anger I experienced during the day. I couldn't really be thankful for everything in my daily life because of my anger, and this hardened my heart. I became very sad about the hardness of my feelings because I couldn't repent.

Some reported feelings of disappointment and anger with the locals whom they served, struggling with discouragement and disappointment. A pastor in his fifties explained:

> The reason that I felt that I was sick was because of the . . . locals whom I served. I would have liked to hear "thank you" from them; I would have liked to feel their appreciation. I have this desire because I had put all of my energy and my heart into them. I was also physically and spiritually hurt by them . . . I ended up hospitalized . . . Emotionally I was very angry and wondered whether I should continue to serve them. This doubt caused me great turmoil and suffering.

Others' emotional wellbeing was affected by colleagues. For example:

> I felt victimized and betrayed by my co-workers and colleagues. Apart from them, I reflected on myself, and whether I perpetrated trouble for my co-workers and team members. They may feel that way about me . . . . I thought I had made a lot of sacrifices to them to raise them in ministry.

Emotional well-being also affected missionary self-identity. The study participants frequently experienced an identity crisis after burnout. These missionaries were not exempt from the struggle to know one's self, to understand their true identity as children of God. Among those who mentioned diminished confidence in their adequacy for the role in the mission field, role confusion, loss of mission vision, and cultural disorientation emerged as prominent symptoms of damage to their identities as NBKM who had been called and equipped by God. Loss of vision caused one missionary to doubt his calling.

> I don't know what to say about Korean burnout? Can it be *Taljin [burnout]*? *Sojin*? Like *Taljin*, I understand and I entered the mission field . . . how to live and do ministry . . . at first they have determination toward their goals and prepare their hearts in faith. However, as time goes by, their belief fades away. I wonder why I am here! What am I doing here! . . . I counseled myself. At that time, my vision became unclear because of burnout *[Taljin, Sojin]*.

Another missionary's depression resulted in confusion about his identity:

> As I shared with you, I received financial support from my church. However, I felt sorry for myself. Am I a good-for-nothing? In the Middle East mission field, many Middle Eastern missionaries experience a big worry . . . due to cultural and language barrier: the limits to evangelism in the mission field. We [I] felt depressed because we couldn't work, as we [I] were used to working in the Korean church context. As a pastor and missionary, I languished and lost of my identity. Am I a missionary? Am I really a pastor?

In his late forties one pastor realized:

> In the mission field, I collapsed. This was because there were no sheep or supporting groups. I left for the mission field alone, with my family. When I did not find my identity in relationship with God, I felt lonely. I think many missionaries do not understand this while they were ministers in Korea.

These NBKMs' self-identity was primarily built on social status, family background, and respectable church status. The mission field, however, was oblivious to these, requiring them to establish new identities and assume new roles and statuses. These changes contributed to their burnout.

Relational Wellbeing

Relational wellbeing involves having a healthy relationship with God and with others, shown through one's mature character. Relationships are crucial. Participants reported, explicitly and implicitly, the inseparable connection between their relationship with God and with others. An inadequate relationship with God precipitated problems in human relationships. In this subsection, I address "relationship with God," then "relationship with others."

Relationship with God

A forty-five year old male missionary to the Middle East shared:

> We [I] were not able to focus on our mission ministry any more during the burnout. As I said, while I was praying and worshipping God, I realized what was very fundamental—my relationship with the Lord. That was what I was lacking. It is somehow shameful. As a missionary you go to a mission field. Coming before God is very fundamental and basic, and should be rooted [in the missionary].

Looking back, he realized that God was doing the ministry, not him. God was carrying out His mission, not him. He was not able to see that blind spot, but now he sees that "God is mission."

Another missionary experienced what others had—that burnout can bring them back to the core of mission:

> As a missionary, I engaged with missions work on my own agenda. However, it was not until I experienced physical burnout that I realized and was able to receive a clear vision and mission from the Lord in regards to my calling. In my weakest moments, I reestablished a deep relationship with the Lord, in which He breathed upon me new life to engage in missions.

This participant, as with others like him, came to understand that his mission was a way of *being*, rather than *doing*, which propelled him.

Relationship with others

Participants often reported peer conflicts as the primary concern and reason for seeking recovery. The data revealed that a frequent cause of conflict with others was the inability or unwillingness of one party or the other to forgive some real or imagined offense. For example, two missionary pastors described "unforgiveness" as a conflict issue. According to the first:

> I was unable to truly forgive those who had wronged me. I knew that in my mind, I tried to forgive them, and kept on telling myself to forgive. This is because I understood that since God is a God of forgiveness, I should also forgive. However, it was hard for me to forgive. I knew that unforgiveness caused a lot of suffering and bitterness in my life. So, I knew that I had to forgive . . . I also knew that it was better for me to stay silent, and not simply express what I was going through to others in order to avoid more problems.

However, during that time, it caused me to suffer despite knowing that it was better for me to be silent. I knew staying silent would be hard for me, yet I chose to do so. Instead, I turned to prayer. This helped me realize that I had to forgive them in my heart, not just outwardly. I started to pray a lot and cried out to God to have mercy on those I could not forgive . . . I couldn't share my unforgiveness with anyone else, apart from God.

The second indicated relational difficulty with the locals:

It took a long time for me to recover because I felt betrayed by a local whom I discipled. This sister betrayed me, which fed my burnout. I couldn't pray. I really hated her. I understood that I needed to forgive her. Although I deeply knew this, I couldn't forgive her for three to four years. It took me a long time before I could truly forgive her. I felt that I needed some special opportunities to release this burden of unforgiveness.

Another participant cited peer conflict as widespread among Korean missionaries everywhere:

Peer conflict is a very common issue in the mission field, most of the time. These conflicts are primarily with co-workers who also work under an NGO, many of whom are Koreans. These conflicts, foremost with other Korean missionaries, but also with local ministers, are a matter of great concern among Korean missionaries. I think that their [my] burnout is largely relational in nature.

The effects of problems in the field on all four areas of life were sometimes evident in the testimony of a single missionary. An unmarried female NBKM shared how burnout affected her emotionally, physically, spiritually, and relationally:

I think spiritual burnout comes first. Even in my preaching, when I tell myself to be thankful and joyful, I know that it is not how I actually feel in my daily life. I was trying to be thankful, but I couldn't do it. I was becoming emotionally sensitive and physically tired. I know my personality is very task oriented and I could not stop working because there was so much to do . . . . One symptom was that I became very angry and was easily offended by people.

Additionally, a single missionary recalled:

What shocked me mentally, what made me weary, was relationships. So, I asked myself what was wrong with me? Maybe I should not be a missionary . . . . Did I listen to God's voice wrong? I thought I definitely listened. What is going on with me? When I confronted my problem, it was hard for me.

Clearly, troubled relationships were a major indicator of burnout. Overwhelming feelings of self-doubt and confusion often arose in relational problems, and a duty-driven relationship with God inevitably affected the missionary's relationships with others, which in turn exacerbated stress on physical, emotional, and spiritual areas.

Chapter Four Summary

This chapter discussed the sources and consequences of burnout among NBKMs. The sources of burnout include problems arising from the culturally dominated religious background of Korean missionaries, the inadequacy of the Korean mission system with regard to training and systematic support, and the lack of self-care. Consequently, NBKMs experienced the physical, spiritual, emotional, and relational effects of burnout. These consequences are interrelated, revealing the NBKM's need for a healthy view of God, others, and self, in order to recover. The next chapter discusses how NBKMs approach recovery through the path of *self-effort* (self-help) or the path of *self-care*.

5
Paths To Recovery

ONCE AWARE OF THEIR problem and desiring change, study participants approached burnout recovery one of two ways: through self-help or through self-care. Self-help (self-reliance) is ultimately ineffective and results in a cycle of burnout, temporary or partial recovery, and repeated burnout (see Figure 16, with its arrow pointing back to the first step to recovery).

Because of culturally engrained self-reliance, resistance to self-disclosure, and reluctance to rely on others, the process leading to relapse was chiefly characterized by independent help, characterized by redoubling efforts in engaging in religious practices. These efforts brought only temporary relief unless the NBKM abandoned duty-centered and work-centered approaches to serving God and recognized God's nurture and the need for outside help, whether human or divine, leading to appropriate forms of self-care. Those who pursued relief through the self-reflection and growing self-awareness of self-care experienced God's intervention and received help (relational support and cognitive transformation) from other sources as essential elements of their process of healing and recovery. They exhibited signs of recovery, and reported healing and renewal through interdependent care. It is evident that in self-care, God's help and the help of others work hand-in-hand, leading to a holistic (physical, emotional, spiritual, and relational) healing process.

While most of the Korean missionaries interviewed first exercised self-help to bring temporary relief, when they saw the futility of self-reliance they were able to open up to God's intervention, leading to inner healing and spiritual transformation (see self-care in Figure 16). The resulting recovery led to lasting change in all areas of life, including foundational changes in perception of mission purpose and behavior.

Burnout (Taljin 탈진) must be cured. As mentioned above, two categories of recovery efforts emerged from the collected data: self-help and self-care. The path to recovery began with recognition that something was so severely wrong that action must be taken. Such awareness led to one of two approaches: 1) self-help, which leads to temporary relief, followed by relapse, or 2) self-care, which leads to healing and recovery. Self-care involved dependence on God and others. The following is a discussion of the two approaches: self-help, and self-initiated care leading to recovery.

Self-Help: Leading to Relapse

Self-help is essentially effort exerted by those who rely primarily on themselves to overcome burnout. Inevitably, as reported by every study participant, self-help does not lead to lasting healing or restoration. In several cases, employing increasingly rigorous spiritual disciplines brought temporary relief, leading sufferers to believe they had overcome burnout. For some time, they were able to function reasonably well, but eventually they came back to the same point of burnout again. Those who took the path of self-help used independent self-help strategies, performed religious activities, and attended seminars and conferences as they attempted to overcome burnout on their own.

Self-help is based on self-effort. For participants, the symptoms of the self-help mentality were characterized by attempts to fulfill expectations through accomplishments and independent effort. Many NBKMs felt hopeless. Although they did their best, they failed, causing disruption even in their inner lives. For example, a male missionary described his self-help mentality, "In the beginning I tried not to rely on others . . . because of that I pushed myself and worked hard and therefore became very tired spiritually, physically, and emotionally sometimes to the point of exhaustion." His fatigue was driven by his dependence on his own abilities and work, as opposed to his relationship with God. After failure, many of these NBKM interviewees made two kinds of efforts to treat the symptoms: religious activities and attending seminars and conferences.

Religious Activities

Religious activities include worship, prayer, Bible reading, and ministry service. NBKMs who engaged in such activities believed they would be restored by clinging solely to God and waiting for him to intervene as they increased their religious activity. This approach may reflect a sense of *noonchi* (i.e., the self-conscious concern for others' views and opinions of them). They seemed to manifest a strong sense of *noonchi* toward God—always checking whether they are in the right stance with God based on their performance as missionaries (as mentioned in chapter two). Religious attempts at self-help included private worship, devotions, and prayer.

Through worship and prayer, missionaries strove to move God to act on their behalf. Such missionaries clung to their spiritual practices during burnout even when their prayer time did not feel effective. For example, a male missionary, looking back on his experience, described the disconnect between religious activities and burnout recovery:

> Spirituality was not increasing. I always had family services, prepared for sermons, and did quiet time . . . because I was not physically renewed, it affected my mentality, and I lost my patience. It was different from my spiritual state. I started getting mad at the stuff that I had brushed off before and not been angry at. But, I strived to heal myself.

When he eventually started seeing a pattern developing in his life and ministry, he finally realized that a problem existed.

A male ordained missionary reported his choice to increase his own efforts at self-help:

> I tried to pray. However, my prayer didn't feel in depth. I would lose my concentration while praying. I would try harder to pray. I didn't feel like my prayers were as effective as they had been, nor did reading the Scripture help. I became very depressed. In looking at my own condition, I was determined to come out of it by trying even harder. Yet it didn't work. Whenever I thought that I had overcome a struggle, other problems started to surface. I did not experience recovery through my self-effort. In my opinion, trying hard on my own did not contribute to any recovery because other problems would come my way.

This missionary realized he had a problem when he experienced lack of intimate connection with God despite repeated attempts to reach Him in prayer.

Until total breakdown, most of the NBKMs interviewed chose to delay the process to true recovery by depending solely on religious activities. Male missionaries especially tended not to admit their need for others' help due to the "face-saving" aspect of Korean culture, wherein missionaries are expected to be strong, especially finding strength in God alone, independent from the help of others. Additionally, some missionaries over-spiritualized their condition, believing God was punishing them. They also sought healing by controlling their thoughts, as well as exercising self-help efforts in prayer. Some participants couched their self-help efforts in terms of "waiting on God." For example, a male missionary reported having simply waited on God for two years, which caused him to become emotionally exhausted and prompted him to go to Korea for a break:

> I believed that burnout was due to spiritual warfare. I continued to pray and communicate with God through His Word. I tried to obey God, and put a lot of effort into listening to God. However, my period of burnout lasted for a long time. It went beyond my patience. In my case, I figured out the ways to overcome burnout on my own. For two years, I talked to God through my self-effort to find God's guidance. However, in seeking God on my own, I became emotionally exhausted and physically tired.

One woman reported she thought serving God and helping others was the same as rest. Believing this, she took no time for herself. She described the inner turmoil and confusion about her need for rest:

> Am I allowed to rest? When I thought about resting, I became very nervous. I felt that people needed me, so would resting be okay? I would feel uncomfortable if I was resting and not helping others. I felt an emotional pull in my heart. For me, working was resting. If I truly rest, I won't feel like I'm resting.

Another missionary, once realizing that she was experiencing burnout, looked back and acknowledged she wrongly decided to engage in too much travel aimed at planting churches. She tried to recover through working, which did not help with her difficult relationships with missionaries. These missionaries kept busy to avoid confronting burnout. Such self-help efforts eventually led to relapse.

Attending Seminars and Conferences

Several participants mentioned attending seminars or conferences as a self-help effort. For example, one burned-out missionary wife recounted:

> In order to recover . . . I tried to attend an annual Chinese mission conference for Korean missionaries working in China. I knew that the problem was with myself. Therefore, I tried to solve it with my

own efforts by attending these mission conferences. However, my self-effort in finding relief did not help me much.

Another female missionary reported a similar experience:

> I exerted a lot of effort at the end. I went to seminars, went to revivals, went to meet people, purposefully made rounds, calling on people, I really tried hard . . . . I made a resolution that I needed to start all over, like a new believer, as I had promised myself, alone before God . . . . I went back to the first steps of my faith.

A male ordained missionary in his forties spoke of the same problem:

> I enjoyed studying endlessly and attended many seminars . . . where I received education and counseling. The counseling had been helpful; yet, I found myself still caving in when facing a crisis or a situation that infuriated me. . . . I couldn't help becoming angry and caving in. I would ask myself, "Why can't I apply what I've learned?" I simply had head-knowledge.

More instruction or information (whether in the form of seminars, conferences, or even counseling), evidently did not contribute substantially to participants' recovery because they represented self-help efforts, leaving unresolved deep issues of the heart. However, the struggle apparently did heighten awareness that their own efforts to change—apart from God and necessary human intervention—were futile.

Conclusion on Self-Help

The NBKMs reported that their efforts to recover solely by helping themselves, at best, brought only temporary relief. But this temporary relief initiated a debilitating burnout cycle unless their self-help efforts led to greater awareness that their initial attempts to help themselves were ineffective. Genuine recovery required self-care rather than self-help. The next section of this chapter explores self-initiated care.

Self-Initiated Care: Leading to Recovery

In clear contrast to self-help, NBKMs who chose the path of self-initiated care recognized their need to care wisely for themselves by relying on *God* and *others* (discussed in subsequent sections), requiring the cooperation of

God, others, and ones' own responsibility. Self-care (see Figure 16), specifically the Self-Care box that encompasses Self-Initiated Care, God's assisted Care, and Others' assisted Care) involves undergoing changes of thinking and behavior. In recovery, NBKMs also reported gaining a healthier sense of self, stating the more they knew God, the more they knew themselves. This section discusses self-care in terms of the forms and sources of assistance. In form, the self-help activities reported, such as prayer, Bible reading, and worship, resemble self-care activities. The missionaries practicing self-help perceived prayer as a daily duty required to fulfill the role of a NBKM. By contrast, those practicing self-care perceived prayer as an intimate experience of God during which they discovered who they were in relation to Him. These two approaches to the same activities looked the same, but moving to the self-care path required a change of perception. This shift in perception was initiated by self-reflection, God's intervention, and the influence of others.

Self-Initiated Care

Self-initiated care functions in conjunction with God's intervention and the help of others. Participants' rate of recovery appeared to differ depending on their personality and areas of neglect. In order to identify the areas of neglect, it is necessary to differentiate among the elements of holistic, personal, self-initiated care. Self-initiated care will be discussed as four interrelated elements: physical, emotional, spiritual, and relational self-care. These four areas of recovery require of NBKMs a willingness to accept God's intervention through others.

Physical self-care

Participants' path to recovery required identification of and attention to their physical health. Many missionaries were driven by spiritual activities to neglect their physical needs. One participant so neglected herself physically that she had to be hospitalized for lack of nutrition and energy. An aspect of her burnout recovery was learning the importance of physical self-care, despite cultural expectations:

> [Korean] people think of missionaries as angels. When I was hospitalized, people wondered why I was suffering. Their interpretation

> of my physical condition made me really sad .... People looked at me differently, and I became really sad ... for the sake of the ministry, I realized I needed to take care of myself. I needed to be healthy to lead the ministry. I ate regularly, and changed my lifestyle to make sure I was healthy.... I believe that good ministry comes from good health.

After being released from the hospital, she practiced self-care by purposefully changing her lifestyle to keep herself healthy. Her increased physical health contributed largely to her burnout recovery. Another missionary's burnout was a result of relentless mission work and not enough rest. After he visited the doctor, he learned to practice self-care by making rest a priority. "I took a four-month vacation at a rehabilitation center surrounded by nature. I spent time there keeping in shape physically and relaxing myself mentally." Regular physical exercise clearly aided another missionary's recovery:

> Through my local friends, I became interested in going to a sports center. Even living 18 years [abroad], I never knew about a sports center. I felt like it was not necessary to spend money on a membership at a sports facility. However, my friends finally dragged me there. I finally signed up for a one-year contract ... I was glad I discovered a new way to make me feel healthy and alive. Exercising made me feel alive. On top of that, exercise and prayer life made me feel alive.

This missionary's friends helped her care for herself physically. She realized how important exercise was for her own physical care. While caring for her body, she was also caring for her prayer life. Both were evidence of emotional self-care.

Emotional self-care

Emotional self-care, in particular, entails having a good understanding of one's affective wants and needs. The following examples are instances of how individuals, upon first realizing their need for emotional care, began to resort to different methods to recover emotionally. One participant found help in gardening and exercising, demonstrating the interconnectedness of the physical, emotional, and spiritual.

> Maybe this was what I had in my mind .... At that time, after getting a missionary psychological test I thought that I might be

in that condition. Because I know that the emotional aspect is important, I made an effort . . . what I usually do is gardening and exercising regularly especially after I was sick. I tried to find a way. I do not do this every day, but once or twice a week . . . sometimes three times a week.

Another participant spoke of his recovery as freedom discovered through renewal of his relationship with God and appreciation of God's creation:

> I enjoy nature. I walk alone . . . I am so into the issues that are intertwined in a chain of relationships between me and God, and me and nature, even in the third world. I am set free . . . I rest in nature . . . and have strength from above . . . when I feel like that, I become big and am changed; I think that I should not be in control of . . . issues.

Yet another participant reported self-care through self-discipline of the mind and body,

> When depression comes and I become tired, I exercise to clear my mind. I would rather go exercise at parks to get rid of my depressed feelings. In these areas, I use my will and self-discipline to keep me going and take care of myself.

Instead of taking self-discipline to the extreme, resulting in exhaustion and burnout, this missionary used self-discipline in a healthy way. She cared for herself by choosing to exercise, rather than ignoring her feelings of depression. Although she presents an example of the self-discipline that could potentially lead to burnout, this relationally-motivated discipline aided the process of the recovery because she valued herself as God does. For another missionary, listening to music and enjoying Korean surroundings were a self-initiated means of self-care to overcome stress:

> It took me a long time before I realized that I really like music. However, I didn't know myself well enough. I automatically turned to music to find relief from my stress. Yet, it never occurred to me that music was my strategy for self-care . . . I decorated the second floor where I lived with Korean decorations. It helps me overcome my fatigue and gives me comfort when there's a whole new strange environment outside.

One enthusiastic participant engaged effectively in cognitive therapy to improve his emotional health:

> Due to my belief in the importance of emotional health, I like cognitive therapy. Through cognitive ability, the power of the Holy Spirit enters . . . the work of healing occurs. The education regarding Cognitive Therapy was of great help. My interest in it led my mission in the direction of family therapy ministry . . . planting a church is very hard if our family is not healthy spiritually and emotionally.

These missionaries initiated burnout recovery on their own, but their connection to God was essential to their healing. Emotional care enhanced NBKMs' faith. Accessing and experiencing the effect helped NBKMs become aware of their need for spiritual care. Cognition played a big part in recovery, in which those suffering from burnout actively perceived and recognized their weaknesses and the need to do things differently.

Spiritual care

Spiritual care is self-care in collaboration with God. Spiritual care leads to burnout recovery through faith, prayer, the Word, and one's relationship with God through the Holy Spirit. One ordained NBKM gave explained how he overcame his emotional burnout via connecting with God through a cognitive processing of faith:

> I didn't want to talk to anyone. However, I used my will to do otherwise. I tried to talk to others and maintained social networking. I know that God gave me the faith to process everything in my mind, and internalize in my heart. I have to connect my faith and cognitive reasoning and thoughts together in order to help me make big decisions to overcome burnout.

Although he initiated his healing by reaching out to others, he did not fully depend on himself to bring about recovery. Instead, he allowed God to give him the faith that he needed to be healed. Through his cognitive interaction with God, he initiated the healing process, but he did not try to complete it himself.

A female missionary in her late fifties indicated that the Holy Spirit enabled her to overcome difficulties through her faith in the Word and prayer:

> God, who has sent us, has enabled us to meet those whom He's prepared and to start a ministry through them. Whenever there are difficulties [burnout], the Holy Spirit opens my eyes towards

God's wisdom and methods. The most important part of being a missionary is being in the word and in prayer—of being an offering of praise to Him alone.

A male ordained missionary in his mid-fifties reported the benefits of a good relationship with God,

> Overcoming burnout happens in relationship with God. If we [I] have a good relationship with God we will be able to overcome, if not we should get help from other people. If their relationship with God is not strong they may need help from others.

Thus, spiritual care involves receiving God's help, which inevitably leads to relational means of recovery.

Relational care

Such care is rooted in three relationships: relationship with God, people, and self. How these relationships develop depends, in part, on inherent and cultural differences between men and women (see Appendix D).

By God's intervention, a missionary pastor was helped through increased interaction with his family and colleagues:

> I tried to talk with my wife and spend time with my family. I hardly did that due to my workload. However, it is all due to God's grace that I'm able to change. I interact more with my co-workers too . . . I try to make time to go traveling with my family to take a break and spend more time with them.

Similarly, both genders demonstrated the cultural habit of respect for the elderly in church. A missionary wife was helped through her relationship with an elder pastor:

> Intercessory prayer, support and encouragement from those around me have been of great help. An elder pastor for whom I had great respect, continued to pray for and encourage me . . . he would strengthen me with the Word and I would experience healing.

Another single female missionary felt loved and helped toward recovery when she shared her life with the community. Her experience is typical of the female study participants in self-initiated relational care:

> When I think about their presence in my life, they make many things happen in life that are exciting. They do not allow me to

feel lonely. With them with me, time flies because I have much to do . . . with them. In the midst of my busy schedule with these short-term missionaries, I was able to feel loved. Although it was uncomfortable at times living in the mission field, these relationships made it better.

These missionaries found help in recovering through personal means of self-initiated care, which encompassed the entire person: physical, emotional, spiritual, and relational. Different areas of the NBKMs' lives contributed more or less to their overall stress levels (See Chapter Two). When NBKMs decreased their stress, they improved their recovery from burnout. Thus, addressing specific elements within the domain of personal self-care, especially in relationship with God, has been shown to be the most significant factor in recovering from burnout.

God-Assisted Care

With regard to self-care, the study participants either initiated contact—non-duty-driven pursuit of God in devotions and humble requests for advice from others—or had God intervene directly by His Spirit or indirectly through people. All means of recovery on the self-initiated care path began with a right perception of God and subsequent relationship with Him, and consequently impacted relationships with others—restored relationship with God led to restored relationships with others.

Intimate relationship with God

Every study participant's recovery path began with an *encounter* with the living God. In this encounter, God reestablished the missionaries' character and reconfirmed their callings. This involved recognition of God's character. Thus, a thriving relationship with God involves encountering God in a process of deep intimacy and transformation.

Encounter with God (God's intervention)

Most participants sought relief through self-initiated self-care: prayer and worship, crying out to God, and faith-driven healing, all of which resulted in an encounter with God. Having recognized his futile dependence on human strength and self-help, a male missionary in his mid-forties reported yielding his will to God and expecting His intervention, for His purpose and His honor, and described living in God's power:

> Often times my network, abilities, and strength solves issues immediately. But, if I depend on those and use them because they help me solve issues so fast, I would never learn how to rely on God . . . if I pray, and learn how to use God's power and also seek answers from God as I engage in the word of God on a daily basis, I think I get to know the Mighty God . . . I realize that with my own power I can't do those things, nor would I see how God intervenes in my life.

Similarly, one female participant reported an experience of inner healing by God:

> The presence of God in prayer gave me peace . . . I had to come before God with my wounded heart again, and I experienced God healing my heart. In the end, I was able to face the unresolved issues in my heart. There was bitterness causing me to not fully embrace the locals in my ministry. But as I brought people to Jesus, I also came to Christ. He finally showed me in my bitterness that the locals I was ministering to had bitterness in their hearts as well. The inner healing process helped me come out of burnout.

She saw God clearly intervening in her life and found healing and restoration. Listening to God's voice, a forty-five year old NBKM in Tibet reported finding transforming hope: "During a prayer time . . . this small hope started to grow into something powerful. Since then, whenever I face problems and trouble, I experience this hope in my heart . . . awareness of God's presence, and it makes me feel alive again."

Participants reported that only after finding an intimate relationship with the Lord, knowing His character, and understanding who they were in Christ did they receive healing. The underlying search for relief from burnout through other human beings, religious systems, or behaviors changed into a desire to seek a deeper relationship with God. This desire, in turn, allowed God to change each missionary's character.

God changes character

For some, the recovery process led to character change. Some of the processes were as follows: change in recognition of the character of God through the life of Christ, trusting in God, experiencing the grace of God, finding higher self-esteem and self-identity in Christ, and practicing self-denial. The first stage is recognition. One missionary reported:

> Knowing how [the Christian world] works, I know that I was not healed by anyone else.... In my reflection on God's word, I came to God and decided to change my character. And then next I was able to discern what is not good [inside of me]. I started to change and recognize [who I truly am].

God's word allowed this missionary to recognize that he needed to change. Once he recognized who God was, and who he was in relation to God, he was motivated to take the steps needed to change his character. A missionary wife described how God changed her character:

> God made me a more humble person. Spiritually, I lowered myself. As I reflected, I realized I needed to change myself, and be transformed. I put my effort to be loyal and faithful to God, and asked God to help me love others.

As the result of seeking God's help, she became more humble, faithful, and loving.

Another way God restored the NBKMs was by improving their self-esteem and self-identity in Christ. This was especially true of single women: "If we have higher self-esteem, people look beyond our singleness . . . however, my self-esteem is grounded in God. We don't care what other people think about us." In contrast, males reported the need for self-denial:

> I believe that self-denial is most important! The more we lower ourselves we are able to overcome . . . We have to acknowledge our weakness before God. That is what I experienced to overcome burnout. I had to acknowledge my weakness before God, and that He is strong. The more difficult the time the more I could see my weakness and acknowledging, how my weakness helped me to overcome my burnout.

Because of the profound influence of religious tradition and values in their upbringing, participants understood that self-denial was obedience and faith in God. They realized that they were nothing apart from God. However, this knowledge was insufficient to bring about recovery. To bring about true, holistic recovery, they needed to allow God to change their orientation through the life of Christ, trusting in God, experiencing the grace of God, finding higher self-esteem and self-identity in Christ, and practicing self-denial. Far from being *nothing*, they recognized that they are *something* with God. Thus, some NBKMs experienced a deep transformation initiated by God. This transformation positioned them for further modification of their work-based and relational activities.

God changes work-based activities to relational activities

Although religious activities are still a major part of many recovering NBKMs' lifestyle, these activities are no longer works-based, but relational—relationship with God brings enjoyment in the activities. The activities may remain much the same, but they are now reported as part of a growing relationship with God. Whereas works-based religious activities contributed to burnout, relational activities (e.g., work based upon a relationship with God) facilitated recovery. Although works-based and relational practices may look the same on the surface, they have vastly different motivations. Works-based activities are driven by performance and personal agenda, whereas the heart of relational activities is to set aside one's own personal agenda in favor of a humble partnership with God. The NBKMs interviewed claimed that relational activities which foster a genuine relationship with God include worshiping God, spending quiet time reading the Bible, waiting in prayer, intimacy in prayer, communication with God, and experiencing the filling of the Holy Spirit.

Worshiping God.

A female ordained missionary in her late fifties stated that worship was the key to enjoying God's presence:

> I always worshipped God, in the morning, in the evening. God gives me wisdom when I worship. Whenever I worship, God would help me move on from my circumstances. He helps me make decisions and come to conclusions about things, and move from there. There is a source deep in my heart that moves me to worship and prayer all the time.

Instead of thinking of worship as an obligation, she chose to humble herself and rely on God, enjoying His presence during worship.

Prayer

A female missionary wife explained:

> No matter how I feel, I seek God just as I am, and make the effort to take time to pray regardless of my feelings. Without this habitual effort I could not have endured the difficult time of burnout ... when I cry out to the Lord, I'm given the power to overcome all my suffering ... I was able to overcome and was healed by prayer.

This missionary initiated the healing process by seeking God, but instead of relying on her own strength for healing (practicing self-help), she trusted God to heal her from burnout (practicing self-initiated care). The religious discipline of prayer became a relational practice for her as she continually waited on God. Therefore, her healing was lasting, because it came from God and not from her own efforts.

Another missionary confirmed that this healing process came from God's power alone.

> I would never learn how to rely on God, especially when you come across difficult times that you cannot use "fist" [my own strength] any more. Even with small issues or problems that tempt you to use my fist, if I pray, seek, and learn how to use God's power and also seek answers from God as I engage in the word of God on a daily basis, I think I get to know Mighty God. And then these regular and repetitive spiritual activities help me provide me with strength and deal with big issues and problems.

This missionary experienced a transformed mindset: before burnout, he viewed his religious activity as the source of his energy. After recovering from burnout by getting to know God's character, he viewed God as his source of strength. With this new paradigm came a shift in the way he lived out the Christian life. Activities that were once ritualistic, draining "chores" became opportunities to experience the life-giving excitement of partnering with God in His work.

As evidenced in these interviews, NBKMs seek to have a relationship with God and connect with him. Having been restored to a right relationship with God, the next stage (reported by about a third of participants: twenty-five out of thirty-nine) was to choose to seek help from other people. Though NBKMs confess and attribute the whole healing process to God, we will see that God enables this process through the appointment and help of other people.

Other-Assisted Care

As previously discussed, all study participants who experienced effective recovery began with a healthy reliance on God, knowing that He had underpinned their efforts. To recover from ill health—physical, emotional, spiritual, or relational—they also recognized His help through others. Although the tendency for most NBKMs was independence, recovered participants found God's recovery methodology involved interdependence. Recovery through the help of others took the form of family, community, mission organization, mentor/counselor, education, and other sources.

Family support

Study participants reported that families were the most important and basic recovery resource. NBKM families encouraged the missionaries to connect to God through simple, restful quality time as a family. Family communication also proved critical for encouraging emotional honesty and well-being. Family members supported married women missionaries, and these relationships played a prominent role in their recovery process. Husbands and families encouraged, advised, shared responsibilities, shared Scripture, prayed, and worshipped together.

THE ROLE OF THE FAMILY IN BURNOUT RECOVERY

While in Korea, the emotional support this next missionary received from family helped fill his physical needs. He recalled, "When I went to Korea, my parents and sisters really supported me with all my decisions. They all stood by me. I felt comforted and encouraged, and gained energy . . . through emotional support from my family."

The emotional support this missionary received from his family gave him the energy he needed to care for his body. He reported feeling motivated by the support of his family to exercise physically. As he experienced this physical renewal, he found spiritual renewal.

A married woman explained her family support:

> Family support helps me a lot. In order to overcome my problems, my husband (pastor) and family give me strength to keep on going. When a tree stands alone, it will not fall if there is another

tree supporting it from the side. The tree that supports is just like the family.]

Similarly, a male missionary in his mid-forties explained how family worship led to recovery:

> I still had anger in my mind, and, at times, my anger exploded... all he [an older missionary] advised me was, "Let's pray." It didn't help me. When I was alone, my anger revealed my relapse into the conditions of burnout. I don't think that I was healed through his counsel... but by praying with my wife and worshiping together every day in family worship.

This missionary felt the limitation of sharing with a pastor who was not an expert at counseling. However, through daily family worship with his spouse, he was helped.

The role of the spouse in burnout recovery

Within the nuclear family, spouses played an especially crucial role. Many study participants credited their spouses with playing an essential role in their recovery. Some of the men described their spouses as supportive and interdependent, as well as being their partners and best friends. For example, a male ordained missionary to China indicated his wife was his best friend:

> My wife is my best friend, co-worker, as well as mentor. She has many roles. She prays for me, and we discuss with each other so that we can move forward in our ministry. Because of her, I don't feel the need to look for support and encouragement elsewhere... my wife, who is with me throughout in the mission field, knows what is happening. She therefore, becomes my best helper for me.

Most women in the study credited their spouses in a different way, explaining how they relied on their husband's leadership and mentorship:

> While most Korean women missionaries are limited to the caretaking of the house and the family, I, on the other hand, was given the opportunity to continually develop myself. This was made possible because of my husband who pushes me through. He supports and encourages me to develop myself, even when it's countercultural. When I experienced burnout, the person I poured my heart out to was my husband. Although Korean men do not usually pay that

much attention to the needs of their wives, or listen to them, my husband was otherwise. He listened to my needs, and ultimately, became my communication partner.

Multiple missionary wives in the study emphasized the role of their husband in their recovery process. The role of husbands—acting as mentors—served as a spiritual influence on missionary wives.

Community support

Community support, consisting of fellow missionaries, local church members and leaders, personnel of sending organizations, and supporters, emerged as a noteworthy help for NBKMs. In particular, the data demonstrated the importance of transparent sharing as a means of recovery.

A sharing community emerged as helpful for both men and women missionaries, helping them through recovery, relieving their stress, and allowing them to receive relational support. NBKMs reported that when stories and struggles were communicated to trustworthy partners in mission, such as other missionaries, prayer partners, and locals, recovery was quicker. A single middle-aged female explained:

> I have good prayer partners here and in Korea. . . . I have friends whom I can talk to. I can share all my thoughts with them. I have friends in America. We talk over the phone and share our prayer requests. We do not package our sharing to make it look good, nor do we cover up or hide anything from each other. We listen to each other full of joy. Whenever I share with these friends, I am able to release myself from hurt and pain build in me. Through my sharing, I am able to recover.

Those who were open-minded and teachable when sharing in a Christian community seemed to go through the healing process more quickly than those who tried alone. For example, one unmarried missionary belonging to a small group in Christian community shared,

> The most important thing as a single missionary is that it's not good to be alone. Therefore, I need to find friendships in the Christian community. In the group, we share our testimonies with one another. Although they are foreigners, we share about how God comes to meet us. I meet many good and mature Christians. I realized that if I left the Christian community, I wouldn't live. The Christian community is such a blessing to me in my life.

The data indicated that, while women were more verbally relational and engaged in two-way sharing of advice and encouragement, men tended to give more advice than they received. Five out of the sixteen NBKM men in this study shared their love in the form of serving others and seeking support. In addition, one missionary pastor in his fifties discovered that he recovered more easily when the locals to whom he ministered shared their love with him: "Through the gospel, the people come to know the Lord, through these people I received God's grace and this helped me to recover."

Mission organization support

Mission organization support is more systematic and less direct than community support, but, as the data revealed, participants found it helpful in the recovery process. The most important factor of mission organizational support that emerged from the research was the need for strong, continuous, personal communication. Other important factors participants identified were organizational prayer support, home church prayer groups, and missionary member care support by sending organizations.

ORGANIZATIONAL PRAYER SUPPORT

The crucial aspect of organizational prayer support involves *awareness* of NBKMs and their needs. Slightly less than half (about fifteen out of thirty-nine) of the interviewees actually pointed out that their Korean mission organizations gave them enough prayer and financial support, yet, there was almost no systematic or interactive personal or relational support. Their prayer supporters and sending churches lacked personal and emotional involvement while interceding. Without such a personal element, prayer supporters lacked insight into the potential problems the NBKM could be facing in their lives and ministries. Representing the other missionaries' experiences, a single missionary in her mid-sixties explained the difference relational interaction made to her:

> Now, I feel like whenever they [the church leadership] pray for me, I become strengthened. Through my church visitations, people consider me to be a missionary, and support me in my ministry continually. I really appreciate these warm support and welcome . . . these networking relationships with community members

allowed me to keep on going. These relationships are from God, and are only made possible by Him alone.

Because of her strong relationship with the church, she reported feeling strengthened by their prayers, implying that prayer and community support are interrelated.

Home church prayer groups

A missionary wife in her sixties reported that intercessory prayer on the part of group members and the church's head pastor helped her relationally and spiritually. An older missionary wife recalled:

> I became strengthened through intercessory prayer. I never realized the power of such intercession, but God opened my eyes to see how he gives me strength through it. When I went to Africa, I would lose communication with people. During those times, God causes me to remember my intercessors and that gives me so much assurance. I begin to realize they are truly praying for us, encouraging us. Our head pastor always sends to me and my husband e-mails whenever we go away. We are reassured, become confident, and are spurred on through such prayer and encouragement.

This missionary found strength through remembering the church members who were interceding for her and her husband through prayer. Receiving organizational prayer support in this way is one crucial expression of another form of missionary support, member care.

The importance of member care

Because many Korean missionaries are sent out by individual churches, the Korean mission system tends to lack unified management and organization, resulting in inadequate member care for field missionaries. For example, one single female missionary who was unable to recover on her own and had no access to systematic member care finally found recovery through her spiritual formation group community. However, it took an inordinately long time.

> I was trying to figure it out by myself. My recovery took time. I was attending classes at a seminary, and through one of my professor's lectures, I received a picture about recovery. It was confirmed that

I was to experience recovery. At a spiritual formation group, my community helped me find healing through fellowship and sharing. While they were able to help me, the recovery process took about five to six years.

A few NBKMs became aware of their need for systematic member care support and acquired it. Systematic member care involves the networking of various churches, agencies, and missionaries, coming together to support missionaries and their families. This support may be physical, emotional, spiritual, relational, and/or material. For example, one single female missionary in her mid-forties commented:

> Thankfully, I came to realize the importance of member care need in mission [field] . . . . Someone who specializes in member-care, upon hearing my story, explained my situation as this: When I was floating in mid-air, God had prepared and placed a mattress at the point of my downward fall. It could have taken me three, five, or maybe up to 10 years for the recovery process . . . . Our mission team needs more professional development and I hope that people can have more interest in such developments . . . . To over analyze and be conclusive especially on one's relationship with God is dangerous.

Because a member care professional offered this missionary a new perspective on her story, the missionary was able to recover more quickly. Most NBKMs interviewed reported wanting to have member care such as private group counseling or one-on-one mentoring, but, because their burnout was considered shameful, they were uncomfortable about opening up and ceased trying. However, a few missionaries who had experienced previous success with mentoring and counseling sought and found help from private group mentors or counselors.

Mentoring support

Many study participants favored the mentorship of close friends or authority figures with whom they had deep relationships over professional counseling. Most of the NBKMs interviewed sought close, trusted friends to keep confidence. These close friends acted as mentors (see Appendix E). A male missionary pastor had this to say:

> Instead of receiving counseling, I tried to go to those who have higher authority than me for consultation. I also am able to open

up and talk with Western missionaries and leaders in ministry. But, as for difficulties faced as a missionary, I go to those whom I can trust, and who hold my situation with confidentiality.

Additionally, a single female lay-missionary naturally turned to mature, trustworthy friends to confide in: "The pastor whom I'm close to in Korea, also my church friend at church . . . I met him at a mission conference. I always talk to him on the phone. He prays over me through the phone and Facebook." This woman who was comforted demonstrated an open perspective and a willingness to share with close, trustworthy friends.

One missionary, a woman in her early forties, reported, "I feel it would be enough to have one person, a partner at the church, in the fellowship the same spirit, through whom you can share, connect and receive enough care . . . I have never ever felt this way before." As in this woman's case, sometimes, close friends often are not available to NBKMs. While some study participants that had experienced emotional trauma benefited from relational counseling, most men still preferred counseling via education as means of recovery.

Counseling support

Many Koreans are not familiar with the concept of counseling. However, those who have experienced it report that counseling was very effective in helping them realistically evaluate themselves and their work (see Appendix E).

The role of a counselor is to change a person's cognitive process through guidance and instruction. A single female in her forties found help with her struggles through a professional counselor:

> For a long period of time, the question that I had was, 'where am I physically and mentally?' Through counseling I got help. It got me to see the areas that I never thought about. As I did so, I was helped . . . I was able to organize my thoughts.

This missionary was able gain a more realistic sense of her situation, which helped her to organize her thoughts and function more effectively. Even though some missionaries are unfamiliar with counseling as a result of cultural stigma, the NBKM study participants tended to be willing to share with trustworthy friends or colleagues.

Formal and informal education

Some study participants found educational endeavors, whether formal or informal, contributed to burnout recovery in that learning contributed to the mindset transformation that fostered recovery. Through education, the participants were trained to think and make choices. They were able to reflect on and process their work, which enabled them to move on. They arrived at a deeper understanding of their circumstances and received guidance toward solving their problems, which strengthened their hearts and minds. By promoting a transformed mindset, formal and informal education (See Appendix F: Education as an Aid to Burnout Recovery) contributed to these NBKMs' cognitive transformation for the sake of healing and recovery.

Assisted by God and Others

While each participant reported individual recovery, primarily through the help of God or the help of others, for the purpose of analysis, each area is discussed separately. However, from the data it should be understood that these two domains are interconnected. This is explicit in most of the participants' accounts.

According to the interviews, healing and recovery from burnout began, most often, first in relation to God—relationship with God was restored. Subsequently, most then sought help from others. A mid-forties single female missionary credited her recovery to God's unsolicited intervention through people, which demonstrates the interaction between participants' perception of relational care and God's help:

> God put good people around me to encourage and pray for me . . . . It was God who orchestrated and placed each person by my side, to encourage me in my time of need. This is how I overcame and recovered.

Another single mid-forties female happily noted how her relationship with God was first restored and how she was subsequently helped by others:

> I restored my relationship with God while I was praying. Through that, I was able to rest and reflect on my life. I gained spiritual recovery . . . my root feelings made a connection with the word of God . . . I am very thankful because I am already seeing three member care specialists, and have been helped greatly by them.

A mid-forties male pastor echoed that God was at the center of his recovery and that his recovery was facilitated by others:

> Although I strongly testify that my relationship with God was foremost in bringing about transformation in me, in truth, it was in my learning in the midst of conversing with my mentoring professors and missionaries where I realized the relationship between God and the inner self.

Another missionary reported needing both God and community to recover:

> When I made priorities to overcome my burnout, I realized that God gave me grace . . . . It was through a long period of sharing my stories with others that I recovered . . . At the time, I thought sharing was subsidiary . . . But, then I realized a different dynamic when I talked to God alone, compared to when I shared with a community.

The content of these reports clearly indicates how vital it is for NBKMs to pursue self-initiated care with God and with others. Through self-initiated care, the interviewees became aware of ways in which their perspective needed to be transformed, and, consequently, they were able to accept God's care and others' care.

Chapter Five Summary

This chapter discussed the two paths of recovery, self-help and self-initiated care. NBKMs who took the path of self-help found temporary relief. However, subsequent relapse(s) resulted in NBKMs' realizations that they needed God's and others' assisted care to help them achieve lasting recovery. Awareness of their burnout prompted study participants to take action through self-initiated care, seeking physical, emotional, spiritual, and relational healing. Data show that recovery—healthy relationship with God, others, and self—came through this path identified as self-initiated care. Mission organizations also had a critical role to play in self-initiated care, through prayer, member care, and mentoring and counseling. The totality of the reports made it clear that recovery is not a one-time event, but a process.

All missionaries who reported recovering from burnout found a new perspective on their relationship with God, learned to live in God's presence, and grew in relationship with the Him, instead of maintaining a self-help mentality. They learned to live in relationship *with* God not work *for* God, acknowledging that they were doing God's work, not their own mission work. They experienced a transformed mindset and began to see life holistically, rather than just focusing on its spiritual aspects. They became more self-aware and learned to prevent future burnout by examining themselves. They practiced interdependent Self-Initiated Care (physical, emotional, spiritual, and relational) and relationship with God. As shown in Figure 16 by the large two-directional arrows, the recovery process includes functional overlaps within Self-Initiated Care: God's help and others' help. The next chapter will discuss the signs of recovery, including transformed thinking.

6

Signs of Recovery

As seen in the previous chapter, the data indicated that recovery started with self-awareness, allowing missionaries to confront their problems, act on interventions, and seek solutions. Once the study participants saw their lives realistically, they were able to reorient their lifestyles according to actual needs. As each missionary recounted the process of recovery, and the helpers involved, they all credited God as the one who brought them to awareness and restoration. This chapter explores the manifestations or signs of recovery in four realms of wellness: spiritual, psychological, physical, and axiological. The last of these has to do with a *transformed mindset* on the part of the study participants.

Spiritual Wellness

Experiencing God's grace through repentance and freedom in Christ, having their relationship with God restored, and exhibiting spiritual growth characterized spiritual wellness. For example, a pastor missionary noticed his spiritual growth as he recovered:

> I feel like Christlikeness is internally established in me. Also, because I went through those difficult experiences, which I can share with others, I think I came to understand others better and can relate to those who go through similar situations to mine... to see them receive comfort from me.

A female missionary likewise noticed increased intimacy with God during her recovery:

> I have always had a relationship with God. However, I always felt guilt before God. But now, I have a different understanding of His love for me—just as I am. I don't gain His love by performing religious rituals and activities.

These aspects of self-initiated care involving the NBKMs' relationships with God led them to experience less pressure to strive to become closer to God and to discover freedom in Christ. A single middle-aged female NBKM also described how the inadequacy and harmfulness of work-driven religious life is corrected by understanding of the meaning of Christian freedom:

> What does it mean to be filled by the Holy Spirit? I believe that being filled with the Holy Spirit produces fruit. I question myself whether being filled with the Holy Spirit means fasting, living in the monastery, or praying. Most people cannot do these. We live in society, in reality. But, I also think we should also be filled by the Holy Spirit. That is why working people go for Morning Prayer. However, when they go to work, they keep on dozing off to sleep. Does this show that they are being filled with the Holy Spirit? I think this is kind of ridiculous and meaningless . . . . Because of this I shifted my view in Christ. I became free in Christ.

This missionary reoriented her views of activities such as praying and spending time with God. These activities became the means to being truly filled with the Holy Spirit, rather than cultural demands. She, like most NBKMs, reported strengthened personal character through a renewed relationship with God. An older middle-aged male ordained pastor described this change:

> As a missionary . . . I experienced spiritual revival from my detrimental physical condition. This was a channel of recovery for me . . . . Through my sickness and recovery; I was able to receive a vision from God. In the midst of my burnout, God gave me a clear message to be humble and meek. God gave me a new vision and mission. I was able to come to God to discover who He is, and who I am in Christ.

In addition to increased freedom in Christ, these NBKMs' spiritual wellness was evident in their reports of being able to accept God's love. One woman discovered true relationship with God and what He truly wanted her to do:

> I just had my own agenda and standard, and I was tired because I was not able to do the things that I wanted to do. I felt guilty before Him because I could not get things done. . . . I was greedy to do more. But, God still loved me, although I did not . . . do QT and pray in the morning. God continued to love me. God is happy

> with me, as I am, whether eating or taking a rest for an hour in the afternoon. That is who He is.

She discovered a renewed relationship with the Lord that changed her attitude. By finding her true self, in Christ, she was healed from burnout. An ordained pastor, who ministered in a culture very different from his own, described how he found his identity in Christ and let go of his spiritual perfectionism:

> I tried to find the meaning of ministry by doing work, but now I find it in "being myself." So, now I do not overdo mission . . . I was a perfectionist before, for example I wanted to memorize a five-page-long sermon. Now I don't do that. Now, I just read it and preach my life comfortably.

This pastor is an example of one who relied on receiving self-initiated care from God's acceptance of his situation. He was freed by this new understanding of his acceptance by God and his identity as His child.

Most NBKMs in this study had tried to find meaning from their work for God, but failed. However, they credited God for their recovery from burnout. Most spoke of God's grace to characterize all the steps of their recovery process. In addition to spiritual wellness, the data also indicates that those who have recovered show improved psychological health, such as flexible defense mechanisms, more positive emotions, and a sense of self-worth.

Psychological Wellness

Psychological wellness emerged as a result of burnout recovery. For example, after having recovered, participants no longer suffered from debilitating fear. They also reported having healthy self-esteem, emotional stability, and a clearer sense of self. With greater self-awareness, their self-initiated care is characterized, in part, by their ability to think through their problems realistically and deal with their emotions effectively.

Burnout experiences inevitably involve psychological problems. However, the reports of post-burnout experiences indicate that these issues had been improved upon. A single female described her return to psychological health:

> God has given me a sense of high self-esteem: don't raise your pride, but your sense of self-worth. He taught me to not raise my

pride toward others, but focus on my identity, "You are very precious person in my sight."

One ordained pastor discovered a more integrated life of faith and reason:

> First of all, when I was burned out, one of my symptoms was to cut off social networking. I didn't want to talk to anyone. However . . . I know that God gave me the faith to process everything in my mind, and internalize in my heart . . . to connect my faith, cognitive reasoning . . . together, in order to help me make big decisions to overcome burnout.

This pastor reported that a feature of his return to health was heightened cognition, which played a big part in the process of recovery. His transformed mindset stimulated his journey to recovery.

Psychological wellness is evident in these participants, in that they reported new, healthy views of God, themselves, and others. Optimism and sensitivity replaced debilitating fear and its counterpart, indifference. They learned how to think realistically, manage their stress effectively, and live confidently.

Physical Wellness

As the NBKMs realized the need to incorporate self-initiated care into their life, they came to appreciate the importance of blending physical wellness with the spiritual. Changes in how they viewed God's expectations of them, how they understood self-denial, and how they cared for themselves, resulted in improved health.

One missionary pastor reported the neglect of his physical health because he had believed there was a conflict between self-care and dedication to spiritual activities:

> I lay down my desires . . . I would pray and read the word of God instead of eating breakfast. But, these days I definitely eat . . . I learned to rest before God . . . I examined myself freely and took care of myself. I lay down my way of thinking. [At first] I could not do a workout, although I liked it. As I did work out, the restoration started to happen little by little . . . and my lifestyle changed too.

This recognition of the need to physically care for one's self was also evident in the report of a single female in her mid-forties:

> I was sick physically . . . . Keeping me healthy is the start of ministry. I have to do that well. I spent a lot of time on doing it. Since then, I started to eat regularly. I tried not to make any lifestyle pattern that can cause any illness.

One male recovered his health through the support of his wife and physical exercise—hiking:

> After coming back on my furlough, my favorite pastime was to go mountain hiking with my wife, or by myself . . . While I became healthier physically; I also regained strength in my heart. I received a new passion for my ministry, and was able to go back to the [mission field] refreshed.

These missionaries and others like them neglected their physical well-being before gaining awareness of their work's detrimental effect on their bodies. Physical burnout was an impetus for self-initiated care, during which the missionaries learned to value themselves as God's children, rather than just as God's laborers. In this way, they gained a new perspective on God's character and learned to do their work *with* God instead of just *for* God. According to the interviews, in the understanding of many there appeared to be a conflict between the importance of physical activities and what they referred to as spiritual activities. In recovery, they were freed from striving in ministry and the perceived need to prove their devotion to God through physical self-denial. Recovery meant lifestyle change—less striving and more resting.

Transformed Mindset

The data reveal that if NBKMs did not experience a mindset shift resulting from burnout and center on their relationship with God, their performance-oriented thinking and lifestyle would lead to repeated burnout. Burnout, whether primarily physical, emotional, spiritual, or relational, precipitated a more mature view of self, God, and others, which in turn led to recovery. When the interviewees became aware of God's work during burnout, they saw their relationship with God more accurately, seeing Him as their nurturing Father rather than as their taskmaster.

NBKMs reported changes in their thinking regarding devotion to God. They described misunderstanding God's agenda as duty driven, the apparent result of Korean cultural religious forces. They spoke of pursuing the character of God and following Christ, and they explained renewal achieved through learning as a part of the process of recovery. These NBKMs gained better understanding of the spiritual aspects and realities of their relationship with God, and, as a result, they acquired new perspectives that made their ministry more sustainable. For example, one NBKM explained:

> God helped me realize the way that the mission . . . should have been. He showed me a view of *being* not *doing*. I realized that it is important not only to go . . . but also how to go. Rather than overcoming my struggles completely, God helped me to realize . . . I am in the process of how I am going to prepare for the mission before I go there again. This would help me not to go through burnouts and maintain a good relationship with the Lord. I think what I am doing is becoming aware of that process, realizing it, and approaching it.

Through character building, some missionaries, such as this one, indicated recovery as a process with the Lord:

> Through my burnout, I realized that I walked with the Lord through every moment. I can rely on Him, and seek Him, be with Him. I was able to slowly transform my character into God's image. I was near death, but now that I've regained healing, I am able to identify with those who are going through similar situations that I have gone through. I overcome with God walking with me. I follow His words, and live as a disciple of Christ.

As this missionary recovered from burnout and God transformed his thinking, he began to understand what it truly means to follow Christ. Before burnout, his Christian life was characterized by trying to obey God with hard work. After his mindset transformation, he was able to understand God's grace and love and to show that grace and love to others.

Another NBKM reported a change of perspective regarding missions:

> I believe in missions, it is important to enjoy life, living happily and healthily. I used to think of missions as a heroic feat that most normal people would not be able to handle, where one overcame extreme pain and hardships, while infinitely working towards the goal and achievements of mission. That was the glorious picture I had of missions. Yet that has changed, for our Father does not desire achievements so much as he is concerned that his children live in happiness and well-being.

After burnout and throughout their recovery process, these missionaries gained a better understanding of the spiritual aspects (relationship with God) and realities (living a healthy lifestyle) of life. One missionary pastor described his change in thinking:

> As I rest (and work as a half-time minister) and look back, I learned a lot so far, but a lot of knowledge and information are not important, what is important to me is to internalize. God still delights in me although I do not know a Bible verse . . . He cannot help delighting in you. He laughs. Why does He laugh? As I think, He supports me because I am His son. Since I feel this, I become liberated now. That is what made me feel free.

One female participant explicitly testified of the change in her thinking: "God brought a paradigm shift, which clears your head into realizing that spiritually, mentally and physically the joy comes from ministry itself. There needs to be this paradigm shift, in order for living; it is key to restoration."

Looking back on their experiences of burnout, many missionaries experienced a mindset transformation allowing them to find meaning and God's purpose during their struggles. This mindset shift emerged as a necessary part of healing and recovery for spiritual renewal and prevention of future burnout. Recovery does not happen all at once; it takes time. Healing and the integration of perspective on the inner self with the view of God and others leads to lifestyle change.

Chapter Six Summary

This chapter further examined the process of recovery. As NBKMs grew in their relationship with God, they experienced a change in their thinking, which led to a change in their behavior. This process of transformation of thought and action led to signs of spiritual, psychological, and physical wellness. As NBKMs continued to more clearly understand their identities in Christ, they grew in the experience of freedom in their lives and ministries. They became motivated by their relationship with God, rather than performing religious duties and activities. The path of self-care resulted in change in the inner self, thinking, and lifestyle. This points to the need for holistic transformation through self-initiated care in order to recover from burnout.

7

Discussion, Implications, Applications, and Recommendations

I BEGIN THIS SECTION by summarizing the findings regarding Korean missionaries seeking recovery through self-help versus self-initiated care. Thereafter, I will discuss my findings in light of what other scholars have contributed to this topic, present the implications of the findings for missionary training and support systems for member care, suggest practical applications, and make recommendations for further research.

Summary of Findings

In this section, I review this study's findings with regard to: 1) the causes of NBKM burnout, 2) symptoms of NBKM burnout, and 3) NBKMs' approaches to burnout recovery.

Causes of Burnout

The data pointed to three primary contributors to NBKM burnout, namely lack of 1) cross-cultural competence, 2) self-awareness, and 3) self-care. Korean missionary training often lacks adequate equipping in cross-cultural awareness, which results in sending out missionaries who are steeped in their own cultural perspective and ill-equipped for cross-cultural engagement. These same cultural ideals that hinder cross-cultural competence can also inhibit self-awareness. Generally, individuals from the Korean Christian culture are deeply influenced by Shamanism, Buddhism, and Confucianism (as reported in chapter two), and therefore may lack a strongly developed sense of autonomy and neglect self-reflection. Consequently, NBKMs are slow to recognize their burnout.

Symptoms of Burnout

NBKMs experience a variety of physical, emotional, and spiritual symptoms, relational difficulties, and problems in their ministries, yet they often ignore these signs of burnout. Rather than acknowledge their problems through effective self-examination, they tend to believe that, even in difficulties, God alone will sustain them if they continue to serve Him as they have been doing—being compulsively devotional rather than lovingly responsive. This conviction translates into a do-it-yourself, self-help approach—ultimately resulting in relapse. Consequently, lack of self-awareness and duty-driven religious efforts in pursuit of success and pleasing God exacerbate the symptoms of burnout. However, this study demonstrates the power of an alternative approach to recovery from burnout: self-initiated care.

Approaches to Burnout Recovery

Missionaries aware they are experiencing burnout proceed in one of two directions: self-help or self-initiated care. In contrast to self-help, which attempts to overcome burnout through self-reliance and independent help, self-initiated care embraces God's help and help from others through interdependent care. Through self-initiated care, an enduring process of recovery develops, beginning with self-awareness and an effort to change with the help of others, rather than with one's own strength alone. This openness to assistance stems from the missionary's recognition that God has provided others to help them maintain a correct view of themselves (self-worth and identity) and the ministry to which God has called them (reconciliation with God). They begin to understand God's gracious, intimate care and their need to care for themselves just as God cares for them. Self-care is a process primarily characterized by cooperative relationships with God *and* others.

By choosing the path of self-initiated care, which is characterized by transformed thinking about one's relationship with God and others, NBKMs experience lasting recovery. Community (including God) is indispensable to the recovery process, because interaction with others through mentoring, biblical counseling, and appropriate education facilitates transformative thinking. Thus, God and others foster NBKMs' restoration; their ministries became acts of love rather than attempts to fulfill personal agendas. In a few cases, burnout has the indirect positive effect of revealing to the sufferers any false identities they may have adopted and with the destruction of these facades, they can come to face themselves as broken persons seeking recovery. Data show that through the experience of burnout, some missionaries seek a more meaningful relationship with Christ. They can thus become stronger in their faith and broaden their perspective as a result of their burnout experience.

Research data revealed differences in recovery depending on gender (see Appendix D) and marital status. Males tend to engage in more isolated self-care through solitary pursuit of God, while females tend to be more relational and rely on collaborative care with others. Married women often find healthy identity in their individual families and recover with the support of their families, whereas single women are more inclined to seek support from close friends within the larger Christian community.

Examination of the recovery process revealed that as some NBKMs recover from burnout, they realize their burnout was not necessarily directly due to difficulties on the mission field. Instead, they see their burnout as the result of an accumulation of various cultural, educational, and family issues from the past, culminating in the burnout they ultimately face. However, NBKM reports pointed to a single factor that resulted from numerous attempts at recovery—the need for a change in thinking that results in transformed relationships.

Ultimately, NBKMs demonstrate a need to see themselves serving as members of God's family—not employees—benefitting from partnership with a loving Father and responsively fulfilling God's mission with a humble heart. Unfortunately, many NBKMs seem inclined toward legalistic ways of serving God. Even worse, after being sent, missionaries are often left to be lonely survivors on the mission field. The data revealed that the roles of community, including mentoring, biblical counseling, spiritual transformation, trustworthy friendships, missionary education, and small group experiences are vital to speeding the process of recovery for NBKMs. Though Korean Christian missionary culture, which is reinforced by Korean religious culture, often fosters an environment in which the individual helper is characterized as unimportant when compared to the sovereignty of God, it is evident in this study that Christian community plays an active role in recovery. Self-initiated care builds upon this foundation of community dynamic and transforms NBKMs' perceptions of God, others, and self, allowing lasting recovery to take place.

Discussion of Findings

Other scholars have studied the causes and effects of Korean missionary burnout, with varied results. This study's findings most closely mirror the following in different respects: An, G. Taylor, Cloud and Townsend, and McBride, regarding spirituality in burnout recovery; E. A. Cho, B. Lee, T. W. Lee, and G. Taylor, regarding sharing in spiritual community; J. S. Park, W. R. Shenk, and S. S. Moon and T. W. Lee, regarding the development of a global missiology; Bosch, D. C. Kim, and K. C. Chung, regarding the re-orientation toward *missio Dei*; and Paul E. Nelson, O'Donnell, L. Lindquist, B. Lindquist, and Minirth et al., regarding pastoral and psychological care.

Spirituality in Burnout Recovery

An, a Korean scholar whose work centers on the problem of Korean missionary burnout, confirms this study's finding that burnout, especially spiritual and physical burnout, is common among NBKMs.[1] He asserts that recovery must come from Christ: "Inner self recovery, the restoration of interpersonal relationships or the recovery in fellowship with God must be rooted in Christ."[2] G. Taylor agrees that wellbeing stems from a healthy spirituality, claiming, "The spiritual life expresses itself in all we do, think, and feel and spiritual health is an integral aspect of well-being. There are spiritual dimensions to our understanding and pursuit of mental health, as well as physical health."[3] While these studies are in agreement concerning the spiritual nature of recovery, differing roles for spirituality in burnout recovery have been emphasized.

An suggested that pastoral counseling is the solution to burnout. "Restoration happens in the rumination of his fervor [sic] for pastoral ministry in the past, his current attitude of faith, and his vision for the future ministry."[4] An's vision of pastoral counseling is similar to this study's depic-

---

1. An, "Burnout Syndrome Recovery."
2. An, "Burnout Syndrome Recovery," 199.
3. Taylor, "Spiritual Dimensions," 75.
4. An, "Burnout Syndrome Recovery," 199.

tion of self-initiated care as self-reflection on the past, acceptance of God's grace in the present, and humility for the future.

However, An's definition of self-care centers entirely around the spiritual aspect of burnout recovery. He asserted, "I found out that recovery from burnout means the recovery of the spirituality."[5] This conclusion comes from survey data, not qualitative research. The qualitative data from my study suggest that his perspective is incomplete. Spirituality is a part of burnout recovery, but psychological, relational, and physical aspects are equally important. An discounts the importance of material aid in the recovery process; for example, he writes, "all the medical treatments have to be achieved by the help of the Holy Spirit."[6] Naturally, the Holy Spirit works through medical treatment, but there is danger in over-spiritualizing the recovery process. NBKMs who saw their health as entirely dependent on the Holy Spirit tended to exacerbate burnout through self-isolation, while those who saw recovery as a holistic process were able to seek help for their bodies, their emotions, their minds, *and* their spirits.

Cloud and Townsend wrote extensively regarding the need for a balanced approach to effective relational, emotional, and spiritual growth:

> We wanted to bring the idea of working on relational and emotional issues back into the mainstream of spiritual growth. Spiritual growth should affect relationship problems, emotional problems, and all other problems of life. There is no such thing as our "spiritual life" and then "real life." It is all one.[7]

In accordance with this holistic approach, NBKMs sought practical solutions to their problems, such as taking medicine, seeking companionship, receiving education, and setting aside time to rest.

Also illustrating the unification of "spiritual life" and "real life," McBride applied this same holistic understanding to spiritual crises.[8] As a pastor, counselor, and experienced therapist, McBride gleaned a wealth of insight into spiritual crises and offered perspective on the role of spirituality in burnout recovery. The diagram in Figure 17 illustrates his understanding of the holistic nature of life.

---

5. An, "Burnout Syndrome Recovery," 201.
6. An, "Burnout Syndrome Recovery," 201.
7. Cloud and Townsend, *How People Grow*, 21
8. McBride, *Spiritual Crisis*.

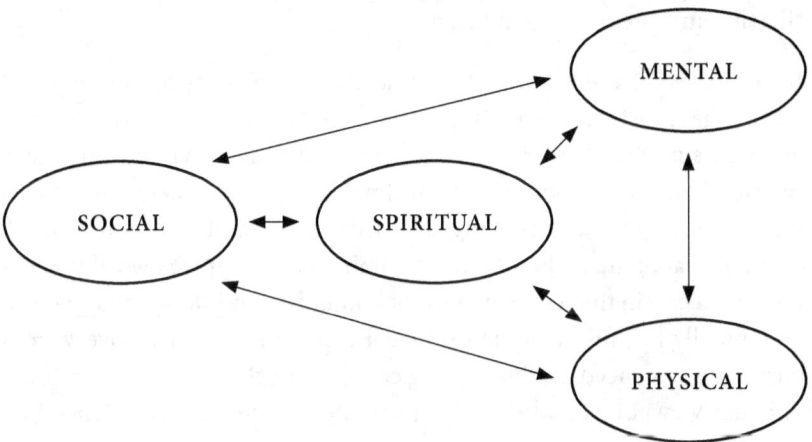

Figure 17. The Synergistic Influences of Being. From J. Lebron McBride, *Spiritual Crisis: Surviving Trauma to the Soul*, 3. Binghamton, NY: Haworth, 2006. Copyright 2006 by Author. Adapted with permission.

He placed the spiritual aspect at the center of the diagram in order to illustrate his belief that the spiritual core of a person is foundational. However, the key to addressing spiritual crises is to see not only the spiritual core but also the holistic nature of life as including the social, mental, and physical components. McBride's findings shed further light on the integration of all facets of life as essential to overcoming spiritual crises. Burnout inevitably involves spiritual crises for NBKMs, and these holistic strategies illustrate how self-care is necessary in this process.

This study's findings indicate that self-initiated care, the road to burnout recovery, must not only be spiritual, but also physical, cognitive, and relational. Minirth et al. stated that recovery from burnout required most importantly self-care in all respects—physical, emotional, and spiritual—and a reliance upon God and others for support.[9] The data conclusively demonstrate that NBKMs need to seek broader healing; restored relationship with God inevitably involved healthier thinking about one's identity in Christ (cognitive healing) and healthier relationships with others (relational healing).

---

9. Minirth et al., *How to Beat Burnout*, 103.

Sharing in Spiritual Community

In self-care, there is a foundational need for a spiritual community that encourages sharing. Cho advised, "It is of vital importance that missionaries make sure that they are provided with relationships within which they can ventilate their emotions and feelings and be genuinely empathized without being prematurely judged."[10] This study's findings confirm Cho's claim, revealing that when NBKMs humbly meet with trustworthy, experienced peers (in the role of mentor or counselor) and show willingness to be mutually helpful in sharing spiritual community, their recovery from burnout is enhanced. In this sharing community, they are able to embrace different viewpoints and thereby "integrate the stressful experience into life and feel ready to move on."[11]

One important source of community support is the sending church. Unwittingly, sending churches may contribute to NBKM burnout through unrealistic expectations and underdeveloped care. B. Lee's claim that sending churches must recognize and abandon the mischaracterization of faith caused by culture and doctrine supports this finding.[12] Korean missionary expert, T. W. Lee, told of many Korean missionaries who were sent from their churches with a misunderstanding of faith and expect to handle all difficulties, hardships, and sacrifices independently.[13] With such extraordinary spirituality and zealous determination, they pioneered church planting without a support system. Although their strong personalities and convictions kept them from giving up easily, these missionaries often let their zeal obscure their ability to think wisely and critically about their own needs and limitations on the mission field. Consequently, their effectiveness on the mission field was limited by their lack of attention to self-care and the absence of support from a fostering community. By contrast, "A theology of care brings the grace and freedom of God into the experience of those who serve in harsh circumstances as Christians care for one another. Biblical caring includes fellowship, edification, comfort, confrontation, strengthening, compassion, leadership, and authority."[14] This study clearly demonstrated that a spiritual community was vital in burnout recovery.

---

10. Cho, "Communal Reflective/Narrative Learning," 151.
11. Lovell-Hawker as cited in Cho, "Communal Reflective/Narrative Learning," 158.
12. Lee, "Philosophical Anthropology," 92.
13. Lee, "Missionary Spirituality and Missiology."
14. Taylor, "Theological Perspective," 55.

Development of a Global Missiology

The adoption of a Western mission model and the syncretistic national absorption of Christianity prevented the development of a missiology that adequately tempered Korean cultural traits. As shown in chapter two, J. S. Park explained, "Some affinity between traditional Korean religions and Christianity made it easier for Koreans to adopt the Christian faith."[15] W. R. Shenk elaborated, "Western theology did not help the non-Western churches grapple with their own cultures and develop an identity that enabled an . . . [Asian] believer to be fully Christian and culturally authentic."[16] As a result, the development of Korean missiology was hindered by unchecked cultural influences that in some ways promoted unrealistic expectations for success and encouraged self-reliance without the support of Christian community.

As this study's findings suggest, NBKMs sought success measured by accomplishments, often in competitive comparison with other mission agencies, rather than finding success in God's free grace and identity in Christ. Korean churches' theology of mission is also weakened by its dependence on traditional Korean cultural values such as reliance on personal strength, suppressing emotional problems, and unquestioning obedience to authority. Weak missiology characterized by self-reliance exacerbated burnout. Developing a missiology that grapples with cultural influence without compromising the grace of the gospel could transform Korean missions and benefit their missionaries, who would get relief from the burdens of certain negative cultural values. S. S. Moon and T. W. Lee advocated this change by suggesting that the Korean church move beyond negative cultural influences and embrace other perspectives so that traditional values can be tempered by global awareness and a new understanding of the local church and its role in the global church.[17]

Re-Orientation Toward Missio Dei

Korean mission as a whole would benefit from a transformed understanding of missio *Dei*, which emphasizes the focal point of missions as God's Trinitarian work in the world, utilizing the church and its mission activities

---

15. Park, "Korean Protestant Christianity," 60.
16. Shenk, "After Bosch," 19.
17. Moon and Lee, "Globalization."

as the chosen agent of his ultimate sending purpose; missiology is not based on the mission of the church, rather, it is based on the mission of the God who sends.[18] As mentioned by D. C. Kim, *missio Dei* (God's mission) involves an attitude of partnership with God; in essence, missionaries should view their calling as *joining in* the work God is already doing, rather than working *for* God.[19] This study's findings agree with Kim's thinking in that NBKMs need to embrace this idea of *missio Dei* in order to prevent and/or recover from burnout. For study participants, re-orienting their perspective toward *missio Dei* was crucial in their spiritual recovery from burnout. Thus, one way in which sending churches can provide for missionaries' needs is to train them in *missio Dei*. K. C. Chung claimed that without an understanding of *missio Dei*, NBKMs and their sending organizations complete their mission work with secular motivations lingering "behind their apparent promotion of God's glory, such as *success-orientation, materialism, megaism and numeralism.*"[20]

Illustrating Chung's assertion, the NBKMs in this study reported being pressured by a success-oriented approach to missions aimed at pleasing God and gaining favor from their sending churches. Their lives were often work-oriented and competitive, characterized by a driving focus on the expansion of their church's mission system. In a period of brokenness during their recovery process, many NBKMs reported being awakened to the perspective that their work was part of God's mission *(missio Dei)*. Consequently, their religious activities took on a new, relational meaning. Before understanding *missio Dei*, these missionaries were working in mission organization systems that are sometimes distracted by secular concerns such as success, materialism, and numbers. After gaining an understanding of *missio Dei*, they completed the same missionary activities, but from a new perspective. Instead of seeing their work as an obligation to their mission organization and to God, they began to see their work as an expression of loving partnership, knowing that they were already loved and accepted by God.

Pastoral and Psychological Care

Introducing a discussion of missionary vitality and, specifically, the need for psychological and pastoral care, Nelson asserted,

18. Bosch, *Transforming Missions*, 389–91.
19. Do Chong Kim, "Member Care Missionaries Missiological Study," 24.
20. Chung, "Missionary Strategy," 47.

> It took godly psychologists ... working faithfully and quietly on a variety of levels to build the trust and credibility necessary to enable the Christian community to extend an appreciation for biblically grounded mental health professionals to the missions community. Missionaries were assumed to be spiritually above the problems that confront ordinary Christians. The precarious pedestal of unrealistic expectations on which missionaries were placed was often the launching pad for devastating brokenness.[21]

In order to avoid (or recover from) such brokenness, missionaries and sending organizations could seek greater balance between work and rest. It is sometimes difficult for Korean missionaries to embrace the "concepts of running with endurance the race set before us (Hebrews 12:1–2) and being diligent to enter into His rest (Hebrews 4:9–11)" because their mission education lacks a strongly developed concept of self-care (as discussed in chapter four).[22] Thus, achieving a balance between active faithfulness to God and realistic attention to the self requires an intentional shift in their thinking from valuing the importance of *doing* (performing religious works, seeking recognition from God and others) to valuing the importance of *being* (embracing identity as God's child, manifesting in a loving response to recognition already received). This transition is catalyzed by pastoral and psychological care.

To accomplish this fundamental shift in their thinking, the data indicate that NBKMs need psychological care. L. Lindquist pointed out, "Psychological care utilizes knowledge of personality and behaviors, an understanding of human development, and the processes of change, and applies theories and techniques of counseling and therapy in helping relationships."[23] One method of psychological care is pastoral counseling. Many of the interviewees, especially women, reported finding a sense of self-worth and restored psychological health through pastoral counseling. L. Lindquist offered advice to the mission community regarding the need for collaborative pastoral and psychological care: "Most of us would benefit greatly from spending personal time under the mentoring and tutorage of both pastoral care specialists and mental health professionals."[24] He added,

---

21. Nelson, "Preface," xi.
22. O'Donnell, "Running Well and Resting Well," 309.
23. Lindquist, "Pastoral and Psychological Caregivers," 53.
24. Lindquist, "Pastoral and Psychological Caregivers," 53.

Psychological care may assist missionaries to enhance their vitality, overcome tensions and conflict, and/or resolve psychological disorders. Helping overcome bruised backgrounds, inner and interpersonal conflicts, trauma and stress, and responding to other issues often involves psychological care.[25]

As this study shows, psychological healing alone is not enough for full recovery from burnout, because all aspects of the missionary's life must be addressed (see B. Lindquist, as discussed in chapter two[26]). O'Donnell's diagram, A Best Practice Model of Member Care (see Figure 7) communicates this same idea: pastoral care and psychological care are an indispensable aspect of holistic member care.[27] Thus, pastoral and psychological care can play a vital role in the systematic support of missionaries, enabling them to reflect on and process their own ministry experiences. These models of pastoral and psychological care are important tools for developing Korean approaches to missionary care that are informed by helpful Western strategies.

Implications

Based on the results of this study, transformed thinking and the development of a more sophisticated Korean missionary support systems are needed for sending agencies, supporting churches, and missionaries and their families to effectively prevent and overcome burnout. This development should not be a direct importation of Western ideals or methodology, but rather the integration of helpful Western strategies with specifically Korean self-theologizing in order to create a truly Korean solution. Transformed thinking begins with reorienting missiology through the mission model of *missio Dei*. This shift necessitates theological transformation of the perspectives of individual missionaries. This holistic change in large-scale missiology through the individual lives of NBKMs in the field must manifest in effective missionary support systems. These systems are constructed through effective member care and self-care training.

---

25. Lindquist, "Pastoral and Psychological Caregivers," 53.
26. Lindquist, "Member Care."
27. O'Donnell, "Going Global," in *Doing Member Care Well*.

Transformed Thinking

In light of the study results, in order to help missionaries recover from burnout, transformation should take place in the way mission agencies, Korean sending churches, and individual NBKMs think about missions. There must be an understanding of *missio Dei*, genuine theological transformation, and a change in individual missionaries' perspectives.

Mission model (missio Dei)

Increased effectiveness in burnout prevention and recovery necessitates a comprehensive change in missiological perspective, beginning with the adoption of the *missio Dei* mission model. Currently, many Korean mission organizations focus on numbers, an attitude that can foster pride and competition between churches, agencies, and the missionaries themselves. This can also give rise to an ethnocentric perspective on the mission field (as mentioned in chapter two). Consequently, this mission model must be replaced by a *missio Dei* model. For lasting change, a genuine transformation of the Korean Christian belief system must occur. Rather than seeing mission work as a duty to God measured by achievement or success, *missio Dei* reorients the missionary's perspective: the NBKM's ministry is a partnership in God's work pursued with faithfulness as a response to his transforming love and grace. This missiological shift necessitates a parallel shift in theology.

Theological transformation

This new missiological model must include theological transformation in order to be successful in preventing burnout and facilitating recovery. This change is essential for the continued growth and development of the Korean church, as articulated by H. J. Lee. Korean church missionary training should seek to transform the way it teaches about God; instead of unwittingly emphasizing the pursuit of blessing through works, the church should refocus its theological training on selfless service in God's mission, irrespective of personal reward or recognition.[28] This change is dependent upon the church's presentation of the character of God. Presenting God as a nurturing and gracious father rather than as a legalistic

---

28. Lee, *Shift the Paradigm*.

and demanding authority will transform the way the NBKMs view God and, consequently, how they view themselves. Avoiding the temptation to use God's name to further a personal agenda for success, they can humbly carry out God's agenda, responding to His call to His mission out of love for Him and for others. As God's children and recipients of His grace, they will be empowered to share the gospel more effectively if Korean missionary training refocuses on the gracious attributes of God. A full picture of the character of God corrects the cultural overemphasis on achievement and fosters a mission perspective that inhibits the development of burnout and encourages recovery.

Missionary perspective

Sending agencies and churches need to be transformed in their thinking, along with their missionaries. Study participants' growing understanding of *missio Dei* clearly contributed to the recovery processes. While most credited God for their recovery, they also described the many means He used to bring it about, especially support from other Christians. Interaction with other people awakened an awareness of the self, an acknowledgment of the problem, and a transformative shift in thinking—spiritually, emotionally, and cognitively. It is this holistic view of the self that needs to be addressed by NBKMs and their supporters.

In light of the fact that there is a primary lack of systematic care, the scope of change and improvement is far beyond the ability of the individual missionary (as shown in chapter four). NBKMs enter the mission field thoroughly educated and disciplined, but often with little practical cross-cultural experience. Although these missionaries are highly educated in Koreanized theology, their lack of cross-cultural communication experience can reduce their effectiveness in sharing the Gospel in other cultures. Spiritual zeal and dedication should be matched with theological education and intercultural preparation. These considerations must be built on the correct foundation. The purpose of mission is not simply to increase church attendance or plant more churches, but to lead people to Jesus. Everyone involved in missions would benefit from the continued reminder that the Gospel is the reason they send and go. Transformed thinking thus promotes comprehensive change, from Korean missiology as a whole to the manifestations of transformed thinking in the mind of a single missionary in the field. The practical outworking of this holistic change is evidenced by and supported through comprehensive missionary support.

Missionary Support

A systematic member care system involving self-initiated care training is a natural expression of genuinely transformed thinking and is essential for prevention of and recovery from burnout. Currently, the Korean education system as a whole struggles with promoting self-awareness. However, transformative learning requires reflection: reexamining our beliefs and their bases and behaving according to understandings gained from the *transformed meaning perspective* that results from such reexaminations.[29] Systematic member care promotes this type of learning. When NBKMs share their struggles in a supportive community, they are able to reflect on their experience and receive healing. Sending churches must take responsibility for placing their missionaries in authentic support groups, instead of assuming that God will take care of these missionaries and leaving them to fend for themselves, as is often the case in an overly spiritualized and culturally bound missiology. Thus, as holistic transformation of thinking takes root, member care can flourish and facilitate true recovery for NBKMs.

Training in member care

Part of holistic transformation must involve training in providing and receiving member care.[30] To prevent burnout and foster recovery, member-care training systems must be characterized by systematic inclusion of individual and group professional mentoring and counseling. Missionaries need to be trained in concrete ways to build interpersonal relationships with the locals and with other missionaries and to handle conflict in a healthy manner. This relational aspect of member care training is essential for combating the relational challenges in the field.

For example, some NBKMs interviewed stated that cooperation among missionaries was difficult because of competition among sending churches. When missionaries envy another's success, they lack the social support and guidance to handle their feelings in a healthy way and begin to

29. Mezirow, "Critical Reflection."
30. Yoon, "Apostle Paul's Mission Strategy."

spread rumors that attack the more successful missionary and damage their witness. To prevent situations like this, churches and mission organizations need to invest deeply in member care research and practice, training missionaries to let go of any competitive attitude and navigate relational conflict in healthy, honest ways.

Member care training must also be characterized by sensitivity to the cultural influences of self-sufficiency and hierarchy, focusing on group dynamics and thorough training in how to relate to one another in humble, supportive ways, without making authoritarian demands. This initiative will require a shift in the NBKMs' beliefs concerning interpersonal relationships: moving from their cultural, hierarchical way of relating to a more open, genuine way of relating. Such a shift will be challenging due to the deeply engrained cultural assumptions regarding relationships, but in most cases should be possible when the NBKMs make a conscious choice to proactively seek and humbly receive care and instruction.

Self-initiated care

Through member care training, missionaries must develop their character, becoming flexible, humble, and teachable, increasing the depth of their relationship with God, proactively seeking community support, and practicing self-initiated care skills. Self-initiated care skills, as discussed in chapters two and four, involve caring for one's self physically, emotionally, relationally, and spiritually. As a part of this practice, Korean missionaries must seek out supportive relationships in their countries to build them up, instead of depending on their own prayer and worship to bring about individual healing miracles.

Self-initiated care relies upon the help of God and others to face the challenges of life in the field and overcome burnout. Many of the NBKMs interviewed stated that finances were a source of stress contributing to their burnout. Currently, when faced with financial hardship, Korean missionaries commonly assume that if they pray and believe enough, God will care for their needs without the help of any other people. Thus, they may practice self-isolating behaviors instead of seeking community support. However, if missionaries are trained through self-initiated care to build interpersonal relationships and to communicate effectively across cultures, they can network and support one another financially as well as emotionally. Member care plays a critical role in facilitating self-initiated care by providing these support structures.

Another critical aspect of self-initiated care is a healthy engagement with family for care and support. As a part of effective member care, missionary families must be trained together, with a shared goal, in order to insure a stable and enduring ministry and to promote health and recovery. Missionary wives, especially, need to be strengthened through education and training. The relationships within the family are an essential aspect of spiritual life, and, therefore, self-initiated care must include attention to these relational dynamics: "Authentic spirituality cannot be practiced apart from a spiritual community, be it the family or the church."[31] Member care can thus facilitate self-initiated care, as mission agencies and sending churches provide Christian family counseling to support communication and teamwork among family members. Agencies need to pay great attention to the dynamic of missionary families, including marital relationships as well as MK education and development, so that healthy family relationships can play a positive role in self-care.

Conclusion on Implications

This study demonstrates a need for holistic, transformed thinking and effective missionary care in order to prevent burnout and facilitate recovery for NBKMs. Korean mission training and education must be focused by *missio Dei*. This focus will transform missiology as a whole and bring about pervasive change, down to individual missionaries. Such a transformation necessitates a renewed approach to theology, encouraging embracing God's grace and his role as father. This theological shift corrects tendencies to over-spiritualize and facilitates a holistic approach to the life and role of a missionary. Transformed thinking thus reaches from the whole of missiology into the practical lives of individual missionaries, changing their perspectives on an individual level. The practical outworking of these changes is a set of mission training programs shaped by all-encompassing member-care. While correcting negative cultural influences member care can utilize the community-oriented lifestyles and strong family values of Korean culture to promote recovery. Fostered by the systematic improvements of member care, missionary-sending organizations and churches must train NBKMs in self-initiated care, the only effective and lasting solution to

31. McBride, *Spiritual Crisis*, xiv.

burnout. These implications demonstrate how this study's findings provide conclusive strategies for recovery from burnout.

Application: Member Care

Korean missions would greatly benefit from mission organizations and sending churches creating missionary care systems grounded in *missio Dei*. Such an approach reflects the broader need to integrate spiritual training, non-syncretistic biblical education, mutual trust and reliance between agencies and missionaries, systematic cross-cultural training, and effective ongoing member care to prevent burnout and assist in recovery for NBKMs. There are many practical ways to advance this strategy.

Member care needs to incorporate holistic strategies to help Koreans avoid and recover from burnout. Member care helps balance the realistic demands of missionary life. It involves emotional, cultural, psychological, and organizational concerns, as well as aspects of the spiritual disciplines. This balanced view embraces spirituality as holistic in nature. In order to effectively combat self-reliance and over-spiritualization, perspectives regarding the role of spiritual life must embrace the social, mental, and physical aspects of the whole person.

The entire system of missionary selection, preparation, and support must be guided by a number of foundational understandings: mission is the spread of the Gospel in cooperation with God, reliance on relationships with God and others is vital, and systematic mission care and self-initiated care are not optional. All mission-related organizations would benefit from including initial and ongoing family and crisis counseling and mentoring, as well as material support. To assist NBKMs in their long-term cross-cultural work, missionary member care should be integrated into churches and mission organizations, developing professional member care personnel who are deeply familiar with practical Korean mission issues and who are able to intervene and help with recovery from and prevention of burnout. These professionals would provide pre-field training, support on site, evaluation, and re-entry debriefing. Member care should be extended to include the many aspects of the overall mission, from the organization to the individual. Again, this comprehensive change should not represent an indiscriminate importation of Western ideas but rather an integration of beneficial Western member care techniques that address Korean mission issues with sensitivity to cultural influences.

Missionary Training

It is essential to provide missionaries with support groups and proper training in order to give them a strong sense of self, which will alter their behavior and allow them to practice self-initiated care. Support for effective self-initiated care also includes training missionary families, equipping missionaries for crisis management, creating a missionary welfare system, and engaging professional member care personnel to conduct training. In addition, mission organizations could pair veteran missionaries with novice missionaries to act as mentors. Before any of this training, however, mission organizations need to screen and evaluate potential missionaries to determine whether or not they are fit and prepared to enter the mission field. They should not only look at a missionary's willingness and abilities, but also character, emotional stability, and family life. In addition, holistic evaluation of missionaries should consider more than education and academic abilities; it should also include practical experience, such as a short-term mission work in the field they are being sent to.[32] If they have no experience, they should be in mentoring partnering relationships with experienced professional member care personnel and participate in pre-field research, biblical counseling,[33] and training.[34] Specific training in spiritual formation is particularly beneficial in addressing the influence of Korean culture on missionaries' understanding of relationship with God and knowledge of self. Training systems would include teaching a correct view of God, self, and purpose in the context of cross-cultural education. Such training should help instill an attitude of open-mindedness, identify potential problems, and thereby prepare Korean missionaries to work knowledgeably with other cultures, reducing relational stress and avoiding burnout.

Suggestions for All Concerned Mission Personnel

Mission agencies and sending churches could provide more strategic, manageable support systems, which should include careful screening of training personnel, extended orientation and intercultural communication training including experience on the field, assistance with adapting to

---

32. Byon, "Missionary Training."
33. Kim, "Depression of Korean Missionaries."
34. Yoon, "Apostle Paul's Mission Strategy."

the new country, ongoing care in the field (via email, Facebook, and other social networking means), personal and supervisory visits, crisis training and intervention, and training and continual support in missionary self-initiated care. One practical way to encourage self-initiated care is to create a manual. Such a manual and the support it prescribes should be provided to all concerned parties and must include access to specialized personnel who are experts in physical, psychological, and spiritual concerns.

Sending organizations

To solve the problem of missionary ethnocentrism, mission organizations should practice cultural sensitivity, training missionaries to be teachable and open-minded and to communicate in ways the people of their mission country will understand. This approach is particularly important for a Korean mission culture that has often neglected thorough training in cross-cultural competence. For pre-field training, professional or volunteer mission experts from other cultures could teach NBKM leaders and candidates in order to develop their cultural awareness. Sending organizations can also utilize psychological testing as objective data to encourage mental health. Despite the potential for cultural aversion to this idea, pre-field psychological testing can prove beneficial for prevention of burnout. Mental health can likewise be encouraged through providing funding for furloughs and self-initiated care, family or individual trips, and rest away from the field. In addition, through training seminars, classes, and/or publications, sending organizations could encourage relational sharing among men, help missionary wives develop a strong sense of worth, and encourage, rather than look down on, single women. Churches should discourage Korean cultural prejudices and gender discrimination in order to educate the next generation of Korean missionaries to more effectively manage burnout. All of these changes require a systematic approach to the mission calling that emphasizes cooperation with (not dictation by) God, the church, and the mission agency.

PARTNERSHIP IN GLOBAL MISSIONS

Korean mission culture has often suffered from a self-sufficiency that inhibits global partnership, and thus sending organizations would greatly benefit from networking with churches around the globe in order to foster

DISCUSSION, IMPLICATIONS, APPLICATIONS, AND RECOMMENDATIONS

cultural sensitivity, inhibit ethnocentrism, and provide in-country support for NBKMs. Denominational missions in the field should humbly end competition, network and cooperate, share information, pray together, support each other, and seek God in order to develop a shared vision for a symbiotic mission relationship. Along with Korean society and churches, sending organizations must also seek cooperation between cultures with different values and engage new perspectives critically and theologically, creating strategies for moving beyond prejudice through the intentional development of cross-cultural communication skills.[35] The integration of these improvements for Korean member care should be interdependently related to Korean culture and theology through a careful attention to self-theologizing and avoiding direct importation of Western models in a way that suppresses Korean culture and identity.[36] Learning from Christians of different cultures will help the next generation of NBKMs better avoid burnout, adapt themselves to non-Korean cultures, seek help when needed, and persevere more successfully in their faith. Reflective of the unity and fellowship of the Godhead, individual missionaries and organizations should seek to abandon all tendencies toward competition and self-promotion in favor of a humble-minded participation in God's mission, in cooperation and fellowship with other missionaries as followers of Christ.

Korean Member Care Team Support

To help in the recovery process, sending agents should provide specialists experienced in biblical and professional counseling related to conflict and crisis management. This involves sending a team of trained member care professionals to the field to counsel the missionaries and educate them in self-care and relational skills. If necessary, these teams can provide spiritual care and assistance in the debriefing process. Spiritual care in particular is essential for this process because Korean religious tradition is somewhat lacking in attention to the gracious, relationship aspect of serving God. Having been trained in specifics issues such as conflict management and spiritual care, these leaders will be in a unique position to support missionaries through direct interaction while they are in the field. Counseling, mentoring, psychological therapy (if necessary), and debriefing must be provided throughout the stages of life on and off the

35. Yang, "Globalization."
36. Moon, *Self-Theologizing*.

field, and the member care team must be the hands and feet of the mission organization in providing care in the field that is specifically designed to address Korean needs and issues.

Korean family support

Sending agencies should provide pre-field training to the entire missionary family (not only the male head of the household), promote healthy husband-wife relationships through non-formal education such as inexpensive retreats and seminars, and create specific, tangible plans for the continuing education of missionary children, recognizing the role of parents as more than guardians. Promoting these healthy family models may help correct potential distortions of the family structure that can result from hierarchical Korean values. Parents should be aware that they must be role models and mentors to their children, and openness and grace in communication can encourage healthy relationships between all family members. As spiritual leaders of the family, their focus should be on building a strong family through intentionally pursuing God together. Spending quality time with the children and communicating with them is highly important. It is vital that parents are sympathetic to the children and their needs as they adjust to new environments and surroundings. Placing children in MK schools, sincerely caring for their wellbeing, and putting an emphasis on family is key. MK families need vacations and time to rest, where they can relax and refresh their minds. There should be MK family networking and family member-care training programs available to them at a reasonable cost, which include provisions for the children to attend with the parents. Not only would this bring the family together, but it would also educate the children. Sending agencies must train missionaries in healthy family life and use member care to support the missionary family on and off the field.

Sending churches

Sending churches need to model a relational and loving Christian community through systematic support of vulnerable members. Sending churches could offer counseling or cross-cultural leadership classes on God, self, servant leadership, mission, and conflict resolution, facilitating member care in the church community. Congregations as well must be educated in cross-cultural perspectives so that the church as a whole, from leadership to membership will be sensitive to the mission of the church and the specific needs and challenges of missionaries. To instill servant leadership, cross-cultural competence, leader integrity, and cooperation between sending churches and agencies of all sizes, regular, the sending church must implement ongoing training.

Helping the congregation as a whole better understand missiological issues will foster healthy expectations for missionaries and stronger bonds of member care between the missionary and the sending church. Churches must realize that missionaries need to be honest about their struggles instead of concealing them for the sake of appearances and then they must strategically arrange and manage support groups so that the missionaries have consistent access to relational and spiritual support.

Mission team leaders

Mission leaders must also be wholeheartedly involved in the spiritual growth and intellectual development of the next generation of leaders. Future Korean Christian leaders must have integrity, functioning as spiritual mentors and pastors with servant hearts. To do this, they must be trained to know themselves as created in the image of God. Many Korean missionary training programs tend to overemphasize cognitive education for the acquisition of missiological knowledge in ways that detract from the development of spiritual growth and maturity.

To correct this imbalance, mission leaders must therefore emphasize the development of spiritual maturity alongside theoretical knowledge.[37] Both formal and non-formal training must include cross-cultural competence, critical thinking, and missiology in a broader scope than solely cognitive training. For example, retreats that re-orient and enhance relationship with God, mission conferences, and mentoring ministries can create an educational environment in which missionaries can reflect, facilitating awareness of actual needs. Fostering community-level training in order to correct weaknesses and develop strengths through collaboration with others also improves cultural competence. Mission experts need to brainstorm together to gather information and funding and to successfully support missionaries through this more holistic approach to missionary education. In the global context, a facilitative style of education, not an authoritative

37. Moon, "Mission from 2012."

style, is desirable. Across denominations, mission leaders should facilitate communication and value analytical and inductive reasoning, pursuing a global as well as a local mission perspective and focusing on the quality of missions rather than the quantity of converts.

One aspect of ensuring quality over quantity is discerning the best match between missionary and mission field. Mission leaders should be aware of the added dimensions of personality when deciding what region would best suit a particular missionary. When placing these missionaries, mission leaders must ensure that they are sent into regions in which their personality type will not become a hindrance and must arrange relocation if necessary.

Individual missionaries

Missionaries need to understand that their overall health is very important. They must get regular health check-ups, maintain good nutrition, get proper rest, set personal limits, have a good spiritual mentor, be involved in a trustworthy support group, and keep each other accountable. Seeking self-awareness through the continual practice of self-initiated care encourages this healthy and balanced lifestyle. NBKMs need to set up emotional and relational boundaries, being true to themselves in submission to God. Resting in Christ should lead to having restful quality time and furloughs without a busy schedule—taking time to reflect, rethink, and evaluate one's ministry.

I do not expect that all concerned parties will follow all these recommendations, but were any number to be instituted, the occurrence and duration of burnout would be reduced and the speed and longevity of recovery would be increased. Systematic member care, missionary training with an understanding of *missio Dei* as central to all its aspects, and cooperation among all concerned should characterize a mission community that anticipates the need for and promotes successful recovery.

Chapter Seven Summary

Study findings indicate that inadequacies in cross-cultural competency, self-awareness, and self-care were the primary causes of burnout. In recovering from burnout, self-initiated care was shown to be the only approach with lasting results. The findings discussed were: spirituality in burnout recovery, sharing in spiritual community, developing mission theology, adopting a *missio Dei* approach to missions, and promoting pastoral and psychological care in burnout prevention. The study findings implied the need for transformation of thinking, along with effective member care and self-care strategies that are sensitive to Korean issues and needs. These outcomes can be applied through member care and missionary training that prevents burnout and promotes recovery. Mission agencies and churches must understand the causes of burnout and develop a holistic approach to member care and training. This includes a supportive and authentic community that encourages confidential sharing through mentorship and biblical counseling (pastoral and psychological). In addition, spiritual formation groups can help missionaries experience God by knowing Him more deeply. This knowledge increases their spiritual maturity and holistically transforms their thinking, enabling them to see God and others realistically. Such training would need to address missiological issues of intercultural sensitivity, interpersonal relationship skills, and a missionary's partnership with God in light of *missio Dei*.

Recommendations for Further Research

Further research should be conducted with those who have recovered from burnout to determine whether there are any additional factors that may have aided or inhibited their recovery (family relationships, shared experiences with other missionaries, education, character development, personal spiritual growth, multicultural insights, gender differences, and missionary evaluation and selection). More research in this field ought to be conducted so that missionary training systems could be improved.

Further, more work could be done on specific aspects of community (church, mission organization, mentors/counselors, friends, and others) that have aided in the processes of prevention and intervention in cases of burnout. How might systematic member care help individual missionaries in preventing/recovering from burnout? For example, is there a standardized way to go about member care, such as creating a manual?

More specific research into the cultural influences on member care would be beneficial for implementing member care effectively in a variety of contexts. While there are many global principles of member care, specific applications are dependent upon various cultural situations and factors. Thus, global member care can be further developed with regard to cultural influence and sensitivity.

Seeking answers to these cultural questions opens the door to other specialized studies. Although Korea is the largest new Asian mission force, China, inheritor of a similar Confucian culture, is mobilizing in a similar way. How might greater attention to member care and burnout recovery benefit Chinese missionaries? How might a global missiology of *missio Dei*, especially in newer mission forces in South Asia, affect the missionary movement arising from that location? This qualitative study, based on Korean missionary self-disclosure, is an effort to discover effective strategies to enable Korean missionaries to recover from burnout, enabling them to share and receive the gospel more effectively in the field. This research could also be helpful for improving 1) Korean mission leaders' and agencies' effectiveness, 2) member care strategies for missionary support systems, including training, mentoring, and counseling, and 3) the development of Korean global mission theology and leadership. Further research into these suggested areas would provide added benefits for Asian missionaries experiencing burnout.

Study Conclusion

While NBKMs' character, culture, and personality made them strong in their devotion to God, they often experienced burnout exacerbated by a works-driven attitude toward their service to God. By following Korean church culture's often hierarchical and success driven ideals, they experienced struggles in the field that were further compounded through inattention to self and fear of shame. As NBKMs were made aware of their situation through experiences of burnout, they took differing paths toward recovery.

Self-help (religious practice in an effort to seek independent help) brought only temporary relief to those suffering from burnout. True recovery proceeded from a correct understanding of the roles of God and others in their lives. Grace-based, interdependent care promoted genuine, lasting recovery through transformed thinking and renewed relationships with God and others. NBKMs recovered holistically through attention to all aspects of self: physical, emotional, relational, and spiritual. Recovery from burnout through self-initiated care revealed the need for improvements within and further development of the Korean mission system, in order to prevent burnout and facilitate recovery through strategies that address cultural influences and encourage healing through self-initiated care.

Appendix A
The Semi-Structured Interviews

All interviews were conducted in Korean. What follows is a rough translation of the interview questions and content.

1. (I heard you had been through burnout, overcame it, and are now in active ministry). What was most effective in helping you overcome burnout? For example, has mentorship (or spiritual guidance) helped you? Or spiritual disciplines (such as retreat, meditation, *lectio divina*, centering prayer, solitude, reflection, and knowledge) or spiritual community? Or attending more church services, worshiping? Or praying harder and fasting? What helped you personally? Tell me in detail the effort that was effective for your recovery (or overcoming).

2. What was your inner healing (pastoral counseling) process of recovery? How did you come to peace and acceptance of who you are? How did you identify as the beloved (Just being as you are . . . not obsessing about constantly doing something without resting)? How long was your process of overcoming burnout?

3. Now, if you were to share your burnout experience with missionaries—what would be most insightful for you to share? How would you help them? Would you share what you did? Or would you share what did not work for you? How would you encourage a missionary going through burnout? What differences can you see in how you approach your ministry having overcome burnout?

4. How did your spiritual community influence your burnout recovery? Who helped you overcome burnout? What role did the church or missions organization play? Did your interaction with your colleagues change? Did you feel alone or supported? Did you experience empathy and compassion from the church? Or did you think you were the only person suffering from burnout? People might have been involved

APPENDIX A: THE SEMI-STRUCTURED INTERVIEWS

in your recovery. How was your family involved? Could your family tell you were burned out? How did they effectively help you?

5. How did education help in your healing? Sometimes having specific education about healing, spiritual development, rest, knowledge of God's love for you as you are, knowledge of cultural discernment, or psychology can help you through the process. What educational supplements produced healing (overcoming) from burnout or hindered you in your burnout process (books, seminars, workshops, or classes)?

6. (Typically, a burned-out missionary is striving to perfect their relationship with God and is living in guilt, shame and moralism). How did you see your striving change for you? Did you feel yourself letting go and laying down your strength to allow God to heal you? Did you experience a new aspect to your relationship with God or a reflection of His character that helped you out of burnout?

Appendix B

Informed Consent Form

Participant's name:

I authorize (   ) of (   ), Biola University, La Mirada, California, and/or any designated research assistants to gather information from me on the topic of Understanding Native-born Korean Missionary Efforts to Overcome Burnout.

I understand that the general purposes of the research are to find out how Korean missionaries recover from burnout, and that I will be asked to describe experiences by answering questionnaires and participating in interviews. The approximate time of my involvement will be 90 minutes.

> The potential benefits of the study are to help future missionaries recover from burnout and for supporters to better provide care for missionaries.

I am aware that I may choose not to answer any questions that I find embarrassing or offensive. I am aware that my participation will be recorded, but that I can decline to have my interview audio-recorded.

I understand that my participation is voluntary and that I may refuse to participate or discontinue my participation at any time without penalty or loss of benefits to which I am otherwise entitled.

I understand that if, after my participation, I experience any undue anxiety or stress or have questions about the research or my rights as a participant, that may have been provoked by the experience, ( ) will be available for consultation, and will also be available to provide direction regarding medical assistance in the unlikely event of physical injury incurred during participation in the research.

APPENDIX B: INFORMED CONSENT FORM

Confidentiality of research results will be maintained by the researcher. My individual results will not be released without my written consent.

Signature   Date

There are two copies of this consent form included. Please sign one and return it to the researcher with your responses. The other copy you may keep for your records.

Questions and comments may be address to (*name of researcher*), (*department*), Biola University, 13800 Biola Avenue, La Mirada, CA. 90639-0001. Phone: (562) 903-6000.

Appendix C

The Protection of Human Rights in Research Committee (PHRRC)

Proposal

Please answer all of the following questions by inserting the requested information. Note that a checked box looks like this ☒

1.0 Give a brief, one paragraph overview of the nature and purpose of the research:

> This qualitative research with native-born Korean missionary (NBKM) participants hopes to discover how they have recovered from burnout, in order to help everyone involved in missions to avoid or recover from burnout.

2.0 Give a full description of participants:

   2.1 General Description: NBKMs who have recovered from burnout and have returned to active involvement in ministry

   2.2 Number of participants: 30 people

   2.3 Age range: Late 20s and older

   2.4 Place of recruitment: Fuller Seminary, Talbot Seminary, Korean Missionary Conference held in Chicago at Wheaton College in July 20th -27th 2012, and others as necessary

   2.5 Are any participants minors?

   ☒ No   ☐ Yes—Please describe

   2.6 Are any participants part of a vulnerable population?

   ☒ No   ☐ Yes—Please describe

3.0 Provide a detailed account of the procedures that will be used in your study. In other words, describe what the participant will experience:

> I will contact mission organizations for referral to potential participants. Participants will receive and sign a consent form and disclosures. They will, subsequently, be interviewed, ideally in person, or, if necessary, by phone, email, or ephone.

4.0 Give a full description of the potential benefits, if any, to the individual, group, and/or society as a result of the research:

> First, this study will provide Korean missionaries with cross-cultural educational strategies to overcome burnout. Second, it will help counselors and home churches provide better member care for burned out Korean missionaries. Finally, in terms of scholarly research, this study will advance research into contextually appropriate paradigms and strategies that are helpful for the majority of cross-cultural missionaries.

5.0 Risk Assessment:

   5.1 Describe the potential risks to the individual, group, and/or society due to the procedures of the study:

> Sharing private information, publicly, can be a sensitive *loss-of face* situation for NBKMs from Korean Confucianism's shame vs. honor culture.

   5.2 Describe risks involved due to the sensitive nature of the instruments being used (e.g., published or researcher-generated questionnaires):

> No instruments or questionnaires will be used in this study. However, I will conduct semi-structured interviews that do not utilize a standardized set of questions.

6.0 Means taken to minimize:

   6.1 General risk minimization strategy

> All interviews will be carefully and confidentially conducted to protect the interviewee's privacy. Specific Korean churches and mission organizations will be referred to by pseudonyms.

   6.2 Describe how the participant's personal privacy will be protected

APPENDIX C: THE PROTECTION OF HUMAN RIGHTS IN RESEARCH COMMITTEE

> The participants will not be mentioned by their actual names. A random alternative name is used in any public literature, email, or communications regarding this study.

6.3 Describe how the confidentiality of the information obtained will be protected

> The researcher will be the only one who will be able to match participants and their narratives. Data collected from participants will be kept on a password protected computer, stored in a locked room.

6.4 Assess the likely effectiveness of these precautionary measures:

> I deem these precautionary measures to be effective.

7.0 Written informed consent:

7.1 Give a description of the procedures to be used in obtaining and documenting the prior informed consent of the participant.

> Each participant will be given a hard copy and/or digital (PDF and MSWord) consent form, dependent on in-person availability. After signing, to indicate consent, participants will return the form (hard-copy original, digitally signed, or scanned signed hard copy). Participant will retain a copy, with the original becoming part of research documentation.

7.2 Explicitly describe whether any of the participants are minors and how parental consent and minor assent will be obtained

> N/A

7.3 Please attach a copy of the following:

7.3.1 Consent Form—Check if attached ý

7.3.2 Verbatim instructions—the exact language you intend to use when you present the instructions and consent form to the participants—Check if attached ý

7.3.3 Minor Assent Form (if needed)—Check if attached ☐ N/A

7.4 If you research involves any of the following see the proposal instructions for further information:

7.4.1 A waiver of informed consent

7.4.2 Minors and/or vulnerable groups

7.4.3 Mandated reporter

APPENDIX C: THE PROTECTION OF HUMAN RIGHTS IN RESEARCH COMMITTEE

    7.4.4 Audio and/or video recording of behavior or interviews

    7.4.5 Medical risks

Participant interviews will be audio-recorded provided participants' consent.

8.0 Attach copies of any questionnaires, surveys, or inventories you are using—Check if attached ☐

> No questionnaires will be used. However, a list of sample interview questions for the semi-structured interviews is attached.

9.0 Are there any special or unusual circumstances regarding the research that you believe could be relevant to the PHRRC's decision in reviewing the project:

☒ No

☐ Yes—Please describe those special or unusual circumstances

10.0 Please check the box most relevant to your research:

☐ **No Risk:** Research involves no risk to human participants if it includes only (1) observation of public behavior or the use of information available to the public, and/or (2) data used in a manner that is strictly statistical and anonymous—information cannot be traced to a specific individual, and (3) meets the criteria for MINIMAL RISK research. (Very few proposals fall into this category.)

☒ **Minimal Risk:** Research involves at least minimal risk to human participants when it includes non-public behavior or data and/or allows for connection of the response to the individual's identity. "Minimal risk" research includes no deception of participants: no sensitive, culturally taboo, or socially controversial material or responses by participants. Also the research procedure is unlikely to impact or change the participants' physical, social, psychological, or spiritual status.

☐ **Moderate Risk:** Research involves at least moderate risk to human participants if the procedure involved deception of participants; sensitive, taboo, or controversial material; is physically intrusive; or may impact the physical,

APPENDIX C: THE PROTECTION OF HUMAN RIGHTS IN RESEARCH COMMITTEE

social, psychological, or spiritual status of the participants. The use of organs, tissues, or bodily fluids may create medico-legal risks, or expose the participant to public embarrassment or humiliation through breach of confidentiality and invasion of privacy.

Please note the following:

1. The proposal, as approved by the Protection of Human Rights in Research Committee (PHRRC), becomes part of the agreement between Biola University and the researchers about the way in which a project will be conducted. Therefore, the proposal must be an accurate description of the research project. The proposal, informed consent documents, and other supporting materials become part of the public record of the PHRRC's deliberations. Any change in the approved proposal, including supporting documents, must be approved by the PHRRC. In order to ensure the integrity of the research study, the proposal will not be available for review by the public until the research project is completed.

    I affirm that this proposal is an accurate description of the way this research will be conducted

                                    Initial   Date

2. It is the responsibility of the principal investigator to supply three (3) copies of the proposal (along with copies of questionnaires, interview schedules, informed consent documents, and other supporting materials) to the PHRRC chair. The copies should be as follows:

    One (1) original copy with required signatures and complete information

        Check if attached ☒

    Two (2) blind copies (all identifying information removed). These blind copies should have blanks inserted at the name of the investigator, supervisor, department, phone number(s), location, country, tribe, or any other identifying information

        Check if two blind copies are attached ☒

Appendix D
Gender Influences

THE STUDY DISCOVERED CERTAIN differences in burnout recovery process for male and female NBKMs. In the course of the interviews men with more than ten years mission experience were relatively open and expressive. NBKM women, however, were even more open than men to personal interaction and sharing with trusted people such as friends, mentors, and counselors. Although men revealed little reliance on mentor/counselor approaches to recovery when sharing their stories, during the interviews these males demonstrated a willingness to discuss very confidential issues. Nearly all men said they appreciated the opportunity to share within a trusting context and expressed a desire for similar opportunities in the missionary support community of sending organizations and churches. At the same time, male missionaries, feeling the need to appear strongly independent, were hesitant to share until assured of the interview's confidentiality.

Most married female missionaries felt dependent on their husbands for burnout recovery. Single females, culturally stigmatized, proactively sought solutions through community networking. Despite these differences, some aspects of burnout recovery were universal for both men and women. Seeking physical care, engaging in emotional connection, deepening intimacy with God, restoring relationship with others, and finding self-worth were essential to overall recovery for all.

Men

Few men in this study found help from family or community. Rather, they tended to look for assistance from mission-related education, self-reflection, and objective group discussion of intellectual issues, along with their regular isolated spiritual practices. Culturally, Korean male missionaries are expected to fulfill their roles as strong, faithful, and enduring soldiers for Christ, even to death. They are to be self-reliant, instead of being open with others and sharing in the community. The exceptions to such reluctance were rare until a man found someone he considered to be a trustworthy confidant. When sharing, men tended to focus more on their spiritual life rather than any physical limitations. They first reported engaging in isolated self-help. Some experienced God's unsolicited intervention. Many would then seek God individually, while a few sought help from others. Surprisingly, most males did not rely on their families as much as females did, unless the relationship with their wife was exceptionally good.

Extra help was needed during burnout for men with trauma from their family upbringing or with personality issues. In some cases, prior exposure to counseling reinforced a sense of self-sufficiency that allowed them to deny burn out. Those who had experienced trauma from their upbringing needed to seek continued counseling. There appeared to be a tendency among these participants to attempt to understand themselves and their problems through education *about* counseling processes, rather than through actual professional counseling.

A small number of men (4 out of 39), who were aware of their own problems, went privately for counseling. These men demonstrated a shift from self in isolation to self-care that involved others. However, counseling is not widely accepted in Korean culture, especially for male public figures. The tendency seen in the study participants was to consult those who were of higher authority than them—those whom they believed they could rely on, and those who had more experience. Among study participants, generally, older missionaries (those who were more religious practice driven) did not rely on counseling to benefit them. These men had a tendency to rely more on their intellect, compared to the women, who tended to be more relational.

Women

Many female participants believed that prayer results in miracles. However, most eventually realized that they also needed to engage in self-care in order to meet their physical needs. Compared to men, women had a more relational approach to the recovery process, having leaned on their husbands, as well as mentors, community involvement, and counseling. Due to lack of independent identity, married women appeared more vulnerable to burnout than men or single women, perhaps due to a confusion of their roles as wives and missionaries. They also appeared more conflicted—trying to find self-identity and self-development. They were generally more willing to seek help outside themselves.

Single women missionaries appeared more community-based and focused on networking with others through ministry. These single women felt inferior, because of the Korean cultural stigma against female singleness and also because of the hierarchy of the mission system. They expressed a need to feel recognition for their work as missionaries and not as secondary helpers.

> Because I am female single [pastor], and because I am woman, when other fellow missionaries, especially men, do not treat me as their fellow coworker, I feel hurt. Since ministry is about giving myself to the people to whom I am ministering, whenever someone treats me unfairly, I try to let it go. But still, when other pastors and my fellow missionaries ignore and belittle me, it is still very hurtful.

This common experience illustrates the unique needs of single, female missionaries. Unmarried females receive help within spiritual communities through Bible study, worship, sharing, and prayer meetings/groups. Single female missionaries, in particular, put a lot of weight on personal relationships and networking with churches and community members.

Appendix E
Group Mentoring and Counseling

For NBKMs experiencing burnout, assistance from others, particularly through group mentoring or counseling, was effective in the recovery process. Group mentoring provided confidentiality and transparency within trusting relationships with friends or authority figures. Despite cultural stigma regarding the potential shame of seeking counseling, some NBKMs were able to gain self-awareness and understanding through the cognitive transformation found in counseling. Both mentoring and counseling promoted healing and proved to be effective means of recovery from burnout.

Group Mentoring

Among those who sought help from others, half of the participants being mentored indicated they made a choice between individual or group care. Self-care provided through group mentorship is cognitively related to NBKMs' relationships with God and others. The data suggests that having human confidants, in addition to confiding in God, is crucial for healing through group mentorship. A single female missionary shared her experience of a mentoring class:

> Through mentoring I realized everyone can face this difficulty [with burnout] . . . I was able to organize my thoughts, ministry, and my mind. Mentoring class gave me a very clear direction of what I am doing and how to continue doing ministry. I was able to see it was a very great time for me.

Her mentoring class helped her to organize her thoughts, to evaluate herself, and to see beyond daunting questions. The experience allowed her to regain a sense that her time was valuable and to understand herself better through mentoring.

APPENDIX E: GROUP MENTORING AND COUNSELING

Group Counseling

While group mentoring emphasizes walking through the Christian life together, group counseling emphasizes personal transformation. As previously mentioned, counseling is very challenging for Korean men. However, participants who went to counseling found help in becoming aware of themselves and their situations. Knowing the *self* was helpful in the recovery process of the NBKMs interviewed. Group counseling was reported by these NBKMs as an effective way to seek help without losing face. An ordained missionary in his mid-forties found healing through group counseling rather than one-on-one private counseling. He shared his positive experience with professional group counseling: "Without the group counseling, I wouldn't have understood why I reacted the ways I did. There were many childhood issues that surfaced when I went for group counseling. It was through this awareness that I found healing."

Younger missionaries seemed more aware of and open to the effectiveness of counseling. Fore example, a male Bible translator lay missionary described his experience:

> I never thought about how these [counseling and understanding of personality] would affect me . . . However, through my burnout, I finally encountered these issues, and discovered that there are more to it than just merely human nature . . . In order to recover, it is a necessary process to think about and get to the roots of problems.

This missionary discovered that his conflicts were more than a product of human nature, and, through understanding himself, he was able to make progress in healing. Counseling, especially in a group setting, gave him an opportunity to know himself by increasing his awareness of and realization of internal and interpersonal issues. Other NBKM study participants have also reported that counseling helped them to connect more deeply with God and others.

Some NBKMs reported they were able to connect spiritual and psychological healing in counseling. A missionary wife in Jordan experienced a release of her own emotional blockages through counseling:

> Since they are connected, spiritual stabilities allow our emotions to be open. But when we are stuck emotionally, how would God touch us? I should have a healthy emotion. If I'm unhealthy emotionally, God would not be able to touch me. Since spiritual

APPENDIX E: GROUP MENTORING AND COUNSELING

encounters have to go through our emotions to get to us, a blocked emotional aspect in our lives would not enable spiritual encounters to move in us.

Study participants who were wounded emotionally were helped through counseling to understand emotional blockage, which can hinder spiritual development and relationship with God. As evidenced by this study's findings, group mentorship and group counseling are both critical contributing factors to NBKMs' healing and recovery from burnout.

Appendix F
Education as an Aid to Burnout Recovery

As mentioned in chapter five, some study participants reported experiencing an effective time of learning, whether formal or non-formal education, during furlough. Education contributed to the mindset transformation that fostered burnout recovery.

For example, a missionary wife in her mid-fifties, leadership training broadened her perspective and strengthened her determination:

> As for me, being a Korean wife, I did not have any adequate [leadership] experiences. While in [that country], I decided that I did not want to stay at home all day, with nothing to do . . . Then one day, I met the president of . . . Seminary and expressed my determination to receive some training for my ministry. Following that, I made a decision to enroll at . . . Seminary to receive some training so that I may serve alongside my husband.

This female Korean missionary's determination for self-development contributed to her recovery. Education helped transform her cognitive processing and transform her mindset. Education helped her develop self-confidence and leadership skills. A similar shift can be seen in this excerpt from an interview with a male in his late fifties:

> I felt that leaving my circumstance and the people would help resolve things. That has led me to have a Sabbatical, which led me to study missiology where I began to understand things. For example, I understood why a certain leader was the way he was. My span of understanding enlarged to include understanding of my leadership style and myself.

Contextualized missionary reeducation was also helpful in dealing with conflict and in broadening traditional leadership styles to be more

APPENDIX F: EDUCATION AS AN AID TO BURNOUT RECOVERY

inclusive of the influence of others. As another ordained missionary explained,

> I didn't know how to deal with conflict. This was the cause of my burnout. God then allowed me to go to a [cross-cultural] leadership school, where I was able to discover my leadership style and who I am... I believe that Korean missionaries undergo disagreements and conflicts due to the difference in underlying Korean theology.

In addition to dealing with cross-cultural conflict, he also experienced transformation in his perspective:

> While taking classes in cross-cultural education there, I had an "aha" moment, which broadened my view about missionary leadership. In that, my perspective of cross-cultural leadership was challenged and widened. I realized my past leadership style was "hierarchical," yet it was okay to lead in a way that is parallel with those I serve alongside.

The Korean pastor missionaries interviewed claimed that leadership in mission and missiology studies helped them become aware of differences and allowed them to be more open minded, broadening their understanding of other nationalities and their cultures. A single woman in her mid-forties asserted:

> Through intercultural studies, I was able to organize my ministry. Through my interactions with other Korean missionaries from all over the world and various ministering backgrounds, I was challenged by their stories and testimonies. I met excellent professors who are knowledgeable in their fields. These people enabled me to undergo a paradigm shift. These meetings with people of various qualifications and experiences broadened my mind.

Those missionaries who used their furlough effectively to learn and meet others tended to recover effectively and to avoid vicious cycles of burnout. They holistically used God's help and the help of others to bring them to recovery. Another NBKM also experienced cognitive transformation through education, allowing her to reflect on herself and her ministry:

> I came to Fuller to isolate myself from my ministry. Before I came, I felt betrayed from people in my community. I raised and discipled them... how could they betray me? My isolation made me aware, allowing me to self-reflect upon my life... I started to listen

> to a lecture about long life development. In this class, I was given the assignment to write about my timeline of life. As I wrote this assignment, a new understanding of my life came to me.

Her realization gave her relief from her negative feelings. Through her education in a "long-life development" class, led by experienced, multiculturally competent mission experts, her cognition was challenged to have a new perspective on her life and ministry.

Many Korean missionaries interviewed allowed no time for self-evaluation, reflection, and realization. They needed time to connect with God and others and to develop these relationships. This development can occur through both formal and non-formal educational experiences. As seen in the interviewees' comments, the non-formal self-learning process is also significant for Korean missionary pastors.

The non-formal education process proved as important as the formal education process, especially for those who minister in remote areas. Attendance at conferences, seminars, and workshops allowed them to recover, learn, and experience connectedness with God and with others. Non-formal education helps remote missionaries change their thinking. In this study, missionaries who had educational support by way of context-driven missions education healed faster than missionaries who tried to figure out cultural differences or dynamics on their own. These missionaries needed more outside input rather than solely relying on devotion to God. According to their comments, there appeared to be three ways to achieve this: attending missionary conferences, obtaining professional advice, and attending lectures by experts in missiology.

A missionary wife in her mid-fifties shared about her experience attending a missionary conference:

> The Korean missionary conference gave me time to examine my spiritual state and what I am lacking, and time of repentance more openly. If I live in the mission field, I focus on the work that I should do, take care of, and serve only, thus I lack having time to reflect myself. I still pray in the mission field, but it is different from now. As I listen to others' words, their stories in the mission fields, and their spiritual journey, I view myself through their sharing, I see my lacking points, and I repent, reflect, and discover.

Through the conference, she was able to reflect and to realize that, with the cognitive input of others, her ability to connect with God and others was increased, helping her to experience restoration. Another missionary wife had a passion for serving, but she was frustrated by her obligation to look after her children. However, she listened to professional advice:

> I was encouraged and challenged by the speaker, Dr. Yang's words that the time spent as a mother and a wife is most precious, as it will not return once it's gone by. Her words really struck me. It gave me a new perspective about my role as a mother and a wife. It made me realize that my role right now is as important as my husband's, although my place in the mission field is currently in the home.

Through seminars, professional advice is reported as cognitively beneficial to missionaries who already have community support in their ministry. For the study participants, spiritual seminars about connecting to the inner self were helpful for recovery from emotional and relational difficulties. One ordained missionary to China in his early fifties explained:

> There is a spiritual conference with an inner healing seminar. It was held for 3 nights and 4 days. I was trying to forgive the one who hurt me. Mentally, I was trying to forgive and move on, but emotionally, I was impacted hard. So during this seminar, God took away a big stone from my heart and laid it down. God opened my eyes to see what was wrong with me, I then also realized that it was [due to a betrayal I felt from a sister whom I disciple.] Through that spiritual conference, I was able to understand that. In front of God, I was able to forgive her, knowing that I'll meet her in the house of God. Then I realized, the person who betrayed me was in trouble as well not only with me, but also with other churches. Yet, when I forgave her, she did not bother me anymore. I was able to let go and release her from my life.

Through the spiritual conference, this missionary was able to find healing as he poured out all that he had gone through before God. He talked to God in his most vulnerable state. He cried like a child, and, at times, lashed out at God. However, in the end, he was able to gain freedom by forgiving. This seminar helped reoriented his thoughts in connection with God, giving him an opportunity to reflect on himself in relationship with God and the word.

The NBKMs interviewed in the study also reported reorienting their thoughts in connection with God through the informal means of books, CDs, and online resources. A single female in her forties reported:

> Books, especially good Christian books, especially those that are faith-related . . . In my opinion, if it wasn't for reading those good Christian books, I will focus a lot on me. But these books broaden my mind. In my experience, with my limited knowledge, we can only live in God. But through books, we can expand what we know, beyond myself, I am able to see other people's perspectives. Books really broadened my perspectives.

As seen in these interviews, general missionary education helps missionaries come to an awareness of their burnout and experience cognitive transformation, which in turn helps their future ministries and lives. In order to experience this cognitive transformation, the study participants reported practicing self-care, supported by God and others.

Curriculum Vitae

NAME   Hannah Kyong-Jin Cho

EDUCATION

    Biola University   Ph. D.
    2013
    Department of Anthropology, Intercultural Education, and Missiology, Cook School of Intercultural Studies

    Biola University   M. A.
    2008
    Department of Christian Education, Talbot School of Theology

    World Mission University   B. A.
    2004
    Department of Biblical Studies

    Calvary Chapel Bible College   B. A.
    2003
    Department of Biblical Studies

EXPERIENCE

    Joy People Church   2009–2013
    Cypress, CA
    Education Assistant Pastor

Mission Dept of the First Evangelical Free Church   2008–2009
Fullerton, CA
Intern

Tiny Tot Christian School   2002–2005
Los Angeles, CA
Teacher

Sa Rang Community Church Korean School   2001–2006
Anaheim, CA
Teacher

Holt Adoption Baby Agency   2002–2004
Seoul, Korea
Volunteer Interpreter

Christian Marriage and Family Ministries   2000–present
http://www.cmfm.org
Volunteer Minister

Youth With a Mission   1994–1999
South Korea, Central America, Tonga
Missionary

References

An, Sung Sam. "선교사 돌봄을 위한 탈진 회복" [Burnout Syndrome Recovery for Missionary Caring]. Unpublished PhD diss., Theological University and Seminary, 2013.
Andrews, Leslie A. "Spiritual, Family, and Ministry Satisfaction among Missionaries." *Journal of Psychology and Theology* 27 (1999) 107–18.
Augsburger, David W. *Pastoral Counseling Across Cultures*. Philadelphia: Westminster, 1986.
Balswick, Jack O., and Judith K. Balswick. *The Family: A Christian Perspective on the Contemporary Home*. Grand Rapids: Baker Academic, 2007.
Barnett, Keri L., et al. "Psychological and Spiritual Predictors of Domains of Functioning and Effectiveness of Short-Term Missionaries." *Journal of Psychology and Theology* 33 (2005) 27–40.
Bergaas, Unndis. "The Relationship of Spirituality to Burnout and Coping among Norwegian Missionaries." PhD diss., Biola University, 2002.
Blöecher, Detlef. "What ReMap I Said, Did, and Achieved." In *WorthKeeping: Global Perspectives on Best Practice in Missionary Retention*, edited by Rob Hay et al., 9–22. Pasadena: William Carey Library, 2007.
Bosch, David J. *Transforming Missions: Paradigm Shifts in Theology of Mission*. Maryknoll, NY: Orbis, 1991.
Buswell, Robert E., Jr., and Timothy S. Lee, eds. *Christianity in Korea*. Honolulu: University of Hawaii Press, 2006.
Byon, Jin Seok. "타문화 사역을 위한 변화와 성장의 기초" [Missionary Training: Foundations of Change and Growth for Cross-Cultural Ministry]. *Mission and Theology* 28 (2011) 35–57.
Carter, Joan. "Missionary Stressors and Implications for Care." *Journal of Psychology and Theology* 27 (1999) 171–81.
Charmaz, Kathy. *Constructing Grounded Theory: A Practical Guide through Qualitative Analysis*. Thousand Oaks, CA: Sage, 2006.
———. "Grounded Theory: Objectivist and Constructivist Methods." In *Handbook of Qualitative Research*, edited by Norman K. Denzin and Yvonna S. Lincoln, 509–35. Thousand Oaks, CA: Sage, 2000.
Cho, E. A. "Communal Reflective/Narrative Learning from the Crisis-Related Experience: A Potential Member Care Practice." *Current Mission Trends* 14 (2011) 143–60.
Choi, Hyung Keun. "선교사 멤버케어 시스템 구축" [Construction of a Missionary Member Care System]. *Mission and Theology* 28 (2009) 86–114.

REFERENCES

———. "Preparing Korean Missionaries for Cross-Cultural Effectiveness." PhD diss., Asbury Theological Seminary, 2000.

Choi, Sang Chin, and In Jae Choi. "The Effects of Korean Cultural Psychological Characteristics on Coping Styles, Stress, and Life Satisfaction: Centering around Cheong and Wellness." *Korean Psychological Institutes* 14 (2002) 55–71.

Chung, David. *Syncretism: The Religious Context of Christian Beginnings in Korea*. Albany, NY: State University of New York Press, 2001.

Chung, Kahp Chin. "The Missionary Strategy of Korean Churches in South Africa." Master's thesis, University of Pretoria, 2005.

Clark, Donald N. "Christianity in Modern Korea." *Education About ASIA* 11 (2006) 35–39. http://www.asian-studies.org/eaa/Clark-Korea.pdf.

Cloud, Henry, and John Townsend. *How People Grow: What the Bible Reveals about Personal Growth*. Grand Rapids: Zondervan, 2001.

Coe, John. "Resisting the Temptation of Moral Formation: Opening to Spiritual Formation in the Cross and the Spirit." *Journal of Spiritual Formation and Soul Care* 1 (2008) 54–78.

Corbin, Juliet, and Anselm Strauss. *Basics of Qualitative Research*. Thousand Oaks, CA: Sage, 2008.

Corby, Joy E., and Linda Stone Fish. "Missionary Ministry Satisfaction Predictors: How Spiritual Attribution Influences the Effects of Stress on Family Communication and Satisfaction." PhD diss., Syracuse University, 2003.

Creighton, M. R. "Revising Shame and Guilt Cultures." *Ethos* 18 (1990) 285.

Creswell, John W. *Qualitative Inquiry and Research Design: Choosing Among Five Approaches*. Thousand Oaks, CA: Sage, 2007.

———. *Research Design: Qualitative, Quantitative, and Mixed Methods Approaches*. Thousand Oaks, CA: Sage, 2009.

Croucher, Rowland. "Stress and Burnout in Ministry." http://www.churchlink.com.au/churchlink/forum/r_croucher/stress_burnout.html

Cumings, Bruce. *The Two Koreas*. Foreign Policy Association Headline Series 269. New York, NY: Foreign Policy Association, 1984.

Denzin, Norman K., and Yvonna S. Lincoln. "Introduction: The Discipline and Practice of Qualitative Research." In *Handbook of Qualitative Research*, edited by Norman K. Denzin and Yvonna S. Lincoln, 1–28. Thousand Oaks, CA: Sage, 2000.

Denzin, Norman K., and Yvonna S. Lincoln, eds. *The Sage Handbook of Qualitative Research*. Thousand Oaks, CA: Sage, 2005.

Dey, Ian. "Grounded Theory." In *Qualitative Research Practice*, edited by Clive Seale et al., 80–93. London, UK: Sage, 2004.

Dodd, David S. "The Missionary Family in Stress and Conflict." In *The Family in Mission: Understanding and Caring for Those who Serve*, edited by Leslie A. Andrews, 263–74. Palmer Lake, CO: Mission Training International, 2004.

Dodds, Lois A., and Laura Mae Gardner. *Global Servants Cross-Cultural Humanitarian Heroes: Volume 1: Formation and Development of these Heroes*. Liverpool, PA: Heartstream, 2010.

———. *Global Servants Cross-Cultural Humanitarian Heroes: Volume 2: 12 Factors in Effectiveness and Longevity*. Liverpool, PA: Heartstream, 2011.

Dodds, Lois A., and Lawrence E. Dodds. "Caring for People in Missions: Just Surviving or Thriving? Optimal Care for the Long Haul." Paper presented at the IFMA/EFMA

REFERENCES

Personnel Meeting, Orlando, FL, December 1997. http://www.heartstreamresources.org/media/Membercare.pdf.

Duhe, Dale Joseph. "When There is No Shepherd: Providing Member Care for Missionaries in Foreign Lands." DMin diss., George Fox University, 1994.

Dye, T. Wayne. "Stress-Producing Factors in Cultural Adjustment." *Missiology: An International Review* 2 (1974) 61–77.

Elmer, Duane. *Cross-Cultural Conflict: Building Relationships for Effective Ministry*. Downer Grove, IL: InterVarsity, 1993.

Enns, Marlene. "Now I Know in Part: Holistic and Analytic Reasoning and their Contribution to Fuller Knowing in Theological Education." *Evangelical Review of Theology* 29 (2005) 251–69.

Eriksson, Cynthia B., et al. "Social Support, Organizational Support and Religious Support in Relation to Burnout in Expatriate Humanitarian Aid Workers." *Mental Health, Religion and Culture* 12 (2009) 671–86.

Fawcett, John, ed. *Stress and Trauma Handbook: Strategies for Flourishing in Demanding Environments*. Monrovia, CA: World Vision International, 2003.

Foyle, Marjory F. *Honorably Wounded Stress Among Christian Workers*. Grand Rapids: Monarch, 2001.

———. *Overcoming Missionary Stress*. Wheaton, IL: Evangelical Missions Information Service, 1988.

Friedman, Meyer, and Ray H. Rosenman. *Type A Behavior and Your Heart*. New York, NY: Alfred A. Knopf, 1974.

Gardner, Laura Mae. "Member Care and Missions: Looking Ahead a Strategy Paper." In *Wycliffe Member Care and Counseling Resource Collection*. Orlando: Wycliffe, 2009. CD-ROM.

Girón, Rodolfo. "An Integrated Model Of Missions." In *Too Valuable to Lose: Exploring the Causes and Cures of Missionary Attrition*, edited by William David Taylor, 25–40. Pasadena: William Carey Library, 1997.

Gish, Dorothy J. "Sources of Missionary Stress." *Journal of Psychology and Theology* 11 (1983) 236–42.

Grayson, James Huntley. "Elements of Protestant Accommodation to Korean Religious Culture: A Personal Ethnographic Perspective." *Missiology: An International Review* 3 (1995) 43–59.

———. "A Quarter-Millennium of Christianity in Korea." In *Christianity in Korea*, edited by Robert E. Buswell Jr. and Timothy S. Lee, 7–28. Honolulu: University of Hawaii Press, 2006.

———. "Religious Syncretism in the Shilla Period: The Relationship between Esoteric Buddhism and Korean Primeval Religion." *Asian Folklore Studies* 43 (1984) 185–98.

Guba, Egon G., and Yvonna S. Lincoln. "Paradigmatic Controversies, Contradictions, and Emerging Confluences." In *The Sage Handbook of Qualitative Research*, edited by Norman K. Denzin and Yvonna S. Lincoln, 191–215. Thousand Oaks, CA: Sage, 2005.

Gudykunst, William B., et al., eds. *Communication in Personal Relationships across Cultures*. Thousand Oaks, CA: Sage, 1996.

Han, Chul Ho. "Korean Sending." In *Perspectives on the World Christian Movement*, edited by Ralph D. Winter and Steven C. Hawthorne, 372. Pasadena: William Carey, 2009.

Hart, Archibald D. *Adrenaline and Stress*. Tulsa: Western, 1995.

REFERENCES

———. "Depressed, Stressed, and Burned Out: What's Going on in My Life?" *Enrichment Journal* (2006). http://enrichmentjournal.ag.org/200603/200603_020_burnout.cfm.
Hay, Rob, et al. "ReMap II Project Methodology." In *WorthKeeping: Global Perspectives on Best Practices in Missionary Retention*, edited by Rob Hay et al., 23–35. Pasadena: William Carey, 2007.
Hayward, Doug. "Defining Culture." In *Encountering Missionary Life and Work: Preparing for Intercultural Ministry*, edited by Tom Steffen and Lois McKinney Douglas, 184–85. Grand Rapids: Baker Academic, 2008.
Herr, Glenn. "Doing Your Job? Does Your Church Care?" *Evangelical Missions Quarterly* 23 (1987) 42–45.
Hiebert, Paul G. *Anthropological Insights for Missionaries*. Grand Rapids: Baker, 1985.
———. *Anthropological Reflections on Missiological Issues*. Grand Rapids: Baker, 1994.
———. *Cultural Anthropology*. Grand Rapids: Baker, 1983.
———. "Cultural Difference and the Communication of the Gospel." In *Perspectives on the World Christian Movement*, edited by Ralph D. Winter and Steven C. Hawthorne, 373–83. Pasadena: William Carey, 1999.
———. *Transforming Worldviews: An Anthropological Understanding of How People Change*. Grand Rapids: Baker Academic, 2008.
———. *Understanding Folk Religion: A Christian Response to Popular Religious Beliefs and Practices*. Grand Rapids: Baker, 1999.
Hofstede, Geert. *Culture's Consequences: Comparing Values, Behaviors, Institutions, and Organizations across Nations*. Thousand Oaks, CA: Sage, 2001.
Hofstede, Geert, ed. *Masculinity and Femininity: The Taboo Dimension of National Cultures*. Thousand Oaks, CA: Sage, 1998.
Hong, Eunice. "Understanding Intergenerational Korean American Church Splits." PhD diss., Biola University, 2010.
Im, Jong-Pyo. "Incarnational Bonding Process in Relation to Effectiveness of Cross-Cultural Adjustment through Field-Based Missionary Training Model for Korean Missionaries." PhD diss., Fuller Theological Seminary, 2007.
Ivancevich, J. M. et al. "Occupational Stress, Type A Behavior, and Physical Well-Being." *The Academy of Management Journal* 25 (1982) 373–91.
Jackson, Anne. *Mad Church Disease: Overcoming the Burnout Epidemic*. Grand Rapids: Zondervan, 2009.
Jenkins, Phillip. *The Next Christendom: The Coming of Global Christianity*. New York: Oxford University Press, 2002.
Jordan, Peter. *Re-Entry: Making the Transition from Missions to Life at Home*. Seattle: YWAM, 1992.
Journal of Psychology and Theology 27 (1999) 107–18.
Jung, Jung Sook. "선교사를 위한 가정 사역" [Family Ministry for Missionaries]. *Bible and Counseling* 2 (2003) 7–40.
Kang, Byung Moon. "선교지에서의 세계관의 갈등과 인격 발달과 성화의 문제" [In the Mission Field in the World of Conflict and the Issue of Personality Development and Sanctification]. *Chongshin Nonchong* 24 (2004) 363–89.
———. "선교사 스트레스 이해와 그 대책" [Understanding the Stress of Missionaries and Multi-Perspective Steps to its Solution]. *Chongshindaenonchong* 22 (2003) 138–58.

REFERENCES

Kang, Sung Sam. "한국 세계 선교의 현황분석과 교회선교 활성화를 위한 갱신방안 연구" [Analysis of the Korean World Missions and Church Renewal Mission Study for Activation]. *Shinhwakjinam [신학지남]* 264 (2000) 243-74.

———. "Missionary Attrition Issues, Supervision: Perspective of the New Sending Countries." In *Too Valuable to Lose: Exploring the Causes and Cures of Missionary Attrition*, edited by William David Taylor, 251-64. Pasadena: William Carey Library, 1997.

Keum, Kyosung. "A Grounded Theory Study on the Emerging Negative Perception and Public Criticism of the Korean Protestant Church by Non-Christian Koreans." PhD diss., Biola University, 2011.

Kim, Andrew E. "A History of Christianity in Korea: From Its Troubled Beginning to Its Contemporary Success." *Korea Journal* 35 (1995) 34-53.

———. "Korean Religious Culture and Its Affinity to Christianity: The Rise of Protestant Christianity in South Korea. *Sociology of Religion* 61 (2000) 117-33.

Kim, Do Chong. "선교사 멤버케어(Member Care)에 대한 선교학적 고찰: 하나님의 선교(Missio Dei)의 통전적 관점에서" [Member Care Missionaries (Member Care) Missiological Study on God's Mission: *Missio Dei*, in Terms of the Holistic]. Unpublished master's thesis, JangShin Theological Seminary, 2010.

Kim, Dong Sung. "Burnout Among Presbyterian (Daeshin) Pastors in Korea." Doctoral diss., Regent University, 2003.

Kim, Eun Young. "How Attachment Styles Relate to Experience of Stress among North American and Korean Missionaries." PhD diss., Biola University, 2009.

Kim, Hyung Jun. "타 문화권 선교사 부부의 탈진과 부부적응" [Burn-Out and Marital Adjustment in the Korean Cross-Cultural Missionary Couples]. Unpublished DMin diss., University of Jangshin, 2009.

Kim, Jae Un. *The Koreans: Their Mind and Behavior*. Translated by Kyung-Dong Kim. Seoul, Korea: Kyobo Book Center, 1991.

Kim, Wonil. "Minjung Theology's Biblical Hermeneutics: An Examination of Minjung Theology's Appropriation of the Exodus Account." In *Christianity in Korea*, edited by Robert E. Buswell Jr. and Timothy S. Lee, 221-37. Honolulu: University of Hawaii Press, 2006.

Kim, Yoon Hee. "한국선교사 우울증과 성경적 상담" [Depression of Korean Missionaries and Biblical Counseling]. Unpublished master's thesis, Chongshin Theological Seminary, 2013.

Kim, Young Ok. "선교사의 자존감과 스트레스 대처방식에 관한 연구" [A Study Between Missionaries' Self-Respect and Stress Coping]. Unpublished master's thesis, University of Chongshin, 2004.

Kim, Yungwook. "Negotiating with Terrorists: The Iterated Game of the Taliban Korean Hostage Case." *Public Relations Review* 34 (2008) 263-68.

Ko, Hyun Ju. "장기 선교사의 탈진 실태와 요인 분석에 관한 연구: 선교사 멤버케어 적용" [A Study about Long-Term Missionaries' Burnout: Missionary Member Care Application]. Unpublished master's thesis, University of Chongshin, 2004.

Korean Statistics Department. "The Korean National Statistical Office of the Christians." Korean Computer Mission, 2011. http://kcm.co.kr/statistics/5/s011.html.

Kraft, Charles H. "Culture, Worldview and Contextualization." In *Perspectives on the World Christian Movement*, edited by Ralph D. Winter and Steven C. Hawthorne, 400-406. Pasadena: William Carey, 2009.

REFERENCES

Lee, Boyung. "A Philosophical Anthropology of the Communal Person: A Postcolonial Feminist Critique of Confucian Communalism and Western Individualism in Korean Protestant Education." PhD diss., Boston College, 2004.

Lee, Chung Soon. "The Pentecostal Face of Korean Protestantism: A Critical Understanding." *Asia Journal of Theology* 29 (2006) 399–417.

Lee, Dong Gwi, et al. "Validation of Korean Version of the Locus of Evaluation Inventory." *The Korean Journal of Counseling and Psychotherapy* 20 (2008) 65–82.

Lee, Hak Jun. 한국교회, 패러다임을 바꿔야 산다 [Korean Church, Shift the Paradigm]. Seoul, Korea: Holy Wave Plus, 2011.

Lee, Helen. "Healthy Leaders, Healthy Households 1: Challenges and Models." In *Growing Healthy Asian American Churches*, edited by Peter Cha et al., 58–76. Downers Grove, IL: InterVarsity, 2006.

———. "Healthy Leaders, Healthy Households 2: Practices and Values." In *Growing Healthy Asian American Churches*, edited by Peter Cha et al., 77–99. Downers Grove, IL: InterVarsity, 2006.

Lee, Jeong Yeong. "Korean Taegeuk Thought: A Paradigm for New Science." In *Korean Studies, Its Tasks and Perspectives*, vol. 2. Sungnam City, Korea: The Academy of Korean Studies, 1988.

Lee, Kwan Jik. "목회자,그들은 왜 탈진에 이르는가?" [Pastor, Why Pastor Burnout?]. *Pastor and Theology* (神學指南) 85 (2000) 40–44.

Lee, Sung Ock. "Korean Mission: Mission in the Age of the Privatization of Religion." *International Congregational Journal* 5 (2005) 75–90.

Lee, Tae Woong. "선교사의 영성과 선교학" [Missionary Spirituality and Missiology]. *Global Mission Training Center* 23 (2004) 71. http://www.gmtc.or.kr/5gmtc_subject.htm.

Lee, Yoo Kyung. "선교사의 스트레스와 탈진에 관한 연구" [A Study on the Stress and Exhaustion of Missionary]. Unpublished master's thesis, Yeonse University, 2001.

Lee, Young Hoon. *The Holy Spirit Movement in Korea: Its Historical and Theological Development*. Oxford: Regnum Books International, 2009.

Lewis, A. "Burnout—Definition and Precipitating Factors Compiled." In *Wycliffe Member Care and Counseling Resource Collection*. Orlando: Wycliffe, 2009. CD-ROM.

Lewis, Tim, and Becky Lewis. "Coaching Missionary Teams." In *Missionary Care: Counting the Cost for World Evangelization*, edited by Kelly S. O'Donnell, 163–70. Pasadena: William Carey Library, 1992.

Lim, David Moo Young. *Korea Missionary Training Model for Cross-Culture: Focusing Global Ministry Training Center*. Unpublished doctoral diss., Concordia Theological Seminary, 2008.

Lindquist, Brent. "Caring for Members." In *Caring for Harvest Force in the New Millennium*, edited by Tom A. Steffen and Fredrick Douglas Pennoyer, 199–212. Pasadena: William Carey Library, 2001.

———. "Member Care in the Service of Mission: What is in the Driver's Seat?" In *Enhancing Missionary Vitality: Mental Health Professions Serving Global Mission*, edited by John R. Powell and Joyce M. Bowers, 33–40. Palmer Lake, CO: Mission Training International, 2002.

———. *Member Health? Thoughts about Contextualization*. Fresno, CA: Link Care Center, 2009.

REFERENCES

———. "Part Two: Counseling and Clinical Care." In *Missionary Care: Counting the Cost for World Evangelization*, edited by Kelly S. O'Donnell, 71–73. Pasadena: William Carey Library, 1992.

Lindquist, Lareau. "Pastoral and Psychological Caregivers Working Together." In *Enhancing Missionary Vitality: Mental Health Professions Serving Global Mission*, edited by John R. Powell and Joyce M. Bowers, 49–54. Palmer Lake, CO: Mission Training International, 2002.

Lindquist, Stanley E. "Prediction of Success in Overseas Adjustment." *Journal of Psychology and Christianity* 1 (1982) 22–25.

Livermore, David A. *Leading with Cultural Intelligence: The New Secret to Success*. New York: American Management Association, 2010.

Ma, Julie. "A Critical Appraisal of Korean Missionary Work: Challenges for Western Global South Missionaries." *Encounters Mission Ezine* 30 (2009) 1–12.

———. "The Growth of Christianity in Asia and its Impact on Mission." *Encounters Mission Ezine* 16 (2007) 1–7.

Marshall, Catherine, and Gretchen B. Rossman. *Design Qualitative Research*. Thousand Oaks, CA: Sage, 2006.

Maslach, Christina. *Burnout: The Cost of Caring*. Englewood Cliffs, NJ: Prentice Hall, 1982.

———. "Stress e Qualidade de Vida no Trabalho" [Understanding Job Burnout]. In *Stress e Qualidade de Vida no Trabalho: Stress Interpessoal e Ocupacional*, edited by Ana Maria Rossi et al., 37–51. Greenwich, CT: Information, 2006.

Maslach, Christine, and Michael P. Leiter. *The Truth about Burnout: How Organizations Cause Personal Stress and What to Do About It*. San Francisco: Jossey-Bass, 1997.

Mathis, Rick Dean. "A Missioning Care Model for the US Foursquare Gospel Church Missionary Member Care System." PhD diss., Fuller Theological Seminary, 2011.

McBride, J. LeBron. *Spiritual Crisis: Surviving Trauma to the Soul*. Binghamton, NY: Haworth, 2006.

Merriam, Sharan B., et al. *Qualitative Research in Practice: Examples for Discussion and Analysis*. San Francisco: Jossey-Bass, 2002.

Mezirow, Jack. "How Critical Reflection Triggers Transformative Learning." In *Fostering Critical Reflection in Adulthood: A Guide to Transformative and Emancipatory Learning*, edited by Jack Mezirow and Associates, 1–20. San Francisco: Jossey-Bass, 1990.

Miller, Susan B. *Shame in Context*. Hillsdale, NJ: Analytic, 1996.

Minirth, Frank, et al. *How to Beat Burnout: Help for Men and Women*. Chicago: Moody, 1986.

Moll, Rob. "Missions Incredible." *Christianity Today*, March 1, 2006, http://www.christianitytoday.com/ct/2006/march/16.28.html.

Moon, Steve Sang-Cheol. *The Acts of Koreans: A Research Report on Korean Missionary Movement*. Monograph, Korean Research Institute for Mission, 2001. http://www.krim.org.

———. *The Korean Missionary Movement and Leadership Issues*. Korean Research Institute for Mission, 2010. http://www.krim.org/files/The%20Korean%20Missionary%20Movement%20and%20Leadership%20Issues.pdf.

———. "Mission from 2012: Slow Down and Maturation." *International Bulletin of Missionary Research* 36 (2012) 84–85.

REFERENCES

———. *Missions from Korea 2013: Micro-Trends and Financials*. Korean Research Institute for Mission, 2013. http://www.krim.org/zbbs/zboard.php?id=openpds&no=97.

———. "Missionary Attrition in Korea: Opinions of Agency Executives." In *Too Valuable to Lose: Exploring the Causes and Cures of Missionary Attrition*, edited by William David Taylor, 129–42. Pasadena: William Carey Library, 1997.

———. "The Protestant Missionary Movement in Korea: Current Growth and Development." *International Bulletin of Missionary Research* 2 (2008) 59–64.

———. "The Recent Korean Missionary Movement: A Record of Growth, and More Growth Needed." *International Bulletin of Missionary Research* 27 (2003) 11–17.

———. *Self-Theologizing*. Korean Research Institute for Mission, 2013. http://krim.org/zbbs/zboard.php?id=news&no=227

Moon, Steve Sang-Cheol, ed. "Missionary Attrition in Korea." PowerPoint, Korean Research Institute for Mission, 2000. http://www.krim.org/files remap_presentation.ppt.

Moon, Steve Sang-Cheol, and David Tai-Woong Lee. "Globalization, World Evangelization, and Global Missiology." In *One World or Many? The Impact of Globalization on Mission*, edited by Richard Tiplady, 253–69. Pasadena: William Carey Library, 2003.

Nelson, P. E. "Preface." In *Enhancing Missionary Vitality: Mental Health Professions Serving Global Mission*, edited by John R. Powell and Joyce M. Bowers, xi–xii. Palmer Lake, CO: Mission Training International, 2002.

Nichols, Thomas David. "An Online Peer-Based Spiritual Mentoring Program for Field Missionaries." DMin diss., Asbury Theological Seminary, 2011.

O'Donnell, Kelly. "Developmental Tasks in the Life Cycle of Mission Families. *Journal of Psychology and Theology* 15 (1987) 281–90.

———. *Global Member Care*, Vol. 1, *The Pearls and Perils of Good Practice*. Pasadena: William Carey Library, 2011.

———. "Going Global: A Member Care Model for Best Practice." In *Doing Member Care Well: Perspectives and Practices from around the World*, edited by Kelly O'Donnell, 13–22. Pasadena: William Carey Library, 2002.

———. "Going Global: A Member Care Model of Best Practice." *Evangelical Missions Quarterly* 37 (2001) 212–22.

———. "An International Model for Member Care." Paper presented at the MANI Africa Member Care Compendium, Nairobi, Kenya, 2006.

———. "Member Care on the Field: Taking the Longer Road; Perspective of the Old Sending Countries." In *Too Valuable to Lose: Exploring the Causes and Cures of Missionary Attrition*, edited by William David Taylor, 287–302. Pasadena: William Carey Library, 1997.

———. "Running Well and Resting Well: Twelve Tools for Missionary Life." In *Doing Member Care Well: Perspectives and Practices from around the World*, edited by Kelly O'Donnell, 309–22. Pasadena: William Carey Library, 2002.

———. "Staying Healthy in Difficult Places: Member Care for Mission/Aid Workers." Unpublished manuscript, 2009.

O'Donnell, Kelly, and Michele Lewis O'Donnell. "Ethical Concerns in Providing Member Care Services." In *Missionary Care: Counting the Cost for World Evangelization*, edited by Kelly S. O'Donnell, 260–67. Pasadena: William Carey Library, 1992.

———. "Perspectives on Member Care in Missions." In *Missionary Care: Counting the Cost for World Evangelization*, edited by Kelly S. O'Donnell, 10–23. Pasadena: William Carey Library, 1992.

REFERENCES

———. "Understanding and Managing Stress." In *Missionary Care: Counting the Cost for World Evangelization*, edited by Kelly S. O'Donnell, 110–21. Pasadena: William Carey Library, 1992.

O'Donnell, Kelly, and Michele Lewis O'Donnell, eds. *Global Member Care*. Vol. 2, *Crossing Sectors for Serving Humanity*. Pasadena: William Carey Library, 2013.

———. *Helping Missionaries Grow: Readings in Mental Health and Missions*. Pasadena: William Carey Library, 1988.

O'Donnell, Michele Lewis. "CHOPS Inventory Supporting A4 Workers" (blog). http://coremembercare.blogspot.com/2012/12/mc-tools11.html.

Oak, Sun Deuk. "Chinese Protestant Literature and Early Korean Protestantism." In *Christianity in Korea*, edited by Robert E. Buswell Jr. and Timothy S. Lee, 72–93. Honolulu: University of Hawaii Press, 2006.

———. "Healing and Exorcism: Christian Encounters with Shamanism in Early Modern Korea." *Asian Ethnology* 69 (2010) 95–128.

Onishi, Norimitsu. "Korean Missionaries Carrying Word to Hard-to-Sway Places." *New York Times*, November 1, 2004. www.nytimes.com.

Pak, Su Yon, et al. *Singing the Lord's Song in a New Land: Korean American Practices of Faith*. Louisville, KY: Westminster John Knox, 2005.

Pan, Shin Hwan. "Development of Group Counseling Program for Seminarian's Maturity on the Basis of the Reality Therapy-Focused on Reducing High Narcissistic Personality Tendency." *The Korean Journal of Counseling* 5 (2004) 151–64.

———. "Pastoral Counseling of Korean Clergy with Burnout: Culture and Narcissism." *Asia Journal of Theology* 20 (2006) 241–55.

Park, Insook Han, and Lee Jay Cho. "Confucianism and the Korean Family." *Journal of Comparative Family Studies* 26 (1995) 117–34.

Park, Jin Sung. "독신 여성사역자의 갈등 해결 패턴에 관한 연구" [Unmarried Single Women Minister's Conflict and the Research of the Patter]. Unpublished master's thesis, Yeonse University, 2003.

Park, Yong Kyu. "Historical Overview of Korean Missions." In *Accountability in Missions: Korean and Western Case Studies*, edited by Jonathan J. Bonk, 1–18. Eugene, OR: Wipf & Stock, 2011.

Park, Joon Sik. "Korean Protestant Christianity: A Missiological Reflection." *International Bulletin of Missionary Research* 36 (2012) 59–64.

Park, Young Hee. "The Great Revival Movement of 1907 and Its Historical Impact on Korean Church." Paper presented at the Presbyterian Church in America (PCA) Korean-American English Ministry Pastor's Conference, January 2008.

Park, Jung Eun. "선교사 멤버케어에 관한 연구" [A Study on Missionary Member Care]. Unpublished master's thesis, Fuller Theological Seminary, 2009.

Pines, Ayala M. "Adult Attachment Styles and their Relationship to Burnout: A Preliminary, Cross-Cultural Investigation." *Work and Stress* 18 (2004) 66–80.

———. "Burnout." In *Handbook of Stress: Theoretical and Clinical Aspects*, edited by Leo Goldberger and Shlomo Breznitz, 386–402. New York: Free, 1993.

Pirolo, Neal. *Serving as Senders*. San Diego: Emmaus Road International, 1991.

———. *Serving as Senders Today*. San Diego: Emmaus Road International, 2012.

Prins, Marina, and Braam Willemse. *Member Care for Missionaries: A Practical Guide for Senders*. Brackenfell, South Africa: Member Care Southern Africa, 2009.

REFERENCES

Richardson, Jarrett. "Psychopathology in Missionary Personnel." In *Missionary Care: Counting the Cost for World Evangelization*, edited by Kelly S. O'Donnell, 89–109. Pasadena: William Carey Library, 1992.

Ryu, Dong Sik. *Folk Religion and Korean Culture*. Seoul, South Korea: HundaiSa Sang Sa, 1978.

Schubert, Esther. "Current Issues in Screening and Selection." In *Missionary Care: Counting the Cost for World Evangelization*, edited by Kelly S. O'Donnell, 74–88. Pasadena: William Carey Library, 1992.

———. *What Missionaries Need to Know about Burnout and Depression*. New Castel, IN: Olive Branch, 1993.

Schulz, Dorris (Dottie). *Why Do Missionary Care?* Missions Resource Network, 2005. https://www.mrnet.org/system/files/library/Why_Do_My_Care_updated_2012.pdf.

Schwandt, Joanne. "Missionary Outreach Support Services: A Qualitative Study of a Model for Online Mental Health Consultation." Diss., Regent University, 2007.

Seale, Clive. *The Quality of Qualitative Research*. London: Sage, 1999.

Shenk, Wilbert R. "After Bosch: Toward a Fresh Interpretation of the Church in the 21st Century World of East Asia." *Mission Focus: Annual Review* 11 (2003) 8–21.

Shim, Il Sup. "The New Religious Movements in the Korean Church." *International Review of Mission* 74 (1985) 103–8.

Silzer, Sheryl Takagi. "Confessions of a Confucianist: Implications for Missions." *Priscilla Papers* 23 (2009) 1–11.

Song, Sung Ja. "Korean Cultural Family Therapy: The Solution Based on Family Healing Application." *Korean Journal of Social Welfare* 32 (1997) 160–80.

Song, Young Hack, and Christopher B. Meek. "The Impact of Culture on the Management Values and Beliefs of Korean Firms." *Journal of Comparative International Management* 1 (1998) 1–18.

Steffen, Tom, and Lois McKinney Douglas. *Encountering Missionary Life and Work: Preparing for Intercultural Ministry*. Grand Rapids: Baker, 2008.

Strauss, Anselm, and Juliet Corbin. *Basics of Qualitative Research: Grounded Theory Procedures and Techniques*. Thousand Oaks, CA: Sage, 1990.

———. *Basics of Qualitative Research: Techniques and Procedures for Developing Grounded Theory*. Thousand Oaks, CA: Sage Publications, 1998.

Strauss, Gary, and Kathy Narramore. "The Increasing Role of the Sending Church." In *Missionary Care: Counting the Cost for World Evangelization*, edited by Kelly S. O'Donnell, 299–314. Pasadena: William Carey Library, 1992.

Sunkyusacarenet [선교사 케어넷]. 땅끝의 아침 [The Morning of the End of the World]. Yong San, Seoul, Korea: Durrano, 2007.

Taylor, Glenn C. "Spiritual Dimensions in Mental Health." In *Enhancing Missionary Vitality: Mental Health Professions Serving Global Mission*, edited by John R. Powell and Joyce M. Bowers, 75–81. Palmer Lake, CO: Mission Training International, 2002.

———. "A Theological Perspective on Missionary Care." In *Enhancing Missionary Vitality: Mental Health Professions Serving Global Mission*, edited by John R. Powell and Joyce M. Bowers, 55–61. Palmer Lake, CO: Mission Training International, 2002.

Taylor, William David, ed. "Prologue." In *Too Valuable to Lose: Exploring the Causes and Cures of Missionary Attrition*, xiii. Pasadena: William Carey Library, 1997.

REFERENCES

———. *Too Valuable to Lose: Exploring the Causes and Cures of Missionary Attrition.* Pasadena: William Carey Library, 1997.

Tippett, Alan R. *Introduction to Missiology.* Pasadena: William Carey Library, 1987.

Tucker, Ruth, and Leslie Andrews. "Historical Notes on Missionary Care." In *Missionary Care: Counting the Cost for World Evangelization*, edited by Kelly S. O'Donnell, 24–31. Pasadena: William Carey Library, 1992.

Van Manen, Max. *Researching Lived Experience: Human Science for an Action Sensitive Pedagogy.* New York: State University of New York Press, 1990.

Whiteman, Darrell L. "Part II: Anthropology and Mission: The Incarnational Connection." *International Journal of Frontier Missions* 21 (2004) 79–86.

Won, Young Jae. "유교문화 영향으로 인한 한국교회의 세속화와 목회자 나르시시즘" [The Secularization of Korean Churches and Pastoral Narcissism Due to the Confucian Culture]. *The Philosophy of Korean Christianity Institute* 8 (2009) 61–86.

Wright, H. Norman. *Winning Over Your Emotions: Helpful Answers That Will Change Your Life.* Eugene, OR: Harvest House, 1998.

Yang, Guen-Seok. "Globalization and Christian Responses: Korea." *Theology Today* 62 (2005) 38–48.

Yoon, Ki Soon. "사도바울의 선교전략과 21세기 한국교회 선교방향에 관한 연구: "훈련된 선교사의 전략"을 중심으로" [A Study of the Apostle Paul's Mission Strategy and Mission Direction of the Korean Church: Based on Strategy of the Disciplined Missionary]. Unpublished PhD diss., Hanyoung Theological University, 2011.

You, Young Gweon. "Shame and Guilt Mechanisms in East Asian Culture." *Journal of Pastoral Care* 51 (1997) 57–64.

Youn, Hee Kyung, and Julian C. Muller. "A Discussion about Difficulties of University Education for Korean Missionary Children." *Nederduitse Gereformeerde Teologiese Tydskrif* 52 (2011) 272–84.

www.ingramcontent.com/pod-product-compliance
Lightning Source LLC
Chambersburg PA
CBHW070329230426

43663CB00011B/2259